14 FEB 2003

Making a World of Difference

Wiley Series in Information Systems

Making a World of Difference

IT in a Global Context

GEOFF WALSHAM

JOHN WILEY & SONS, LTD
Chichester · New York · Weinheim · Brisbane · Singapore · Toronto

Other Wiley Editorial Offices

John Wiley & Sons, Inc., 605 Third Avenue,
New York, NY 10158-0012, USA

WILEY-VCH Verlag GmbH, Pappelallee 3,
D-69469 Weinheim, Germany

Jacaranda Wiley Ltd, 33 Park Road, Milton,
Queensland 4064, Australia

John Wiley & Sons (Asia) Pte Ltd, 2 Clementi Loop #02-01,
Jin Xing Distripark, Singapore 129809

John Wiley & Sons (Canada) Ltd, 22 Worcester Road,
Rexdale, Ontario M9W 1L1, Canada

British Library Cataloguing in Publication Data

A catalogue record for this book is available from the British Library

ISBN 0-471-87724-7

Typeset in 10/12 pt Palatino by C.K.M. Typesetting, Salisbury, Wiltshire.
Printed and bound in Great Britain by Bookcraft (Bath) Ltd, Midsomer Norton, Somerset.
This book is printed on acid-free paper responsibly manufactured from sustainable forestry,
in which at least two trees are planted for each one used for paper production.

Wiley Series in Information Systems

*To Jenny, Peter,
Matthew and Thomas*

Contents

Series Preface

The information systems community has grown considerably since 1984, when we began publishing the Wiley Series in Information Systems. We are pleased to be a part of the growth of the field, and believe that this series of books is playing an important role in the intellectual development of the discipline. The primary objective of the series is to publish scholarly work that reflects the best of the research in the information systems community. We are specifically interested in those works that are also relevant to the practice of IS. This volume by Geoff Walsham entitled *Making a World of Difference: IT in a Global Context* is an excellent example of the strong scholarly work with a challenging relevance for the practice of IT that we strive to publish.

Walsham offers a comprehensive overview of the issues surrounding globalization as it relates to information technology. He presents a truly outstanding synthesis of the major theoretical perspectives in globalization and information technology. Leading theorists of globalization, such as Giddens, Castells and Beck, are presented in a concise and thorough way, reflecting Walsham's deep understanding of their writings. He presents a careful analysis of the many levels at which globalization must be approached, ranging from the individual, the work team, the organization, the inter-organizational, the cultural and the transcultural. Walsham unpacks the complexities and subtleties of the globalized individual, firm and culture, revealing the intertwining role of identity and technology at each level. He uses case studies from around the world to dramatically portray the human and social problematic of IT in a world of globalization, arguing for technology development that enhances rather than destroys diversity.

Dick Boland and Rudy Hirschheim

Preface

I first started using computers as an operational research analyst, over 30 years ago. In those days I worked on producing models of petrochemical operations, running boxes of punched card through batch-processing mainframe machines. Despite the technical focus of much of this activity, I was concerned even then with the degree of realism of the models, how the outputs from them were being used, and whether this changed the world for the better in some small way. In other words, I was interested in the relationship between computers, organizations and society.

Later, in the 1980s, I started looking at the social aspects of computerization as the main thrust of my work. This primarily involved in-depth case studies of the development and use of computer-based information systems in organizations. The results from this work were brought together in an earlier book in the Wiley Series (Walsham 1993). In that book I focused on processes of human interpretation around the design and use of information technology (IT). I argued the need to take account of, and to manage, the diversity of views and attitudes surrounding the role and value of particular technologies and systems.

I continued this strand of work throughout the 1990s, a period of further rapid change in the world in general, and in the use of IT in particular. For example, in terms of IT-related change, the massive upsurge in the use of the Internet in the latter half of the decade is an event of major importance. I remain, however, concerned about the human aspects of the use of information and communication technologies, where many issues are problematic despite technological advances. An enhanced ability to collect and process data, or to communicate electronically across time and space, does not necessarily lead to improved human communication and action. In this volume I continue to explore these human aspects of computerization, as I did in my earlier book, but using a wide range of more recent case materials. For analytical purposes, I divide the issues into a set of levels of analysis, investigating the role and value of IT at the levels of personal and professional identity, the work of groups or teams, organizational connectivity and restructuring, and inter-organizational networking.

There is a second set of personal motives that have led me to writing this book. I have, in some senses, led a double life for many years, since in addition to my work on IT in mainstream Western economies, I have worked extensively in the so-called developing countries. My earliest professional experience was a year spent teaching mathematics at a university in the southern Philippines. I lived and worked for four years in Kenya in the 1970s. Since then, I have worked extensively in India and Malaysia, and for shorter periods in other developing countries around the world. In this book, for the first time, I aim to bring together my double life, and to look at the role of 'IT in a global context', the subtitle of the book. Of course, I cannot personally cover the whole world, but I use a range of case studies from a wide range of countries and all the continents. I describe and analyse the case studies carried out with my own research collaborators where possible, but I supplement these by drawing from the work of others to provide a more global coverage.

I have a particular bias with regard to the world, reflected in the main title of the book, and in its core content. The world is highly diverse in terms of human characteristics such as gender, race, religion and culture. In my view, this diversity is largely something to be celebrated and to learn from. I do not subscribe to the view that Western societies, such as my own, represent the pinnacle of human achievement, and that the goal of Third World countries should be simply to follow this development path. There are positive and negative features in all societies, and the goal of all of us should be mutual learning from the 'other'. This applies, in particular, to the use of information and communication technologies, where we should be concerned with learning how to use IT effectively, but in a way that recognizes personal, organizational and societal diversity. IT makes a 'world of difference' in the sense that it is important in the contemporary world, but I also hope that we can use IT to support a world of 'difference', one in which diversity is respected.

Not all aspects of diversity are to be welcomed however. For example, stark asymmetries of wealth and power in the contemporary world severely limit the ability of some people to lead a full and rewarding life. The challenge for the use of IT in the future is to try to ensure that existing inequities are not reproduced or indeed magnified. The Internet has enormous potential in this respect, offering possibilities for connectivity and access to less privileged groups and societies. However, the worry is that its use will be monopolized by those who are already advantaged, and that the gap between the 'information rich' and the 'information poor' will be widened still further. I will explore this issue in some detail in the book.

The book is organized into four parts. Part 1 focuses on theoretical views of the contemporary world, paying particular attention to the role of information and communication technologies. Part 2 presents empirical material at the different levels of analysis mentioned above, with case studies drawn mainly from the rich countries of the world. Theory from Part 1 is drawn on for analytical purposes where appropriate. Part 3 has a similar goal to Part 2, but with a specific emphasis on non-Western cultures. Some overall conclusions are summarized in Part 4. The book presupposes a reasonable level of prior knowledge on organizations and IT, and is thus aimed primarily at postgraduate students, research communities concerned with IT in organizations and society, and practitioners involved in the development and management of information and communication technologies.

The ideas behind this book reflect the work of many people, including all those referenced in the text, and those who collaborated with the research endeavours reported here. I would, however, like to name some people for particular contributions. I have worked directly over the last decade with a range of research collaborators, mostly as my PhD students in the first instance, but later as my academic colleagues. I have drawn on their work extensively in the main text, and I am immensely grateful for their contribution to my own learning. They are, in alphabetical order: Michael Barrett, Maria Hayes, Niall Hayes, Kaewta Rohitratana, Sundeep Sahay, and Susan Scott.

I am also grateful to the following people who read the first draft of the whole book and offered valuable comments: Dick Boland, Matthew Jones, Dan Robey, and two anonymous Wiley reviewers. As mentioned above, I have drawn on the work of others who were not my direct research collaborators, and they are of course fully referenced in the book. However, some of these authors kindly read an early version of the material which referred to their work, and offered me some helpful comments that I have tried to incorporate appropriately in the final version. They are as follows: Simon Bell, Jørn Braa, Sirkka Jarvenpaa,

David Knights, Mikko Korpela, Ole Hanseth, and Bjørn-Erik Munkvold. I would also like to acknowledge the help of Diane Taylor at Wiley. My wife and family are essential support for all my work.

Geoff Walsham
Cambridge
February 2001

Part 1
IT in Society

1
Introduction

It is widely acknowledged that major social transformations are taking place in the contemporary world. For example, although the term globalization is hard to define in any precise way, it reflects the increasing interconnection of societies in terms of their economic, political and cultural life. Organizations in both the public and private sectors are changing, sometimes in a radical way. Many large organizations have de-layered, and undergone other processes of major change such as those associated with business process re-engineering. The detailed work life in these organizations, and in small- and medium-sized enterprises, is often significantly different in style and content from that of even 10 years ago. In addition to changes in work and work life, the norms and values of society outside the sphere of paid employment have also shifted, often dramatically. Attitudes to gender, the environment, race, sex, family life and religion have been transformed over the last few decades in many countries of the world.

It is relatively easy to catalogue changes as outlined above, but it is important to remember that there has also been continuity and stability. Societies remain clearly distinct, despite increasing interconnection, and their citizens normally pursue a lifestyle that would be broadly recognizable to their ancestors of 50 years earlier. Organizations have transformed themselves in many ways, but the human processes involved, for example, in leadership, team working, and the pursuit of personal aspirations retain many similarities with the past. Individuals may work or socialize in a different way, and some social norms and values have shifted, but we all need self-respect, a community or communities to which to belong, and ways of giving meaning to our lives.

The specific role of information and communication technologies in the interweaving of the stability and change that has taken place, and that might take place in the future, is the subject of much debate. Some commentators argue that these technologies are the driving forces for change, whilst others would see them in a more supporting role. It is, however, generally accepted that they are a fundamental element in the changed nature of work processes, in organizational restructuring and in societal transformation. Terms such as the 'information society', or even the 'information revolution', are relatively common in the academic and business world, and are increasingly recognized by the ordinary citizen. However, they often reflect a wide variety of different views on the precise nature of these phenomena, and thus obscure more than they reveal.

To investigate the role of information technology in more detail, which is the primary goal of this book, it is necessary to go down from the level of broad generalizations to the more specific level of organizations, groups and individuals. However, in doing this, we are confronted by a bewildering array of ever-changing technologies, work processes and organizational forms. Much current debate in business organizations centres around technologies such as groupware, the Internet and enterprise systems; and around topics such as e-commerce and knowledge management; although we can be sure that these will be supplanted in due course by the as-yet-unknown technologies and topics that will be considered central a few years hence.

In addition to the shifting multiplicity of technologies and topics, there are multiple levels at which we can analyse the role of information technology. For example, we can focus on the individual level of personal or professional identity, on the level of teams and group working, on the level of the organization, on inter-organizational networks, on a given society, or on the inter-societal level. All these levels can be investigated separately, but they are, of course, inextricably interconnected, and indeed their separation is largely an analytical device.

Much of the literature in the English language that addresses the wide range of issues outlined above has a strong 'Western country' bias, both in terms of the subjects of study normally being located in these countries, and in terms of the nationalities of the authors. However, what is happening in the countries of Asia, Africa or Latin America is important for the whole world, both from an economic and a wider social perspective. The cultures of these countries are often radically different from those of the Western countries, and insights from work in the latter do not necessarily apply to the former. Japan presents one obvious example of such a difference, and one where significant amounts of published work exist in English. However, much less has been written about, for example, the nature of work and organizations in India or China, countries that together account for over two billion people.

So, is it possible to make sense of the role played by information technology in this multi-technology, multi-level, multicultural arena? Most research in this domain has been carried out by selecting one part of the mosaic and exploring issues in depth in one country, one organization, one group, or even with respect to one individual. Indeed, I have done this myself over a number of years, working with a group of research collaborators in a range of different organizations, sectors and countries. Much of this work has been published as articles or conference publications, where the connectivity of the various pieces of work cannot be elucidated due to space constraints, whereas this book will attempt a more comprehensive and integrated analysis.

Thus, the purpose of this book is to reflect on these experiences of managing and working in multi-level, multicultural contexts, mediated by information and communication technologies; and also on the experiences reported by other researchers and practitioners in these domains. However, the aim is not only to examine individual cases in some detail, but also to develop a degree of synthesis. For example, what links can be made between the role of information technology (IT) at different levels such as that of the individual, the group and the organization? How do broader societal themes such as globalization relate to evidence from these lower levels of analysis? What can be said about the similar and different usage of IT in a multicultural world? What are the implications of these analyses for organizational and management research and practice?

This is not a how-to-do-it book in any direct sense. It does not contain a set of formulae, rules, methodologies or prescriptions as to how to develop, use or manage IT in a specific context. The aim of the book is to provide up-to-date material on the adoption, use and management of IT and computer-based information systems, supported by relevant literature and cases from a wide variety of organizational and cultural contexts, and situated within an analysis of the broader arena of global stability and change. I hope that the reader will find that this material, and the concepts through which it is presented, will aid his or her own processes of learning and reflection on the topics and issues considered, and thus that the book will support thoughtful future practice on the role of information and communication technologies in the evolving world.

STUDYING IT IN A GLOBAL CONTEXT

I have briefly outlined the purpose of the book in the introductory paragraphs above, and in this section I set out the broad approach I have used to achieve this. In particular, I discuss issues of style of study, methodology and the role of theory in the material that follows. In the final section of the chapter, I then show how this broad approach translates into the specific structure of the book.

Style of Study

Kling (1994) discussed five styles of analysis and writing about computerization. 'Technological utopianism' and 'anti-utopianism' are self-explanatory, relating to views that information technology is 'good' or 'bad'. Writings of the former kind are common in the popular management literature, for example when extolling the virtues of the Internet. The latter are associated with forms of technophobia, seeing machines as a bad thing. I will not devote any further space to either of these here, since they share similar characteristics of over-simplification and misplaced enthusiasm, either for a brave new world of technology or one with no technology. 'Analytical reduction', according to Kling, is a style of analysis based on reducing the complexity of the world to a few key concepts, and carrying out empirical work within that limited space, often using the instrument of a survey, and normally reported in academic journals. Whilst such studies may have some value, they do not allow in-depth analysis of the subtle inter-linking of the social and the technical in specific contexts, and again they will not be used extensively here.

The remaining two of Kling's genres are 'social realism' and 'social theory', and the approach adopted in this book can be related to these latter two categories. Social realism refers to the use of detailed empirical studies of 'computerization as it is actually practised and experienced'. Kling argues that a common weakness of the work of authors in this genre is that they are rarely explicit in drawing concepts or themes that generalize across technologies and social settings. In contrast, authors in the 'social theory' genre develop concepts and theories that transcend specific situations, but Kling argues that their use of specialized terms and abstractions can make their work difficult to access for many readers.

In addition to the five genres outlined above, Kling identifies 'hybrid discourses' that combine features of two or more of the basic genres. The approach adopted in this book can be considered to be such a hybrid discourse. The work of social theorists will be complemented by 'social realist' empirical studies, although 'socially grounded' studies might be a better term, avoiding the implications of a single truth implied by the word 'realist'. The purpose of this combined approach is to explore the relationship between micro-studies of computerization and various theories concerning individuals, groups, organizations and societies. This hybrid approach is aimed at generalizing results from micro-studies through the development of theoretical concepts derived from the studies, but which are also linked to broader social theories.

Methodology

Most of the case studies reported in the book, including those from my own research and that of my collaborators, can be broadly classed as 'interpretive' (Walsham 1993). This umbrella term can obscure as much as it reveals, since many different types of study are labelled this way. However, I take an interpretive study to mean that multiple perceptions are provided by participants, and thus that the interesting data from the study cannot be 'triangulated' to provide a 'true' interpretation, since whose truth should be chosen? The interpretive researcher filters participants' statements and actions through the lens of his or her own subjectivity, and then produces a 'story' about the events that have occurred and some reasons for them. The purpose of the story, again, is not to tell 'the truth' about the case study but to tell 'a truth', namely the researcher's own thoughts and ideas concerning the phenomena at issue. This book as a whole provides such an interpretive view, namely one particular rendering of my current ideas and feelings about the subject of the role and value of IT in the world at the time of writing.

Some of the case studies in the book have been drawn from secondary published sources, where I was not involved as one of the researchers or in a research supervisory capacity. For these studies, there is a further layer of interpretation, since I am deriving my own views by re-analysing the authors' original studies. It is worth noting, however, that I normally sent draft copies of my own case descriptions to the original authors, and I frequently received substantial comments. I have modified the text of the book to respond to these comments, but the interpretations remain my own, and they do not necessarily represent the views of the original researchers.

I have written extensively on the subject of methods for interpretive studies elsewhere (Walsham 1993, 1995), and this is not the place to go into the topic again at length. However, it is worth noting a few general points here, which will be supplemented by further details in the individual case descriptions. Almost all the empirical work drawn on in the book involved in-depth field studies, based on talking to a wide range of respondents using face-to-face semi-structured interviews, or engaging in action research with practitioners in their organizational context. This was usually supplemented by detailed study of secondary data in the form of internal documents or databases, or external reports in newspapers and the trade press. The reason for the in-depth nature of such studies is that this permits access to the diverse array of complex human perceptions and actions that form the basis of organizational activity. Many of the studies reported in the book were longitudinal, namely research was carried out at intervals over a significant duration, normally years, giving access to changing perceptions and actions over an extended period of time. In order to preserve confidentiality, the names of the case study organizations, and individual respondents, are often disguised.

The Role of Theory

Finally in this section, I would like to make a few comments on my view of the role of theory in interpretive case studies in general, and in particular in this book. Theories about social life do not describe the way that the world 'is' in any full sense, since the overall complexity of even the simplest 'real' situation is beyond the reach of any theory. However, theory provides a point of comparison with the world, offering insights at various stages of a research study. For example, theory can be used as an initial guide to research design and data collection, as part of an iterative process of data collection and analysis, or as a final product of the research.

In this book, I will be focusing mainly on the last two of these categories: where theories help in case analysis; and where the case studies enable theoretical concepts to be developed as part of the 'final product' of the research. However, the results from a case study cannot all be neatly captured in this way. Insights from a particular study may enable the researcher, or the reader of a subsequent description, to connect to aspects of their own experience in a novel way. I suggest that the reader of this book should approach my efforts at case description and theory development from this perspective. Namely, that the theories are offered as possible ways of making sense of the complexity and variety that is observed in the real-life situations described, but that the reader may be able to derive other and perhaps better insights by relating the case material to their own knowledge and experience.

A final comment on the theory in this book is its very broad and rather eclectic nature. It would have been tidier to have one theoretical perspective that ran through the whole book, and within which all the material could have been 'fitted'. However, the topic of IT in a global context at multiple levels of analysis is enormously complex, and empirical material is very varied. In my view, no single theory is able to do reasonable justice to this diversity. I have, therefore, drawn from a range of theories, some of them focused at the broad macro-level, and others addressing specific issues or levels of analysis. I aim throughout the book to provide some implications from the theories used, and some reflection on their value.

THE STRUCTURE OF THE BOOK

Figure 1.1 outlines the structure of the book. Part 1 is concerned with 'IT in Society' and contains three chapters. Its main purpose is to provide some theoretical views of the world in the present era, paying particular attention to the role of information and communication technologies. Chapter 2, following the current introductory chapter, describes and discusses contemporary society seen from the perspective of a range of leading writers. The themes that result from this analysis are very broad in nature, and it is necessary to go down to a more micro-level to examine the role of IT in contemporary society in detail. The purpose of Chapter 3 is to introduce and discuss four conceptual areas, which provide analytical constructs for such an examination. Part 1 provides a theoretical and analytical backdrop for the empirical material in Parts 2 and 3.

Part 2 addresses 'Changing Ways of Working' and contains four chapters, Chapters 4–7, which explore the role of IT at different levels of analysis, concerned with personal and professional identity, the work of groups or teams, organizational connectivity and restructuring, and inter-organizational networking. Each chapter is centred on in-depth case material. Many of the case studies in Part 2, although not all, are focused

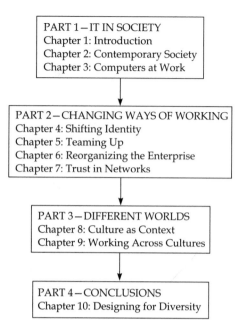

Figure 1.1   *The structure of the book*

on the economically advanced countries. The analytical focus of each chapter is provided by a set of key questions, which are introduced at the beginning of the chapter and then addressed directly in the final analysis and conclusions section. These concluding sections draw on all the case material of the particular chapter, and use specific analytical themes and concepts derived from Part 1 of the book.

Part 3 is entitled 'Different Worlds', and it continues the examination of the role of information and communication technologies and systems in contemporary society, in a similar way to Part 2, but with a specific emphasis on non-Western cultures. Chapter 8 looks at relationships between the culture of a particular society, and its ways of working and organizing using information and communication technologies. The case illustrations in this chapter are drawn from Asia, Africa and Latin America. Chapter 9 continues the focus on non-Western cultures, but addresses the important topic of cross-cultural working. As with Part 2, some key questions are introduced at the beginning of each chapter in Part 3, which are addressed directly in the concluding analytical section.

The final chapter of the book, Chapter 10, presents some overall conclusions on designing and using IT systems in a world of diversity. First, the four conceptual areas concerned with IT in society, introduced in Chapter 3, are revisited in the light of the extensive empirical chapters, and some synthesized conclusions are presented in each of these areas. Second, the future role of the researcher of IT in the contemporary world is discussed, and agendas of relevant research are outlined. Last, I offer some personal views on the question as to whether we can make a better world with information and communication technologies, interpreting this in a wide sense of helping people all over the world to fuller and more rewarding lives.

2
Contemporary Society

This chapter provides a broad context for the later material of the book, being concerned with overall views on the nature of contemporary society. To attempt a complete coverage or synthesis of writing on this topic would be an immense task, but what is presented here has a more modest purpose. A limited selection is made of leading writers, key concepts from their work are summarized, and a first consideration is made of the role of information technology in their analysis or conclusions. In some cases, the writers identify IT as a key element in their analysis, whereas in others the role of IT is largely implicit.

I will start with some influential work in the early 1990s, which can be classed under the label of 'reflexive modernization'. This section includes the work of Giddens on high modernity, and Beck on the risk society. In the subsequent section of the chapter, I will examine the increasing body of writing on globalization, followed by a section on the recent work of Castells on the 'information age'. Finally, I will conclude with a summary of themes from the chapter as a whole, and a brief critique of the relevance of these ideas to the examination of IT in a global context.

REFLEXIVE MODERNIZATION

The sociologist Anthony Giddens is a well-cited writer on social transformation in this epoch. In particular, two of his books (Giddens 1990, 1991) identify some features of contemporary life that, in his view, distinguish it from what has gone before. He emphasizes that these features are not an abrupt change from the modern period, viewed as roughly the post-feudal period in Europe, but rather the intensification of particular modes of thought and behaviour, and the extension of the related institutions of the modern age. He uses the term 'high modernity' to characterize this view, in contrast to the broad stance of post-modernism, for example, which emphasizes discontinuity with earlier periods. Giddens rarely refers to IT explicitly in his books, but information technologies are deeply involved in many of the transformations that he identifies, and illustrations of this are provided below when appropriate.

A first key feature of high modernity, according to Giddens, is time–space distanciation. This refers to the separation of time and space, which in traditional societies were linked through place, and their recombination in forms that permit the precise time–space zoning of social life. Many of the common examples of this principle in the current world are based on the use of IT. For example, e-mail offers the ability to interact with people in different places at times chosen by the sender and recipient, and e-mail users can set aside time zones in their day to carry out this form of social interaction.

A second, but related, feature of high modernity identified by Giddens is the disembedding of social relations from local contexts of interaction. This does not necessarily imply that the social interaction is at a distance, although this might be the case, but that non-local elements mediate the interaction. For example, the interaction between a bank manager and a customer for a loan, which traditionally involved face-to-face interaction and local managerial judgement, is now often conducted, face to face or remotely, using a credit-scoring computer system. The latter system provides an example of what Giddens calls an 'expert system', which acts as a disembedding mechanism. He argues that increased trust is being placed in such systems in contemporary society, although he defines them rather more broadly than computer systems as 'systems of technical accomplishment or professional expertise that organize large areas of the material and social environments in which we live today'.

Time–space separation and recombination, coupled with disembedding mechanisms and shifting bases of trust, provide a basis for breaking away from the hold of pre-established rules and practices, or what Giddens calls institutional reflexivity. He argues that knowledge in contemporary society is provisional and mutable, and is constantly being assessed and revised. Traditional societies relied on rules, procedures and rituals which remained relatively constant over time, whereas knowledge in modern society, whether scientific or social, is regarded as open to continuous revision. The explosive growth of the Internet, providing rapid access to a huge range of new information sources, is likely to intensify this trend still further.

Giddens (1991) made a major attempt to link the key features of contemporary society, as outlined briefly above, with the changing nature of self-identity. He argued that the 'integral relation between modernity and radical doubt' implied by the chronic monitoring and utilization of new knowledge can create existential anxiety in the individual, or even a sense of personal meaninglessness. The reassuring certainties of rules, tradition and ritual are no longer a satisfactory basis for living. Many older workers, in Western countries at least, were brought up to see their work as a 'job for life', that one learnt through apprenticeship and then practised through rules or procedures linked to established norms and values. Much of this basis has been blown away in a relatively short space of time. Giddens argues that individuals need actively and chronically to construct and revise a story of their own self-identity as a basis for personal security and a sense of self-worth. This issue of personal identity is examined further in Chapter 4, using specific examples and case material.

Beck on 'the Risk Society'

A second major thinker on contemporary society is the German sociologist, Ulrich Beck. His book on the risk society (Beck 1992) has been widely cited, and his ideas have influenced the later work of other social thinkers, including Giddens. Beck argues that modern society, in its vigorous and sustained pursuit of wealth production, has produced new risks. These are not solely personal risks as in traditional societies, such as death by misadventure or disease, but global risks that have been manufactured by modern society. Examples of such risks include nuclear disasters such as Chernobyl, global warming, AIDS, so-called mad cow disease, and genetically modified foods. Beck argues that these risks affect us all, and that we do not have adequate institutional mechanisms in the world through which these risks can be monitored and appropriate action taken.

In considering these types of global risks, there are no certain answers, and scientists with 'expert' knowledge frequently disagree, often in a fundamental way, on the seriousness of the risk involved, and what action should be taken. Thus, science does not have a monopoly on rationality, and we must all form our judgements on the competing claims of diverse opinions. Beck is not the only writer to observe the irony that science, which was developed in the pursuit of truth, has helped to create a world where all truth is regarded as provisional, possibly to be undermined by the next set of scientific results.

From the perspective of the individual in Western society, Beck argues that food and survival are no longer the key goals, but that the communality of need has been replaced by the communality of anxiety. This concept refers not merely to the anxiety of personal or global risks, but an undermining of the traditional formations of class, stratum, occupation, sex roles, nuclear family and business sectors. There is a need for individual self-formation to negotiate a new role in this ever-changing world, a theme having strong resonance with Giddens' ideas on the changing nature of self-identity.

Beck sees information and communications technologies as having a key role in the processes outlined above. First, he notes the important role of micro-electronics-based technology in the changing nature of businesses, occupations and economic life generally. However, he also links these technologies to future possibilities for political action. Beck takes a strong view that sub-politics, the involvement of individual citizens in decisions that affect their future and that of the planet as a whole, should provide a means for shaping society from below. Feminism and the environmental movement provide obvious examples of what Beck has in mind. Beck believes that information and communication technologies are, potentially, enablers of this revolution from below:

> ... microelectronics is introducing a stage of technical development which refutes technically the myth of technological determinism. For one thing, computers and control devices are programmable. ... Thus, technology no longer prescribes how it is to be employed in detail; quite to the contrary, this can and must be fed into the technology. ... Thus it becomes a key question who gets what information, by what means, and in what order, about whom and what, and for what purpose (Beck 1992, pp. 216–218).

Beck (2000) has developed his theme of political involvement further. I will review this material in the next main section on globalization.

A Brief Critique of Giddens and Beck

The work of both Giddens and Beck in the early 1990s attracted much interest, but also much critical attention. A few specific comments or criticisms are given here, chosen for their direct relevance to later material in the book. First, it will be clear, even from the brief summary of their work given above, that Giddens and Beck have much in common in their writings. Indeed, although they worked separately on the books referenced above, they later collaborated on a co-authored book (Beck, Giddens and Lash 1994) on 'reflexive modernization', a term coined by Beck to characterize the contemporary age.

The third author of this book, Lash, whilst supportive of many of the concepts developed by his co-authors, criticizes both Giddens and Beck for their relative neglect of the sense-making processes of the ordinary person, outside of scientific debates, institutions and their politics:

> ... their conceptions of 'sub-politics' or 'life politics' focus on experts with relative neglect of the grass-roots. It means for them a concentration on the formal and institutional at the expense of the increasing proportion of social, cultural and political interaction in our increasingly disorganized capitalist world that is going on outside of institutions (p. 200).

A related comment is made by Wynne (1996), who also concentrates on the ordinary 'lay person', but focuses on attitudes to trust. He criticizes Giddens (1990) as taking for granted public trust in 'expert systems', whereas he notes that Beck argues that public trust in scientific knowledge, for example, has declined. However, he differs with both authors in pointing out that the lay person's lack of overt dissent or opposition towards expert systems or scientific knowledge does not necessarily imply public trust. He cites a number of empirical examples of ecological cases where residents in particular communities affected by environmental hazards such as nuclear contamination, felt unable to oppose the 'experts' due to various forms of economic and personal dependency: 'The residents effectively had to behave *as if* they trusted the experts because it would have been socially and psychologically unviable to do anything else when they were so dependent on them' (p. 52).

I will return to such issues in later chapters when examining the way in which employees in business organizations sometimes feel obliged to 'accept' new computer systems as part of their working life, even though they may have serious reservations about the value of such systems. They feel compelled to restrain any dissent due to their dependency on the organization for job security, for example.

Two further observations on the earlier work of both Giddens and Beck are of direct relevance to the topic of this book. Although both writers referred to information and communication technologies and systems in their analyses of contemporary society, it is perhaps surprising that they did not give them any sort of centrality, and little theoretical or conceptual attention. This does not make the concepts that they have developed less relevant *per se*, but it has been argued (Barrett, Sahay and Walsham 1996) that there is a need to extend such sociological theory to add in the IT dimension. A second observation on the work of both Giddens and Beck, at least that referenced above, is that it is highly Western-centric, or even Euro-centric. In other words, no detailed attention was paid by them to other areas of the world such as Asia, Latin America or Africa, and the ways in which contemporary society in such places may differ from that in the West. Again, this is not a criticism in itself, since the authors may have had little knowledge of these other cultures. However, for the purposes of this book, I am interested in IT in the world as a whole, and thus need to include a non-Western dimension. The topic of globalization offers the promise of a wider picture of the world, and this is the subject of the next section.

GLOBALIZATION AND DIVERSITY

The term globalization has achieved the unusual status, in a relatively short time, of becoming fashionable in academic debates in the social sciences, in the business world, and to some extent in the popular media. However, even a cursory examination of these sources would demonstrate that the term is highly ambiguous, and that it masks a wide variety of opinions on what is happening in the world. The purpose of this section is to summarize and critique some of these views. Mention will also be made of the role of information and communication technologies in the processes being analysed, although the book as a whole will go into this subject in rather greater depth.

What is Globalization?

Robertson (1992) wrote an influential book on globalization in which he says that: 'Globalization as a concept refers both to the compression of the world and the intensification of consciousness of the world as a whole' (p. 8). The first of these two points relates directly to the time—space compression, largely mediated by IT, that I have discussed in the previous section. The second point is, however, somewhat wider than the earlier material, since it refers to the world as a whole rather than Western society. The widespread accessibility of communications media such as television, even in remote rural villages in the Third World or underprivileged urban communities anywhere, means that news of happenings in the world as a whole is available to the great majority of the world's population. This does not necessarily imply a well-informed world, since the 'news' is chosen, condensed, filtered and manipulated by a host of complex mechanisms. However, it does mean that remoteness and isolation are not the same in the contemporary age, and that most people are more aware than they were of a wider global arena within which their own community forms only a small part.

Beck (2000) refers to this change in global consciousness using the term 'globality', defined as follows: 'Globality means that we have been living for a long time in a world society, in the sense that the notion of closed spaces has become illusory. No country or group can shut itself off from others' (p. 10). Beck reserves the term globalization for processes of interconnection and influence between national states and international actors such as the transnational corporations (TNCs). Beck argues that the TNCs are 'bidding farewell to the framework of the national state and refusing loyalty to its actors', through such devices as minimizing their taxes, but externalizing the costs of unemployment to the nation states.

Giddens (1999) argues that global financial flows are a key element of these globalization processes:

> Geared as it is to electronic money—money that exists only as digits in computers—the current world economy has no parallels in earlier times. In the new global electronic economy, fund managers, banks, corporations, as well as millions of individual investors, can transfer vast amounts of capital from one side of the world to another at the click of a mouse. As they do so, they can destabilize what might have seemed rock-solid economies—as happened in East Asia (website).

Global financial flows are one element in trends towards more global business as a whole, although we need to be wary of simplistic generalizations here. Although there is much talk in the business world, and the management schools, of global businesses, global markets and global supply chains, the degree to which this has occurred to date, and the degree to which it might occur in the future, remain in dispute. For example, Doremus *et al.* (1998) investigated a range of multinational corporations, mainly in Germany, Japan and the United States, and argued that such companies, who after all should surely be at the fore-front of the move towards globally minded enterprises, remained tied to approaches derived from their unique national identities: 'However lus-tily they sing from the same hymn book when they gather together in Davos or Aspen, the leaders of the world's great business enterprises continue to differ in their most fundamental strategic behaviour and objectives' (quoted in Kogut 1999).

Cultural Diversity

This leads on to one of the most controversial issues in the globalization debate, namely the issue of homogenization and diversity. The broad question is whether the globalization phenomena that we have outlined above, such as time–space compression, an increased awareness of the world as a whole, and movements toward global business, will inevitably lead to a decrease in cultural difference among nations, companies and/or individuals. There is a school of thought, prevalent amongst the Western business community, for example, that takes this for granted. The argu-ment runs that there is only one economic system now, capitalism, and that enterprises need to compete globally under this one set of rules. Therefore, all companies that wish to survive will need to adopt the practices of the winners, leading towards more homogeneous ways of doing things and, by extension to the wider society, to a less-diverse cultural world.

A range of writers have taken exception to this conclusion of the inevitability of homogenization. For example, Robertson (1992) dis-cussed the way in which imported themes are 'indigenized' in particular societies, with local culture constraining the receptivity to some ideas rather than others, and adapting them all in specific ways. He cited Japan as a good example of this blending of the 'native' and the 'foreign' as an ongoing process. Whilst accepting the idea of time–space compression facilitated by information technology, Robertson argued that one of its main consequences is an exacerbation of collisions between global, soci-etal and communal attitudes.

Beck (2000) defined the ideology of global homogenization as 'glo-balism': 'By globalism, I mean the view that the world market eliminates or supplants political action—that is, the ideology of the rule by the world market, the ideology of neoliberalism' (p. 9). Beck argued strongly against this ideology, citing many different reasons. For example, he argued that globalism reduces the complexity of globality and globaliza-tion to a single economic dimension, showing no understanding of the importance of specific political and cultural meanings in particular contexts. Globalism also 'sings the praises' of worldwide 'free trade', but Beck argued that we live in a world far removed from any fair model of free trade due to enormously skewed initial conditions.

Appadurai (1996), coming from a non-Western background, argued against the global homogenization thesis on the basis of cultural considerations. Societies have different cultural histories and will appropriate global trends in a local way:

> ... globalization is itself a deeply historical, uneven and even localizing process. Globalization does not necessarily or even frequently imply homogenization or Americanization, and to the extent that different societies appropriate the materials of modernity differently, there is still ample room for the deep study of specific geographies, histories, and languages' (p. 17).

The term 'glocalization' reflects the ways in which the global, macroscopic aspects of contemporary life are appropriated locally. According to Robertson (1992), the term originated in Japan as a translation of the Japanese word *dochakuka*, roughly meaning global localization.

Globalization and the Self

The debate about the extent to which various processes linked to globalization may lead to homogenization in terms of business processes or national cultures rests to a significant extent on the effect of the processes on the individual member of society, whether in the Western or developing world. The argument will be made here that there is no strong evidence of any simple standardization of humanity, and indeed that global forces may, somewhat paradoxically perhaps, have some effects which tend towards the exact opposite.

Returning to the work of Giddens and Beck, both these writers about contemporary Western society talk about the need for individual life projects, specific to a person's own past history and context, and to his or her future trajectory and aspirations. The world of relatively set rules, traditions, social classes and job roles has been undermined. The new uncertain world requires active navigation. Authors such as these have sometimes been criticized as emphasizing individual freedom of action, in societies where the underprivileged can be thought to have little choice. It is certainly true that some people's choices are more constrained than others, and that life chances are very different at birth dependent on one's parentage and background. Nevertheless, any individual growing up and working in the twenty-first century will need to chart their own course with some vigour, within the range of possibilities available to them, or risk being carried away by the waves of change which will undoubtedly continue to roll.

Robertson (1992) talks about this issue related specifically to globalization, and he adds a subtle distinction regarding concepts such as life projects themselves, which can be seen to be Western individualistic constructs. More group-oriented societies, such as many of those in Asia, and religions such as Islam, which place great emphasis on community, would tend not to see the world as composed of distinct individuals with discrete life goals, opportunities and problems.

Appadurai (1996) took these arguments on cultural difference further, with specific reference to self-identity, and in particular using the concept of imagination. He argued that people draw on contemporary sources, such as the media, and their own cultural histories, to 'annex the global' into their own 'practices of the modern' through their imagination. Thus, even conventional objects such as T-shirts and music become transformed differently in different contexts: 'T-shirts, billboards, and graffiti as well as rap music, street dancing, and slum housing all show that the images of the media are quickly moved into local repertoires of irony, anger, humor and resistance' (p. 7).

Gopal (1997) quoted Appadurai's arguments against global homogenization, and the role of imagination, with a specific focus on IT. He argued that the vision of an IT-driven world of progress, efficiency, unlimited markets, individualism and the superiority of the Western developmental trajectory needs to be challenged, not least because the effects of the use of IT in the West itself have not always been benign. He argued that each developing country must forge its own path in the future, and not try to imitate inappropriate Western models:

> They (developing countries) have different pasts; their historical trajectories have led to different configurations of valences, patterns of trust, responsibilities, and allegiances. They have, as a result, different presents: priorities, voices, capabilities, and capacities are arranged in patterns quite unlike those of the societies from which the technologies originate. And, in spite of the attempts of a few to sediment in the popular imagination a singular vision of prosperous IT-driven existence, they have different imagined futures (Appadurai, 1996); their varieties of aspirations and expectations bear little resemblance to the visions embedded in the technology (p. 140).

The Role of the Nation State

A key topic identified by many writers about globalization concerns the changing role of the nation state in an increasingly globalized world. Is the nation state a redundant entity, at the mercy of international forces that it cannot control, to be replaced by large federal groupings or even world government? What policy measures and other actions remain within the control of the individual nation state, and can these be effective in improving the lives of the citizens of that country, and protecting them from the worse effects of the cold winds of global competition and the actions of the transnational corporations?

The answer to the first of these questions is a qualified no, in my view, leading us to the details and complexities of the second question, which will be country- and context-specific. The nation state is not redundant, although its influence is more conditional than in some previous eras. Hirst and Thompson (1996) adopt the stronger view that the rhetoric of globalization is often used to attack the concept of the nation state as a strategy from the right of the political spectrum to undermine the welfare gains that have been achieved in most Western economies. They argue that this rhetoric should be opposed, and that the state should continue to pursue approaches to counter asymmetries of privilege within its borders.

Clark (1997) also supports the importance of the nation state, and argues that globalization tendencies should be analysed in conjunction with tendencies towards fragmentation, the latter referring to the multiplicity of diverse interests within the state that need to be accommodated. In addition to challenges to the welfare state, globalization brings with it political costs such as high levels of unemployment in a country as a whole, or in particular regions. The state is required to mediate between increasingly potent international pressures and heightened levels of domestic discontent from those affected negatively as a result of such pressures. Clark argues that:

> In the circumstances, it is to be expected that fragmentationist policies will have renewed appeal amongst the motley groups and peoples who have most to lose by continuing globalization: employment sectors in the First World felt to be threatened by the 'export' of jobs to low-wage areas of globalized production; embattled politicians who see globalization eroding their own sources of power and control; traditionalist societies within the Third World disenchanted by the empty promises of development but subject none the less to its seemingly pervasive effects; ethnic identities which may

seem to be the only stable anchors in the fast-moving tides of cultural change (p. 202).

Beck (2000) is deeply concerned with the type of issues raised in the above quotation, and he places great emphasis on the need for new forms of political action that cross national borders as a means of moulding 'responsible globalization'. He argues the need for collaboration among nation states, for example to limit or obstruct the 'horse trading' whereby global firms minimize their tax obligations and maximize state subsidies. Using Europe as an example, he argues that a new transnational federalism would enable states to have a new life as 'individual glocal states', limiting the power of transnational centres. Turning to the wider world, Beck points to the need for political action in the form of a social contract against exclusion, and a sense of global responsibility in the face of enormous inequity: 'The share of the poorest fifth of humanity in world income fell from 4 to 1 per cent between 1960 and 1990. By contrast, 358 dollar billionaires possess more than what a half of humanity put together currently earns' (p. 153). Beck's overall argument, therefore, is the need to oppose the hegemony of 'globalism', and to develop a new transnational politics that engages with the issues of globalization, particularly those concerned with social consequences.

THE INFORMATION AGE

A major analysis of contemporary society, which addresses many of the earlier issues that I have discussed in this chapter, including the topic of globalization, is contained in the three-volume magnum opus of Manuel Castells (1996, 1997, 1998), *The Information Age: Economy, Society and Culture.* It draws on a wide range of empirical data, much of it collected by the author and his research collaborators over a period of more than a decade. The geographical coverage of the work is impressive, with major material on Latin America and Asia, for example, in addition to Europe and the United States.

Castells assigns a central role to information and communications technologies in the societal transformations that have taken place in the modern world. He is not, of course, the first major author to do this, and he acknowledges a debt to the earlier work of 'informationalist' writers such as Bell (1973) (see Webster 1995 for a review of some others). However, the depth of his analysis and supporting evidence makes it particularly compelling.

The basic thesis of Volume 1, Castells (1996), is that a new 'network society' is emerging from current processes of change that is both capitalist and informational. The latter is defined as follows: '...the term informational indicates the attribute of a specific form of social organization in which information generation, processing and transmission become the fundamental sources of productivity and power, because of new technological conditions emerging in this historical period' (p. 21). Castells believes that globalization is real, in the sense that the markets for goods and services are becoming increasingly globalized. This does not mean that all firms sell worldwide, but that the strategic aims of all firms, large and small, is to sell wherever they can throughout the world, either directly or via their linkage with networks that operate in the world market.

However, in the informational economy, there is complex interaction between historically rooted political and social institutions, and increasingly globalized economic agents. There is, therefore, wide variety in the way in which individual countries and regions act as part of the globalized world. Castells argues that the global economy is characterized by its interdependence, but also by its asymmetry, and the increasing diversification within each region. In this sense, Castells supports the theory of glocalization, discussed in the previous section.

With respect to organizations, Castells argues that major organizational changes have taken place over the recent period. He identifies these as including a transition from mass production to more flexible production, the emergence of small and medium firms as major agents of innovation and sources of job creation, and new methods of management such as total quality management and other ideas imported into the West from Japan. Other key changes involve networking: the multidirectional networking of small and medium businesses, the licensing–subcontracting model of production under an umbrella corporation, and the intertwining of large corporations in strategic alliances.

Castells places great emphasis on networking, and indeed argues that firms have become network enterprises, and that we are in the era which forms the title of Volume 1, namely the network society. Information technology is assigned a key role: 'While the networking form of social organization has existed in other times and spaces, the new information technology paradigm provides the material basis for its pervasive expansion throughout the entire social structure' (p. 469).

It is interesting to note that this first volume was published in 1996, and that no doubt the material was developed rather earlier. Although the Internet has existed for a relatively long time, it is only in the last few years that its enormous potential impact has started to be exploited. Castells anticipated the network society before these developments, and the growth of the Internet lends further support to his thesis here.

The processes of change to a network society have been accompanied by a transformation of work and employment but not to a unified global labour market. However, according to Castells, there is increasing inter-dependence of the labour force on a global scale, through three mechan-isms. These are global employment in the multinational corporations and their associated cross-border networks; the impact of international trade on employment conditions, both in the North and in the South; and the effects of global competition and of the new mode of flexible production on each country's labour force. Castells argues that information technol-ogy is deeply implicated in these change processes, but that there is no simple structural relationship between the diffusion of IT and the evolution of employment levels in a particular economy taken as a whole.

Finally, in keeping with his roots in urban geography, Castells argues that the 'global city' plays a key role in the network society. However, he defines the global city not as a place, but as a process. This process connects centres of production and consumption of advanced services, and their ancillary local societies, in a global network, whilst simulta-neously downplaying the linkages with their hinterlands. The megacities, in particular, provide a linkage for informational networks and concen-trate the world's power. However, they also provide a depository of all those segments of the population who fight to survive, as well as those groups who want to make visible their dereliction.

Castells (1997) starts Volume 2 with an impassioned plea for a multi-cultural world view of globalization:

> There is in this book a deliberate obsession with multiculturalism ...
> This approach stems from my view that the process of techno-eco-nomic globalization shaping our world is being challenged, and will eventually be transformed, from a multiplicity of sources, according to different cultures, histories and geographies ... I would like also ... to break the ethnocentric approach still dominating much social science at the very moment when our societies have become globally interconnected and culturally intertwined (p. 3).

The challenges to techno-economic globalization come from people's search for communal or collective identity, according to Castells. Reflexive life-planning, of the type discussed earlier in the work of Giddens, is only possible for the elite, or the 'globapolitans'. For those people excluded from the global networks of power and wealth, cultural communes of religious, national or territorial foundation provide the main alternative for the construction of meaning in society.

There are clear links here with Appadurai's arguments on the diversity of imagination, and Castells (1997) provides detailed material on 'resistance movements' to the global order, both within particular national contexts, and in wider arenas. With respect to the former, three examples are given. First, the role of the Zapatistas in Mexico in fighting what they defined as a conjunction of American imperialism and corrupt, illegitimate national government. It is interesting to note their use of the media and Internet-based alliances to publicize and support their resistance. The second example is of the American militia of the far right opposing what they see as the excessive power of the US federal government, with the Oklahoma bombing as a stark example of their resistance. Finally, the Japanese movement Aum Shinrikyo, responsible for the Tokyo subway nerve gas attack, defined the global opposition as unified world government representing the interests of the multinational corporations, and enforced by the Japanese police.

In addition to these dramatic and violent examples of social resistance to the perceived global order in particular national contexts, Castells also analyses more cross-cultural resistance movements, who use largely peaceful means to pursue their opposition. The first of these is the environmental movement, representing the widespread fear of people concerning the uncontrolled pursuit of science and technology without an adequate consideration of long-term consequences:

> The ecological approach to life, to the economy, and to the institutions of society emphasizes the holistic character of all forms of matter, and of all information processing. Thus, the more we know, the more we sense the possibilities of our technology, and the more we realise the gigantic, dangerous gap between our enhanced productive capacities, and our primitive, unconscious and ultimately destructive social organization (p. 133).

The second widespread opposition to the established order, cited by Castells, is feminism or, more generally, the transformation of women's work and women's consciousness. Castells argues that the decline of patriarchalism, coupled with the change in women's roles and attitudes, requires a reconstruction of the family under more egalitarian relations. However, organizations and institutions have not in general adapted to this new world.

This leads on to Castells' analysis of the role of the state. He argues that the state is losing its power, in comparison to earlier eras, but not its influence. Nation states have been transformed from sovereign subjects into strategic actors. There is a paradox in their role, in that the more that they emphasize communal identity, the less effective they become as co-agents of a global system of shared power. However, the more that they triumph in the planetary sphere, in close partnership with the agents of globalization, or what Beck would call globalism, the less they represent their national constituencies. In particular, they must cope with those groups who are largely excluded from the power and resources of the globalized production networks, whether as producers or as consumers. There are strong echoes here of the arguments of Beck on the role of the nation state, although Beck is perhaps more positive about what could be done to counteract the power of globalism and its agents.

Castells does, however, end Volume 2 on a relatively optimistic note concerning the possibilities for 'informational politics' in the information age. He argues for the recreation of the local state, using the opportunity offered by electronic communication to enhance political participation and horizontal communication among citizens. He believes we have entered the era of 'symbolic politics' in which: 'The new power lies in the codes of information and in the images of representation around which societies organise their institutions, and people build their lives, and decide their behaviour. The sites of this power are people's minds' (p. 359).

In Volume 3, Castells (1998) uses the conceptual analysis of the previous two volumes to explore specific issues, phenomena and regional groupings at the end of the millennium. These include the collapse of the Soviet Union, which Castells ascribes to its inability to make the transition from industrialism to an information-based society. He also explores the disturbing phenomenon of the global criminal economy, brought about by the networking of powerful criminal organizations, and their associates, in shared activities across the planet.

Castells' analysis of the excluded 'fourth world' is an important feature of this volume. He argues that the development of the complex set of linkages of informational capitalism has been accompanied by the rise of inequality, social polarization, poverty and misery in much of the world. Globalization proceeds selectively, including and excluding segments of economies and societies in and out of the networks of information, wealth and power that characterize the new dominant system:

. . . a new world, the Fourth World, has emerged, made up of multiple black holes of social exclusion throughout the planet. The Fourth World comprises large areas of the globe, such as much of sub-Saharan Africa, and impoverished rural areas of Latin America and Asia. But it is also present in literally every country, and in every city, in this new geography of social exclusion. It is formed of American inner-city ghettos, Spanish enclaves of mass youth unemployment, French banlieues warehousing North Africans, Japanese Yoseba quarters, and Asian megacities' shanty towns (pp. 164–165).

An analysis of two major regional groupings form most of the rest of this volume. Castells considers whether the Pacific region could provide the basis for a new economic and political superpower in the new millennium, leading to a Pacific era. He concludes that this will not happen, since the process of development in the region has been enacted by parallel nationalisms, which are not ready to downplay their very distinct identities. However, Castells argues that the region has provided new sources of economic growth and technological innovation with planetary reach. The Pacific economies are interdependent in the region, and intertwined with economies around the world. Thus, the rise of the Pacific region is a prime example of the multicultural foundation of the new global economy.

The analysis of Europe that follows develops the concept that it provides an example of a network state. A network, by definition, has nodes and not a centre. Nodes may be of different sizes, and may be linked by asymmetrical relationships. Regardless of these asymmetries, no node can afford to ignore the others in the decision-making process. To take European integration further requires the development of a European identity that, Castells argues, does not currently exist. He believes, however, that it could be built, not in contradiction, but complementary to national, regional and local identities. It would be based on a blueprint of social values and institutional goals that appeal to the majority of citizens across the continent as a whole.

Castells ends Volume 3, and the work as a whole, with an appeal for conscious, purposive social action, supported by information, in order to address the many problems and challenges identified in the books.

If people are informed, active and communicate throughout the world; if business assumes its social responsibility; . . . if political actors react against cynicism, and restore faith in democracy; . . . if humankind feels the solidarity of the species across the globe; if we assert intergenerational solidarity by living in harmony with nature ... then, we may, at last, be able to live and let live, love and be loved.' (p. 360).

Although Castells' work is relatively new at the time of writing, it has already received significant critical attention. For example, Stalder (1998), whilst applauding its ambition and achievement, argues that no clear coherent theory emerges from it, and that it is singularly silent on specific courses of action that should be followed. Fuller (1999) comments favourably on many aspects of the volumes, but considers that Castells has largely ignored the prior theorizing of others on the role of information technology in society, leading to a reduction in the quality of analysis of this issue. He also criticizes the statistical methodology as over-detailed but too willing to extrapolate the future from current trends. Nevertheless, Castells raises many serious issues of the contemporary world, provides substantial empirical backing for his arguments, and supports many of the other writers reviewed earlier in emphasizing the need for new forms of conceptualization and political action in the changed world of today.

CONCLUSIONS

This chapter has introduced a wide range of important ideas and concepts of some key thinkers about contemporary society in a relatively short space, and necessarily has done some injustice to them. It is hoped that the interested reader may be encouraged to pursue some of these authors further by going back to the source documents. What about linkages between the writers? It is impossible to try to synthesize these connections into some overall model of contemporary society. Four points of connection only will be mentioned here, chosen as themes that broadly unite many of the authors that I have examined. A summary of these four themes is given in Table 2.1.

First, the contemporary world is undergoing major processes of change, labelled in various ways such as high modernity, the risk society or globalization. In addition to the evident increase in interconnection between societies, there is an increased consciousness of the world as a whole. This consciousness includes an awareness of the production of global risks that transcend national boundaries. The transnational corporations have increased their power in this new globalized world, a

Table 2.1   *Major themes on the contemporary world*

Major change processes are taking place	• High modernity (Giddens): time–space distanciation; disembedding; trust in expert systems; institutional reflexivity • Risk society (Beck): production of global risks; inadequate institutional control of these • Globalization (Robertson, Beck, Giddens): increased consciousness of the world (globality); increased interconnection between societies; increased power of the TNCs
Information and communication technologies are deeply implicated	• Time–space compression and zoning (Giddens, Robertson) • Information age (Castells): information generation, processing and transmission fundamental to organizational and societal change; IT enables pervasive expansion of networking throughout social structure • Potential for IT to aid political involvement (Beck, Castells)
Change processes are not uniform in their effects	• Indigenization in particular societies—glocalization (Robertson) • Ample room for deep study of specific geographies, histories and languages (Appadurai) • Excluded 'Fourth World' (Castells): much of sub-Saharan Africa; impoverished rural areas of Latin America and Asia; inner-city regions in First World; the urban poor in the Third World
There is an increased need for reflection and action	• Individual life projects (Giddens, Beck) • Important role of imagination in self-identity (Appadurai) • Opposition to the ideology of rule by world markets—globalism (Beck) • Resistance movements (Castells): environmentalism; feminism; religious movements • Role of the transnational state to limit power of agents of globalism (Beck)

cause of major concern to the writers in this chapter if issues of social inequity and exclusion are not tackled.

A second theme is that information and communication technologies are deeply implicated in the global changes that are taking place, through their ability to enable new modes of work, communication and organization across time and space, IT enables networking across wide reaches of time and space, and is intimately involved in changes in economic and social activity. This change process can have profound effects on self-identity, the nature of work and employment, organizational structure and networking, and the nature and governance of the nation state.

However, the change processes are not seen as uniform in their effects, and organizations and societies are likely to remain distinct and differentiated, although increasingly interconnected, through a process that has been labelled as glocalization. This arises through indigenization, meaning the selective appropriation of new ideas by different individuals, organizations and societies. We are entering an age of globalization and interconnection, but also one of multiculturalism, in the sense that many cultures with specific geographies, histories and languages will be involved, and will affect the nature of the future world. Unfortunately, there are many excluded segments of all societies, not solely in the Third World, who do not have access to the networks of information, wealth and power that characterize the new world order.

A final theme taken from the work of the writers reviewed in this chapter is an increased need for reflection and action on the part of individuals and groups, in order to address new issues in their lives and in the world as a whole. This can take various forms, such as the concept of active individual life projects. For those with limited choices or those searching for more communal identity, identification with cultural or religious groupings offers opportunities, and all individuals draw on their imagination to mould global elements to their local lives. Broader international networks such as the ecological movement and feminism also provide means for individual involvement, action and identity formation. A more directly political stance argues the need for opposition to the ideology of the rule of world markets, globalism, and for the important role of the state in this opposition.

There are many important and interesting ideas here, the work of what may be loosely labelled macro-sociologists. They provide a thoughtful overall picture or pictures of the contemporary world, but the detail is missing. Although they do usually discuss the important role of information and communication technologies, no specific evidence is normally provided. Little detail is given on real organizations, and certainly not on individual lives, with a few minor exceptions. It is rather like seeing the world from a plane, a much neater and tidier picture than the messiness of life on the ground. A key purpose of this book is to go down to ground level and to look in detail at the role of IT in the changing world.

The aim is not to contradict the broad claims of the macro-thinkers, but rather to unpack them somewhat. In trying to gain a detailed understanding of IT in a global context, it is necessary to examine some of the enormous diversity of what constitutes the individual, firm or society in the contemporary world. This is the focus and purpose of the empirical chapters in Parts 2 and 3 of the book. To go down from the macro of this chapter to the micro of the empirical chapters, and to connect the two together, some conceptual tools for analysis are needed, not provided by the macro-theorists. This is the purpose of the next chapter.

3
Computers at Work

I argued in the previous chapter that information and communication technologies are crucial elements in the changes that are taking place in contemporary society. The authors whose work has been discussed so far have largely considered the issues of societal change and the role of IT at a broad level of generality. I move in Parts 2 and 3 of the book to detailed analyses of specific topics, such as IT in teamworking (Chapter 5) or in cross-cultural enterprises (Chapter 9). In this final chapter of Part 1, I introduce some further conceptual tools that will be drawn on in these later empirical chapters.

Four broad conceptual areas are developed in the sections below, designed to provide analytical constructs to examine IT and contemporary society at the more micro-level. The four areas are, however, linked to the broader macro-themes from the previous chapter. The first conceptual area concerns *data, information and knowledge*. Information and knowledge were identified as of increased significance in contemporary society, for example by Castells in his description of current society as the 'information age'. But how should we conceptualize information and knowledge? What analytical tools are available to think about issues such as knowledge generation, sharing and transfer? Do different societies view information and knowledge in different ways?

The second conceptual area concerns the specific *role of information technology*, which was identified as a crucial feature of contemporary society by all the writers discussed in Chapter 2. But how should we conceptualize information and communication technologies at the micro-level of analysis? Should these be seen as neutral resources or, as argued later in this chapter, as deeply implicated in change processes, both reflecting and forming the attitudes and aspirations of their designers and users?

To investigate information and knowledge, and the role of information technology, at the micro-level, it is necessary to examine situated work practices, and the third conceptual area concerns the nature of *improvisation and appropriation* in work situations. The first of these refers to the non-routinized nature of work practice, and the second to the way that information technology is appropriated to support particular work activity. Standard approaches to work practice, such as business process re-engineering, and specific information and communication technologies, such as groupware, have an increasingly wide reach in a more globalized world. But how does this reflect in similarity and difference in actual work practice in particular contexts? Analytical tools concerned with improvisation and appropriation can help to examine such a question.

Finally, new trends in contemporary society can be analysed in terms of *power and politics*, as discussed at the macro-level by the authors reviewed in Chapter 2. But how do power and politics manifest themselves at the more micro-level of analysis? For example, what approaches are attempted to increase surveillance and control through IT in the globalized world, but also what opportunities exist for resistance? The penultimate section of this chapter will provide some conceptual tools concerning power and politics as ways of addressing such questions. The final section of the chapter will outline how the various conceptual areas developed below will be used in the rest of the book.

DATA, INFORMATION AND KNOWLEDGE

Data are the most fundamental elements of the digital age, normally represented, manipulated and transmitted as 0s and 1s in computers and telecommunications systems. They are a formalized representation of elements of the real world: facts, concepts or instructions. Two different observers will normally agree on the content of a particular datum, such as the numbers in a particular table, but their meaning is an altogether different matter. There may be a dispute as to why these particular numbers were selected in the first place to represent a specific real-world situation, whether they have been calculated 'correctly' in methodological terms, and what significance should be attributed to them in analysing a particular situation.

This brings us to information. The terms data and information are often used synonymously in everyday English, but most academic authors make a distinction. Checkland and Holwell (1998) provide a useful summary of the variety of definitions of these terms in the information systems field, and on the basis of this review they argue that there is a partial consensus that data are transformed into information when meaning is attributed to them. If we take information then as a particular person's interpretation of specific data, one can attempt to transmit this 'in-formation' to others (Boland 1987), but the meaning for others may well be different. In addition, the same data may be interpreted differently by a particular person at different times.

An illustration of the above can be given by the example of the monthly sales figures for a particular product at a specific point in time. Setting aside the possibility that these have been calculated incorrectly, Person A may interpret the figures, which are higher than the previous month, as indicating an upturn in sales for the product. Person B may point out that there are seasonal effects that normally make this a high sales month, and thus may derive the information from the sales data that underlying sales are actually declining. It is, of course, possible that the two people may 'agree' after further discussion, but it is likely that there will be shades of different meaning in their two positions. At a later stage, several months later, when further sales data are available, showing, for example, a significant decline in sales, both parties will probably assign a new meaning to the data for the original month. The information or meaning conveyed by particular data is personal, often contested, and mutable over time.

The third basic term that is widely used in connection with data and information is knowledge. This has become a fashionable concept in recent years in the business world, and is used in all sorts of phrases such as knowledge workers and knowledge management. However, the meaning of the term knowledge is even more problematic than that of information. It can be argued that individual knowledge enables a person to interpret data and thus derive information. But what about the non-individual knowledge contained in books, embedded in systems, or implicit in shared ways of doing things? The rest of this section will summarize some theories of knowledge, and will introduce the problems of generating new knowledge and sharing knowledge with others, these latter issues being of key concern to organizations. A summary of key conceptual tools in this area is given in Table 3.1.

Table 3.1   *Some key conceptual tools on knowledge*

Types of knowledge	Embrained, embodied, encultured, embedded, encoded (Blackler)
Processes of knowing	Knowledgeable organizational practice derives from: role-related expectations; prior dispositions; interactive–situational dimension (Tsoukas)
Knowledge conversion typology	Between tacit and explicit knowledge: socialization; externalization; internalization; combination (Nonaka)
Sharing knowledge across cultures	Different attitudes to nature of knowledge and approaches to sharing knowledge (Lam)

Theories of Knowledge

Blackler (1995) provides a valuable categorization of five common types of knowledge in the literature as embrained, embodied, encultured, embedded and encoded. Embrained knowledge refers to individual conceptual skills or cognitive abilities. Mathematicians or financial analysts provide archetypal examples of individuals who possess valued mental knowledge of this type. The knowledge is reflected in the person's ability to use these mental skills to prove a theorem, or to carry out a complex financial transaction.

A second category of individual knowledge is that which is embodied in the person, reflected not in terms of cognitive capabilities necessarily, although these play a part, but in their ability to carry out particular actions with the body. A footballer or other skilled sports person provides an example here. The execution of effective play is largely instinctive, based on bodily skill and extensive practice. Skilled craft workers also have embodied knowledge that is not easily learnt by others, and may indeed be impossible to learn for some individuals, being partially reliant, as with cognitive abilities, on innate ability.

Encultured knowledge refers to the process of achieving shared understandings, which can take place at any number of levels, including groups, organizations and societies. Shared knowledge, as discussed earlier in the context of shared information, will normally reflect subtle individual differences as well as agreements. However, the concept of encultured knowledge is that it reflects shared meaning on 'how we do it here' in a particular group or organization, or how to act in a particular cultural context.

Embedded knowledge is a second category of shared knowledge, which is reflected in routines. It could be taken to be a sub-class of encultured knowledge, but it places emphasis on taken-for-granted routines and interactions that enable shared action on the part of a team or larger organization. An example here would be a team of programmers who follow sets of implicit or explicit routines to coordinate their activity of software production. The flying crew of an aeroplane use routines, only partly explicit, that reflect embedded knowledge on how to fly a plane safely.

Finally, encoded knowledge refers to the explicit knowledge representation in books, computer databases, or web sites. It is this type of knowledge which has, of course, seen an explosion in quantity and interest in the 'information age'. Much attention is focused on how to generate, capture, combine or transfer it. However, referring to the earlier discussion in this section, the data contained in these repositories reflect a particular representation of the real world that is highly selective, and they are open to different interpretations and may convey different information to particular individuals, groups or organizations.

Blackler uses his categorization of different knowledge types to argue that traditional conceptions of knowledge as abstract, disembodied, individual and formal are unrealistic. However, his different knowledge types are themselves overlapping and interacting, a point that Blackler argues is important to further work in this conceptual area:

> Knowledge is multi-faceted and complex, being both situated and abstract, implicit and explicit, distributed and individual, physical and mental, developing and static, verbal and encoded. Analysis of the relationships between different manifestations of knowledge ... is at least as significant as any delineation of their differences (pp. 1032–1033).

Finally, Blackler argues that the very concept of knowledge has a rather static feel about it, and that it would be desirable to focus more on the processes of knowing. Knowing is situated in a particular context, provisional in its nature since new data become available and new interpretations of the world are made, pragmatic in the sense that it is mostly valued for its immediate practical application, and often contested since others will have different knowledge of the same phenomena. Following on from this latter point, relations between power and knowledge will be discussed in the final section with specific reference to the work of Foucault.

Tsoukas (1996) focuses on processes of knowing, and provides a thoughtful account of organizations as distributed knowledge systems.

He argues that knowledge is distributed both in terms of it being scattered and not able to be brought together in any full sense, but also in terms of the inability to capture what is needed in any particular circumstances. Knowledgeable organizational practice then, according to Tsoukas, derives from three sources. First, role-related social expectations impose broad normative expectations on individuals in terms of what is expected from them in their work. For example, a stock controller is expected to replenish stocks to appropriate levels when they run low. Second, any individual has a dispositional dimension, namely the system of mental patterns of perception, appreciation and action, which has been acquired by that individual via past socializations. Finally, there is the interactive—situational dimension, namely the specific open-ended context of a social activity within which normative expectations and previous dispositions are activated. I will say a little more about this dimension later in this chapter when considering the concept of improvisation. Tsoukas concludes that organizational members do follow broad rules, but that they do so in an inseparably contingent-cum-local manner. He argues that the role of management should therefore be concerned with facilitating knowledge between purposeful individuals, rather than in 'collecting' knowledge together:

> Given the distributed character of organizational knowledge, the key to achieving coordinated action does not so much depend on those 'higher up' collecting more and more knowledge, as those 'lower down' finding more and more ways of getting connected and inter-relating the knowledge each one has (p. 22).

Knowledge Generation and Sharing

The work of Nonaka is well known in the knowledge management field, and the dynamics of knowledge generation and sharing is the focus of Nonaka (1994). In this article, he argued that knowledge is created and shared through conversion between tacit and explicit knowledge, and he discussed four such conversions. He called the process of sharing tacit knowledge 'socialization', such as that obtained through apprenticeships. 'Combination' refers to the processes of combining explicit knowledge sources, in intranets, for example. 'Externalization' is the attempt to convert tacit knowledge into explicit knowledge, a process of knowledge capture. Finally, he describes 'internalization' as the processes of becoming in-formed from explicit knowledge sources, which is related to traditional theories of learning.

Nonaka's work is helpful in providing a relatively simple conceptual scheme in which to examine various processes of knowledge generation and sharing in specific organizations. Blackler (1995) converts Nonaka's ideas to his own terminology, and argues that Nonaka is suggesting that encultured knowledge, in an organization, for example, is intimately related to the development of embodied, embrained and embedded knowledge, and the links through which they are created. Blackler does not mention encoded knowledge here, which is surprising since Nonaka places considerable emphasis on this in his categories of combination and externalization, as well as in internalization to some extent.

Tsoukas (1996) considers that typologies such as that of Nonaka have advanced our understanding of organizational knowledge by showing its multi-faceted nature, but that such typologies have certain limitations from the 'formistic' type of thinking inherent in them. For example, Tsoukas argues that Nonaka's distinction between tacit and explicit knowledge is too rigid, since these knowledge types are mutually constitutive. The tacit knowledge of individuals underpins any action that they take, even if they are using a source of explicit knowledge as an input to that action, and thus tacit knowledge is a necessary component of all knowledge.

Authors such as Blackler, Tsoukas and Nonaka are valuable in forcing us to think carefully about the meaning of knowledge and the processes of its creation and sharing. The popular management literature has taken up this theme, but the same analytical precision is not always present. For example, the paper by Hansen, Nohria and Tierney (1999) is interesting in discussing the knowledge management strategies of companies in several US industries, including management consulting firms. The paper argues that two distinct strategies are pursued. In the first, the codification strategy, knowledge is 'carefully codified and stored in databases'. In the second, the personalization strategy, knowledge is closely tied to the person who developed it, and is shared mainly through direct person-to-person contacts. Hansen and his co-authors found that all companies used both strategies, but they argue that effective firms focused mainly on one of the strategies and used the other in a supporting role.

Whilst the above analysis has some interest, it avoids many of the more complex issues in knowledge management. For example, in talking about codification, knowledge 'is extracted from the person who developed it, made independent of that person, and reused for various purposes'. This begs the question as to whether any of these processes are feasible, and to what extent. Tacit knowledge, for instance, cannot necessarily be extracted or made independent of the person who developed it. Its 'reuse' by someone else presupposes that the information provided to another person, by the externalized data, is the same as that for the original generator of the 'knowledge', a view that we have challenged throughout this section.

Sharing Knowledge Across Cultures

The complexity of the processes of knowledge generation and sharing takes on a further dimension when we consider work in more globalized contexts needing to take place across cultures. Lam (1997) provides a fascinating grounded case study of the nature and methods of transmission of knowledge in a Japanese and a British high-technology firm, attempting to collaborate on particular joint ventures. In particular, Lam examined the education and on-the-job training of Japanese and British engineers in the two firms, and analysed why they worked in very different ways that made cooperation and knowledge-sharing difficult.

The engineers in the British firm based their specialist expertise primarily on abstract theoretical knowledge acquired through formal university training. In contrast the Japanese engineers relied heavily on practical know-how and problem-solving techniques accumulated in their workplace. Product development in the British firm was organized on a sequential and hierarchical basis, so that the knowledge required for each stage tended to be relatively self-contained. In contrast, product development in the Japanese firm was typically undertaken by a multi-functional team, consisting of members with diverse backgrounds, and took in all the stages of planning, design and development, quality assurance and production.

These differences in educational background, bases of skills, and approach to coordination of work were reflected in different methods of knowledge transmission through the product cycle. In the British firm, coordination across the functions was achieved by passing on detailed documents and full specifications from one stage to the next. This required 'externalizing' knowledge and coding and structuring it into procedures, guidelines or specifications for transmission to others. In contrast, the Japanese firm was highly dependent on intensive human-network-based communication. Knowledge required for overall project achievement was stored 'organically' in team relationships and behavioural routines.

Attempts were made to get the British and Japanese engineers to work together and to share knowledge, but these were largely unsuccessful.

The mutual incomprehension is nicely captured in Lam's paper by two quotes from a British and Japanese engineer respectively:

> You've got two ways of doing something. You are either very much more rigorous about the way you design it and try to ensure you do it right, or you just have a scatter-brain effect and just hope something will work. This is the way I see the (Japanese firm) ... A lot of people do lots of little things and it's like waiting for revolution (p. 982).

> They [the British Engineers] can read the specifications but I am not sure they have the ability to make the product. I think we have far more technical capacity—we've got the know-how. On this project, we have to supply them with a lot of our know-how but it's really difficult. There's so much of it which simply cannot be captured only by reading the documents (p. 982).

In the end, the management of the British and Japanese firms abandoned attempts at genuine joint development work between their respective engineers, and divided the work on projects into compartments, leaving each team to pursue its own part of the projects in its own way.

In the language of Blackler's analysis of knowledge work, the knowledge of British engineers tends to be embrained and embedded in routines. Major attempts are made to translate this knowledge into an encoded form for the purposes of knowledge sharing. In contrast, the knowledge of Japanese engineers tends to be more embodied and encultured, the latter referring both to specific organizational cultures and to the more general 'way of doing things' in a Japanese context. Much of this knowledge is considered difficult to encode, and knowledge sharing mostly occurs in face-to-face contact rather than through explicit codified knowledge bases. It is not surprising that this lack of match between the British and Japanese engineers resulted in major problems of communication and inhibited effective knowledge transfer.

Lam's analysis of this attempt at cross-cultural working can be complemented by a separate study of 'knowledge works', an elite group of factories in the Toshiba group. Fruin (1997) carried out a five-year intensive study of the Yanagicho factory, and he argued that the superior performance of the factory was related to its culture and methods of organizing. According to Fruin, energy, vitality and creativity are expressed in a culture like Japan's through 'knowledge of forms'. In terms of work routines, this implies the following: 'Do what those before you have done, only do it at least as well or perhaps just a little better. One may supersede but never displace the established forms of experience and knowledge' (p. 27).

Traditional knowledge in a particular factory or work site is learnt and passed on through on-the-job processes of socialization and acculturation, and is not normally codified and formalized in written documents. The implicit process of passing on site-specific knowledge to the next generation relies on low levels of turnover in personnel and high levels of functional interdependence. Thus, although Yanagicho is a highly successful factory, any attempt to emulate its achievements in a different cultural context would be very difficult. This is not to say that lessons cannot be learned from Yanagicho of value outside Japan. Rather, it suggests the need for a sophisticated approach to thinking about the nature of knowledge and organization in specific sites such as Yanagicho, in order to consider whether and to what extent the successful aspects of work at the site can be translated to different organizational and cultural contexts.

THE ROLE OF IT

I have touched above on the role of IT in the processes of generation and use of data, information and knowledge. In this section I address this issue as a central theme. Is IT a neutral element in work and organizations? Or does it contain essential features that determine the way that it is used, and thus its effects are not neutral? The broad position that is adopted in this book is neither of these. Information technologies have properties that can and do influence their adoption and use, but there is considerable flexibility in how they are interpreted and used. Grint and Woolgar (1997) emphasize that what we know about technology is a social interpretation: 'Our knowledge of technology is ... essentially social; it is a construction rather than a reflection of the machine's capabilities. Of course, not any construction is possible; the construction of technological capacity is not itself unconstrained' (p. 10).

The technical and the social must be considered together, and in specific contexts, in order to investigate the role of technology in work and organizations. The rest of this section is a development of this thesis, and is focused on some specific concepts and theories that provide analytical support to the broad approach.

Social Construction of Technology

An influential approach to the conceptualization of the role of technology in micro-studies was provided by the group of writers whose work can be broadly classified as the 'social construction of technology (SCOT)' (Bijker, Hughes and Pinch 1987). Their work emphasized that technology is developed and implemented by social groups, and that its final form is the product of a complex social process of interaction of these groups. There is nothing inevitable about this process, in the sense that it is not predetermined that a particular technology will take a particular form, but that this depends on the contingencies and politics of the social process. The early studies that used this approach concerned material technologies such as bicycles, bakelite and light bulbs. However, the methodological approach of tracing the history of the interaction of the relevant social groups surrounding a developing technology can be applied to information technology (e.g. Sahay and Robey 1996).

The early SCOT studies were criticized on a number of grounds. A key criticism was that final closure is normally arrived at in such studies when the artefact gains general acceptance. However, an artefact in use remains open to some degree at least of interpretation by users. This criticism is highly relevant to the domain of information technology, where the merits and demerits of a computerized information system remain open to debate on a continuous basis, and discussion and reinterpretation does not cease on system delivery, or even when the system is in regular use. A further criticism of the SCOT methodology was that it underemphasized the role of individual actors compared with the influence of broader social structures.

One of the original SCOT pioneers developed a later approach that took account of these criticisms (Bijker 1995). He replaced the concept of closure by the idea that a technology sometimes reaches high levels of stabilization, but that this is not irreversible. He added the concept of a 'technological frame' to SCOT studies, this being all the elements that influence the interactions among the actors of a relevant social group, and that lead to particular attribution of meanings to technical artefacts. These elements include attributes of the technology itself, organizational constraints, and the norms and values of that social group.

An example of a study of information technology that drew on the SCOT literature, and the concept of technological frames, is Orlikowski and Gash (1994). They used an empirical study of a groupware technology to analyse the different technological frames of the relevant stakeholder groups in the study: managers, technologists and users.

They showed how the interaction of the various groups, based on their frames, resulted in outcomes that deviated from those expected. They argued that technological frames offer a valuable analytical perspective for investigating actions and meanings surrounding a specific information technology.

Actor-Network Theory

Actor-network theory (ANT) is an alternative approach to that of SCOT for conceptualizing the role of technology in micro-studies. These theories share some common origins, in the sense that there has been regular interaction between members of the two schools of thought throughout their development. ANT has been taken up by a relatively wide range of researchers carrying out interpretive studies of the role of information technology, and I comment on some of this work later. First, a brief overview of the theory is provided.

The initial development and application of actor-network theory was concerned with the sociology of science, and was pioneered at the Ecole des Mines in Paris by Callon (1986) and Latour (1987). Later work has included a strong focus on technology (Latour 1996). The theory is not a stable body of knowledge that can be drawn on by researchers in an unproblematic way, since its developers themselves have frequently revised or extended elements of it. However, some basic aspects of the theory have remained relatively stable over the last decade or so of its development and use, and Table 3.2 provides a brief summary of key conceptual tools in the theory.

Actor-network theory examines the motivations and actions of actors who form elements, linked by associations, of heterogeneous networks of aligned interests. A key feature of the theory is that actors (or actants as they are sometimes labelled) are taken to include both human beings and non-human actors such as technological artefacts. A major focus of the theory when applied in particular contexts is to try to trace and explain the processes whereby relatively stable networks of aligned interests are created and maintained, or alternatively to examine why such networks fail to establish themselves. Successful networks of aligned interests are created through the enrolment of a sufficient body of allies, and the translation of their interests so that they are willing to participate in particular ways of thinking and acting that maintain the network.

Bloomfield *et al.* (1992) point out that the analysis of the various stratagems employed, such as the use of persuasive rhetoric to construct

Table 3.2 *Some key conceptual tools in actor-network theory*

Actor (or actant)	Both human beings and non-human actors such as technological artefacts
Actor network	Heterogeneous network of aligned interests, including, for example: people, organizations and standards
Enrolment and translation	Creating a body of allies, human and non-human, through a process of translating their interests to be aligned with the actor network
Delegates and inscription	Delegates are actors who 'stand in and speak for' particular viewpoints that have been inscribed in them
Irreversibility	The degree to which it is subsequently impossible to go back to a point where alternative possibilities exist
Black box	A frozen network element, often with properties of irreversibility
Immutable mobile	Network element with strong properties of irreversibility, and effects that transcend time and space

and maintain network allegiances, draws much from Machiavelli. However, they note the addition in actor-network theory that non-human resources, such as a graph in a scientific paper, can be used to 'stand in and speak for', or be delegates for, particular viewpoints or truth-statements that help to maintain a particular network of alliances. Bowker and Star (1994) make a similar representational point with respect to computer systems and software:

> Modern information technologies embed and inscribe work in ways that are important for policy-makers, but which are often difficult to see ... arguments, decisions and uncertainties ... are hidden away inside a piece of technology or in a complex representation. Thus values, opinions and rhetoric are frozen into codes, electronic thresholds and computer applications. Extending Marx, then, we can say that in many ways, software is frozen organizational discourse (p. 187).

The idea of software as frozen discourse is an example of an inscription that resists change and displays properties of irreversibility. Callon (1991) says that the degree of irreversibility of a particular element of a network depends on the extent to which it is subsequently impossible to go back to a point where alternative possibilities exist, and the extent to which the particular frozen element shapes and determines subsequent inscriptions. A frozen element that is not 'opened' to question by the actors in the network is termed a black box. Actor-network theory uses the concept of immutable mobiles to describe network elements that display strong properties of irreversibility and are mobile across time and space; various software standards provide illustrations of immutable mobiles.

The philosophy and concepts of ANT have become much more widely known in recent years, and an increasing number of IS researchers are making explicit use of the theory in their work. Three examples are mentioned here. Bloomfield *et al.* (1992) describe an interesting case study of the development of a particular set of resource management information systems in the UK National Health Service. They use actor-network theory to illustrate their argument against the view of technology as a given, but instead illustrate how the boundary between the technical and the social, and the relationship between them, is the subject of ongoing struggles and trials of strength in creating 'facts'.

Boland and Schultze (1996) adopt the vocabulary of ANT to describe activity-based costing as an accounting technology that has been made 'true', and has been established as a widespread practice through a process of translation. Allies have been enrolled, black boxes have been constructed to enshrine the approach, and arguments have been built up into many layered defences against adherents of traditional cost-accounting techniques. The authors undermine the certainties of this fact-construction process by telling a different story, or anti-narrative, where the merits of the two techniques are reversed.

Monteiro and Hanseth (1996) focus on the role of standards, particularly those embedded in infrastructures, in prescribing and proscribing forms of interaction with information technology. Their examples involve EDI systems in the Norwegian health sector, and concern the definition of a message standard for identifying a drug prescription and one for exchanging test results. In both cases, they illustrate the processes of translation and inscription that were taking place, and they contrast the relative successes of the network building in the two cases.

ANT has its critics, like any theory. Walsham (1997) summarized a range of criticisms, two of which I will mention here. First, the theory has been challenged for addressing local and contingent effects, but paying little attention to broader social structures that influence the local. This contrasts, for example, with structuration theory (Giddens 1984), which deals directly with social action and structure at multiple levels, and which has been drawn on to inform studies of the development and use of computerized information systems (for a summary of this work, see Jones 1998). However, structuration theory has itself been criticized as offering nothing specific on how to conceptualize the role of technology in social process. One way forward here is to use structuration theory to guide broader social analysis of a micro-case study, combined with the methodology of ANT to analyse the detailed socio-technical processes that took place.

A second criticism of ANT, forcefully articulated by Winner (1993), is that the social constructivists, and this includes SCOT proponents also, show 'almost total disregard ... for the social consequences of technical choice'. In other words, that too much attention is paid to the detail of what choices were made and why in the development of a particular technology, but not enough to the moral and political consequences of those choices. Bijker (1993) responded directly to the critique of Winner by arguing that an amoral stance is not a necessity of the social constructivist approach.

Latour (1999) also provides a counter to the argument of the amorality of the ANT type of studies of science and technology. This later book by a key founder of the genre provides a substantial restatement of his philosophical position, illuminated by interesting empirical material. He uses many of the conceptual tools referred to in Table 3.2, but adds some new ideas, and takes a quite political stance in advocating the need for citizen engagement in debates about science and technology in society. The broad philosophical position adopted by Latour and others in the actor-network theory tradition, and the specific concepts discussed in this section, will be used in the analysis of the empirical material in some of the later chapters.

IMPROVISATION AND APPROPRIATION

The importance of people's interpretations and attitudes regarding information technology is emphasized by all the theories outlined above. Their perception of the technology influences its use in action, and theories such as SCOT and ANT describe this to some extent. However, the detailed way in which people carry out their work in everyday practice is not a central feature of these theories. In this section we examine some conceptual approaches to an understanding of day-to-day work practices, and in particular the ways in which people use information and communication technologies as part of that practice. A summary of key conceptual tools in this area is provided in Table 3.3.

Table 3.3   *Some key conceptual tools on improvisation and appropriation*

Local, situated nature of work practice	• Plans and situated actions are related but distinct (Suchman) • Key role of local community in situated work practice (Star)
Improvisation: the non-routine nature of work and action	• Order and control mixed with innovation and autonomy (Weick) • Improvisation as fundamental (Ciborra)
IT needs to be appropriated to support improvisation	• Many contemporary IS not designed to support improvisation (Ciborra) • Need to fit IT to situated work practice through bricolage (Büscher and Mogenson)
Appropriation of Western IT likely to be more difficult to achieve in non-Western contexts	• Different models and conceptions of reality • For example, no need for active externalization of meaning in Nepal (Malling)

Routinization and Situated Improvisation

We are all familiar with the concept of routine and the way in which it provides a basis for many of our day-to-day activities, including those in the workplace. Giddens (1984) connected this routinization to feelings of personal security and anxiety reduction. However, Giddens also emphasized that people are reflexive, in the sense that we monitor and reflect on our own practice and that of others, on the planned and unplanned effects of our intentional actions, and on changes in our environment. This reflexivity forms the basis for our subsequent actions, which are therefore not necessarily repetitions of what we have done before.

Further challenges to the centrality of routine in understanding work practice come from authors who focus on the local, situated and contingent nature of that practice. Suchman (1987) argued that plans and situated actions are distinct, illustrating this divergence using an extended example of the local practices of technicians repairing copying machines. Star (1995) emphasized the role of local community in situated work practice, providing illustrations from a range of settings including 'routine' factory work, in which workers broke up the boredom of repetitive activities with various forms of community-based humour and story-telling. Star argued against individualistic explanations for cognition, feeling and remembering, seeing such activities as situated within a local 'web' of people, their perceptions, and their actions.

Improvisation is a word that expresses aspects of the non-routine nature of work and action. Weick (1998) discussed improvising in organizations, using jazz improvisation to provide a 'source of orienting ideas'. He used the definition of improvisation given by Berliner (1994): 'Improvisation involves reworking pre-composed material and designs in relation to unanticipated ideas conceived, shaped, and transformed under the special conditions of performance, thereby adding unique features to every creation' (p. 241).

An important point to note here is that improvisation in this sense is not an alternative to routine, but is reliant on it. The precomposed material is the solid basis, and the improvisation works with this. Order and control are mixed with innovation and autonomy. There are clear links here with Tsoukas' ideas on the inseparability of tacit and explicit knowledge, as reviewed in the earlier knowledge section of the chapter, and their use together in specific interactive situations.

Weick investigated parallels with non-jazz settings, and quoted the work of Mangham and Pye (1991) in this domain. He noted that the process of managing shares with jazz improvising such features as simultaneous reflection and action, simultaneous rule creating and rule following, and the continuous mixing of the expected with the novel. He thus derived some characteristics that are needed by groups with a high capability for improvisation, including a willingness to forego planning in favour of acting, an openness to re-assembly of and departures from routines, and a preference for process rather than structure. Weick cautioned that improvisation may benefit only some organizations under some conditions, but may be a liability under other conditions. An example that springs to mind is the flying of a plane, where passengers would prefer the pilots to rely primarily on routines, with improvisation reserved for the occasional unexpected occurrence.

Ciborra (1999) also writes interestingly about improvisation in organizations. His approach is broadly compatible with that of Weick, but he adopts a stronger view than Weick in seeing improvisation as more fundamental than routine:

> Improvisation is fundamental, while structured methods and procedures possess a derived and de-rooted character. A formalized procedure embeds a set of explicit in-order-to's, but the way these are actually interpreted and put to work strictly depends upon the actor's in-order-to's and because-of motives, his/her way of being in the world ... (p. 85).

Ciborra is arguing that improvisation is much closer to our natural being in terms of who we are and how we read the world, whereas routine works with predigested bits of the past, or lumps of experience that have been made explicit. In terms of the knowledge management concepts introduced earlier, Ciborra is saying that encoded or embedded knowledge is less fundamental to a person's being-in-the-world than other forms such as embrained, encultured or embodied. It does not necessarily follow, however, that the former knowledge types are less important for organizational life as a whole, a conclusion that could perhaps be inferred from Ciborra's work.

Appropriation of IT

If we now consider the role of IT in the support of work practice, the above discussion would suggest that IT can be used to support routine processes or improvisation or both. However, the type of systems needed to do this may well differ, and it is important to consider which type of work practice is being supported. Ciborra (1996a), in line with his other work discussed above, places an emphasis on information systems to support improvisation. Indeed, he argues strongly that if IT is used to automate structured, planned decisions, then the risk is to automate ungrounded organizational processes, i.e. ones that do not reflect the reality and variety of actual work practice:

> What is missing in the design of many contemporary IS is an effective link between the planned, automated decision process and all those tacit aspects, such as the because-of motives, or past experience, which give meaning to the development and implementation of a decision. This is why automated procedures tend so often to be underutilized, for they do not match changing circumstances, badly mimic the know-how of even a novice, feel unnatural and clumsy, seem to lack meaning and be out of context, and are full of loopholes which have to be filled by [improvised] human intervention (p. 375).

Ciborra argues that different types of information systems are needed to support improvised practice as compared with routine. He suggests examples of groupware systems to support interaction between teams, and organizational memory systems to store aspects of past experience.

Büscher and Mogensen (1997) provide a specific case study of the work of interpreting, mediating and shaping involved in the processes of 'technology transfer', or the fitting of particular technologies to actual work practice. They use the term *bricolage* (Lévi-Strauss 1966), a term borrowed from anthropology:

> ... designing immediately, using ready-to-hand materials, combinations of already existing pieces of technology—hardware, software and facilities (e.g. Internet providers)—as well as additional, mostly off-the-shelf ones. It therefore involves design as assembly. It is most important, however, that this is not just an assembly of technical components, but also of appropriate work practices, skills, training, communications ... (p. 79).

Their case study involved the work practice of a company of landscape architects. They describe, for example, how the fitting of a graphical software package encountered problems of time constraints and lack of technical skill. These were worked around using simple manual procedures such as passing on of lists of colours, and the rebooting of systems each time a particular unexplained error occurred. They provide other examples of the improvised fitting of computer-aided design systems and an Internet link for communication between branches.

The processes I am talking about here involve the appropriation of information technology by particular individuals, groups or organizations, and the need for work and technology to co-evolve in order that the information systems can be made genuinely to support work practice. However, whilst agreeing with the above authors on the need to support improvisation, they perhaps downplay the role of systems to support routinized activities. The booking of an airline ticket, the generation of an invoice, or the calculation of a set of sales figures from raw data, do not normally need the same amount of fine-tuning to particular work contexts. This is not to say that any two work contexts are the same. However, differences between an effective airline booking system in Tokyo and Toronto may well be smaller than, for example, a system to support group decision-making in the two countries, since approaches to the taking of decisions differ significantly in different societies.

Appropriation in Different Cultures

This leads on to the appropriation of information technology in different cultural contexts. Most of the developments in information technology have taken place in Western countries. The adaptation of the technology to work practice in a specific organizational context in a given country, particularly the improvised elements of this, is difficult as noted above. However, an obvious hypothesis is that problems are likely to be greater in a cultural context far removed from that where the technology was originally developed.

Lind (1991) explored this issue in some depth, using a detailed example of the introduction of a computerized production control system, COPICS, into an Egyptian car manufacturing company, NASCO. His basic conclusion was that the model of a production system implicit in COPICS was a poor match with the actual functioning of the production system in NASCO, where the rationality was based on Egyptian norms and values. In the language of the social construction of technology, the computer system contained embedded elements reflecting the social context and process of its development, and many of these elements were not easily reversible. In actor-network terms, COPICS can be viewed as a non-human actant, standing in and speaking for the viewpoints of its Western developers.

Specific examples given by Lind of the mismatch between COPICS and NASCO included the assumption that users of the computer system would react instantly to problems that arose in their area, and would take action to correct things. However, middle-level supervisors and managers were not given the responsibility to do this. Lind argues that systems like COPICS are designed around a Western approach to decision-making with respect to delegation of authority, whereas in Egypt decision-making tends to be highly centralized. A second example concerned the more uncertain external environment of an Egyptian company, factors that were not present in COPICS. These included the availability of imported material, great fluctuations in lead times, and changes imposed by government. Lind summarizes his conclusions as follows:

> This book is an attempt to point out how computer programs, developed in the more advanced industrialized countries and based on models and conceptions of reality that are prevailing in these countries, tend to be inappropriate under different conditions in developing countries. The reason, so it is argued in the book, is that models do not have the same explanation value in different cultures (p. xiii).

Kluzer (1991) points out, in a review of Lind's book, that the reader might be misled into thinking that it deals only with the transferability of production-oriented applications, a relatively minor area of computer use in developing countries. In fact, Kluzer notes that this choice shows that even a process like car production, which many would think to be subject to relatively universal functioning criteria, cannot be properly understood, modelled and managed by abstracting from the context within which it is set.

A related theme was developed by Malling (2000) in the context of Nepal. He argued that IT is grounded in the need of Western countries for an active externalization of meaning, while in Nepal such a need is not prevalent. He illustrated this argument using a case study of a computer systems development project in a Nepalese government department. The project was initiated in conjunction with a large Danish non-governmental organization. The main objectives of the project were the establishment of a system for collection and dissemination of information, including the implementation of a management information system. However, even though literacy levels were high, there was no tradition of using written language for internal communication. It was not common to use writing to plan or evaluate activities. The systems developed by the external consultants were not in keeping with the form of communication and action in the Nepalese cultural context, and were not used to any extent. Individuals saw information as a resource which they were reluctant to 'give away':

> Information is frequently seen as a resource, as a commodity, you only give away if you get something back ... The safest way to secure full right over the information is naturally not to externalise it at all. The moment that it is put on paper, it is possible for another to get hold of it. Storing it on IT is even more chancy, as copying it is that much easier. Putting the information on an intranet, or even the Internet, causes it to lose its market value as it becomes accessible to the public (p. 16).

The two examples cited above on the difficulties of transferring IT between Western and developing country contexts are typical of the literature written by those who have spent time analysing such processes (see, for example, Avgerou and Walsham 2000). However, the conclusion should not be drawn that IT is wholly inappropriate to developing country contexts. Rather, the inference is that processes of appropriation of IT into work practice in such contexts must take account of the additional complexity of the norms and values of a non-Western culture. I will investigate this phenomenon in some detail in the empirical chapters of the book, particularly in Part 3 focused on non-Western cultures.

POWER AND POLITICS

The fourth conceptual area in this chapter focuses on power and politics, and their relationship to information technology. It is of fundamental importance to analyse such issues, which can be considered to underlie all individual, organizational and societal practices, since power is endemic to all human activities. The issues considered in the book to date can all be viewed from the perspective of power and politics. Referring back to Chapter 1, the forces of globalism can be thought of as opposed by a range of resistance movements, and indeed the process of globalization as a whole is concerned with ideas and values, sometimes in conflict. In this chapter, power and politics have been present implicitly in much of what has been discussed so far. For example, the relationship between knowledge and power was touched on earlier, and actor-network theory considers the political processes of enrolment and translation. The Nepalese resistance to giving away information, and thus rejection of Western-origin IT systems, as discussed above, can be seen as a political action designed to maintain or reinforce existing asymmetries of power relations *vis-à-vis* those without access to the information.

Although the topic of power and politics has been present implicitly in much of the earlier material, the purpose of this section is to address it directly. The stance taken here takes a relational view of power, in the sense that power is not conceived as something that one possesses in an absolute sense, by virtue, for example, of position or access to resources, but as manifested in shifting power relationships with others. This is not to argue that attributes such as job status or wealth are unimportant to power relationships, but that relations between two individuals, for example, are not determined in some fixed way by those attributes. Other aspects of the history of the situation, such as their past encounters, and the current context of interaction, will also affect their relationship, and this can and does change over time. Politics will be viewed here as attempts to use resources, including power relationships, to achieve particular ends. A summary of key conceptual tools on power and politics discussed in this section is given in Table 3.4.

IT and Political Action

The literature on computer-based information systems has included a political stream for the past 20 years or so. For example, a classic case study by Markus (1983) described power and political action over an

Table 3.4 *Some key conceptual tools on power and politics*

Underlying importance of power relations and political action with respect to IT systems	• Relational view of power: manifested in shifting power relations with others • Politics as attempt to use resources, including power relations, to achieve particular ends
Power–knowledge inseparability	• Regimes of truth (Foucault): intermeshed sets of techniques, procedures, knowledge and power • IS contain representations of knowledge of use in political contexts
Surveillance and control	• IT informates (Zuboff): makes events, objects and people more visible. May be used to discipline conformance or enable creativity • Disciplinary society (Foucault): individuals in contemporary society self-regulate their behaviour to conform to materialistic norms, reproducing the technologies of the powerful • Surveillance can produce multiple forms of resistance in specific contexts (Lyon; Attewell)

extended period of several years in the introduction of a financial information system in an organization. The system had significant effects on both the divisional and central accounting functions, and was a major source of conflict between them. Kling and Iacono (1984) described the post-implementation politics related to a material requirements planning system. They discussed how key actors used the language of efficiency to help push the information systems development in a direction that increased their own capacities for control in the organization. Walsham and Waema (1994) described political actions and the exercise of power in the formulation and implementation of information systems strategy in a UK building society.

This stream of work has continued up to the present time, sometimes in the context of newer technologies. Brigham and Corbett (1997) described a case study of the introduction of electronic mail into an organization, and analysed political action and shifting power relations mediated through e-mail, using actor-network theory for analytical purposes. Brown (1998a) described the implementation of a hospital information support system by focusing on the narratives employed by individuals and groups in giving meaning to the technology in their lives. The paper illustrated how such narratives can be deployed in political actions designed to legitimate individual or group interests.

Berg (1998) discussed a wide range of work on the design of information technologies to support work practice, under such labels as computer-supported cooperative work and participatory design. He focused on the politics of technology, and argued that this does not involve the absence or presence of predetermined impacts, but a fully-fledged realization of technology as a crucial, never fully predictable and potentially creative force. Thus, there are no such things as 'democratic' technologies, for example, but the technology is one element in the specific network of power relations in a particular context. Participatory design involves a search for improved socio-technical configurations within this context:

> As active actants, whose teleology is never given, technologies become political agents through and through, touching upon any other constituent in the configuration they are part of. Here, a critical position implies immersing oneself in the networks described and searching for what is or can be achieved by new interlockings of artefacts and human work (p. 482).

Power–Knowledge Relations

In a number of the above references, a key role is assigned to language in enabling individuals or groups to express particular viewpoints on 'truth' and through this medium to exercise power. For example, Kling and Iacono wrote of 'the language of efficiency' being used to push computer systems that increased control. Brown's case study concerned the deployment of narratives in political action. This link between 'knowledge' of a situation or technology expressed through language, and power relations, has been the subject of significant theoretical analysis. I outline some of this analysis below, and indicate its relevance to work on information technology and systems.

A key writer in this area is Foucault (1980), who emphasized the inseparability of power and knowledge. According to Foucault, knowledge is something that can be expressed in language, and truth is knowledge that is held to be true. Being the possessor or interpreter of accepted knowledge enables the exercise of power. Thus, Foucault talks of institutions or societies having 'regimes of truth':

> ... that is, the types of discourse which it accepts and makes function as true; the mechanisms and instances which enable one

to distinguish true and false statements, the means by which each is sanctioned; the techniques and procedures accorded value in the acquisition of truth; the states of those who are charged with saying what counts as true (p. 131, cited in Introna 1997).

Regimes of truth are thus intermeshed sets of techniques, procedures, knowledge and power relations. Their relevance to an analysis of information technology is that, as we have seen earlier, technology itself can be regarded as a political actant in the production and reproduction of knowledge, truth and power. For example, one can interpret the resistance of Nepalese government officials to adopt new computerized information systems as an attempt to retain and reproduce an existing regime of truth in which information is the property of an individual and is not made available to others except at a price, thus enabling power to be exercised by its possessors. The attempt of an outside agency to introduce new computer systems could undermine this regime by legitimizing the concept of information as a shared resource, thus having a perceived negative effect on the position of such officials.

Haraway (1991) carried out work on scientific knowledge in research on primates, and also on the human immune system. Her analysis used the ideas of Foucault and the actor-network theorists, and she argued that information technology is a similar contested domain in which power and knowledge are inextricably intertwined. Information systems contain data that are themselves particular representations of knowledge and truth, and that are open to various interpretations and use in political contexts. Haraway provides a definition of 'rational knowledge' as an ongoing process of power-related interpretation:

> ... rational knowledge does not pretend to disengagement, to be from everywhere and so nowhere, to be free from interpretation, from being represented, to be fully self-contained or fully formalizable. Rational knowledge is a process of ongoing critical interpretation among 'fields' of interpreters and decoders. Rational knowledge is power-sensitive conversation ... (p. 196).

Surveillance and Control

A particular topic in the context of IT and its use in organizations and society, with strong power-sensitive aspects, is that of surveillance and control. The classic book by Zuboff (1988) coined the term 'informate' to describe the way in which computer-based information systems produce new information, or data in the terminology of this book, that makes activities, events and objects, and thus people, more visible. The positive side of this capability can be considered as offering additional insights on organizational process, and thus potential gains in efficiency and effectiveness. A possible negative side is the potential for increased surveillance and control, which could be considered harmful to the freedom and autonomy of the individual worker.

Zuboff drew on the earlier work of Foucault to refer to the architectural plan for a 'panopticon'. This was conceived by Bentham in the eighteenth century (Harrison 1983), 'consisting of a twelve-sided polygon formed in iron and sheathed in glass in order to create the effect of what Bentham called "universal transparency"'. Zuboff applied this to the concept of an 'information panopticon' whereby computerized information systems may have the potential to make human behaviour in organizations universally transparent. She did not, however, adopt a technologically determinist position, and believed that the degree to which this vision of centralized dominance through information systems would occur is a matter for social choice. Indeed, in a later article (Zuboff 1996), she argued that the real promise of 'informating' could only be realized if organizations broke away from hierarchical approaches to control, and tried to liberate the creativity of employees through new, more egalitarian, structures. She conceded, however, that there was little sign that this was happening.

Although Zuboff drew on Foucault's work, his analysis (Foucault 1979) was rather darker. He argued that contemporary society can be labelled as a 'disciplinary society' in which individuals self-regulate their behaviour to conform to various materialistic norms, and in turn this reproduces technologies of control by the powerful. The enormous emphasis on consumerism in the Western world and the richer developing countries, mediated by technologies such as television, provides an example that is even stronger than when Foucault carried out his analysis. In an organizational context, the work of Foucault relates directly to the visibility and surveillance capabilities of computer-based information systems, even though that was not his original focus:

> He who is subjected to a field of visibility, and who knows it, assumes responsibility for the constraints of power; he makes them play spontaneously on himself; he inscribes in himself the power relation in which he simultaneously plays both roles; he becomes the principle of his own subjection (Foucault 1979, pp. 201–202).

Lyon (1993) provided a thoughtful review of the work of Foucault in this area, and its relationship to electronic means of surveillance. He argued that the metaphor of the panopticon has obvious relevance in the direct monitoring of subordinates within the workplace that is highly prevalent in contemporary organizations, at least in a Western context. Interestingly, Lyon also cites an increase in consumer surveillance as a further example, and the growth of the Internet and associated consumer monitoring through e-commerce has strengthened this argument in the time since it was written. However, Lyon makes the point that the rise in consumerism, for example, was very rapid before the growth of electronic means of surveillance, and that one should not exaggerate the power of electronic media.

Lyon also touches on a further qualification to Foucault's analysis in that surveillance often creates resistance, or what Lyon calls 'outrage' against the panopticon. I have discussed processes of improvisation and appropriation of technology earlier in the chapter, and I noted there the ability of human beings to carry out specific situated action in context, and to appropriate information technology in sometimes unpredictable ways. People are not cultural dopes (Giddens 1984), although they are aware of power relations. They are often able to resist the imposition of surveillance that they consider excessive, part of a broader effect of what Giddens calls 'the dialectic of control', whereby the less powerful can try to evade, divert or change the nature of the control that others attempt to exert on them.

Attewell (1991) made a set of related points when discussing computer-based surveillance in the automated office. He argued that it has not been lack of technology that has prevented high levels of surveillance in the past, but there have been other reasons why work measurement has not been used more forcefully by managers to monitor employees. These reasons include concerns about office morale, a preference for group rather than individual measures, a trade-off between speed and quality, labour market explanations, organizational constraints on intervention and punishment, and the threat of sabotage. Attewell is not complacent about the possible dangers of increased electronic surveillance in the workplace. However, he supports a view that the levels of surveillance in a particular case are determined by the social choices made by managers and others, within a social context of considerable complexity that constrains and enables the various choices. An exploration of the specific features of a particular context requires detailed case study work, such as that contained in the empirical chapters of this book.

CONCLUSION

Four conceptual areas have been developed in this chapter, and a summary of key conceptual tools is provided by Tables 3.1–3.4. How will these tools be used in the forthcoming empirical chapters? Each chapter in Parts 2 and 3 deals with a specific topic, namely identity, teamworking, organizational change, inter-organizational processes, working in non-Western cultures, and cross-cultural working. The conceptual tools described in this chapter will be used to support analysis of these topics, but not in a mechanistic way. In other words, I will not use all of them explicitly in all the chapters, but rather use the conceptual tools selectively to illustrate specific analytical points.

The broad themes of Chapter 2 on contemporary society and the more micro-level conceptual tools developed in this chapter are interlinked, as described at the beginning of the chapter. Thus, in the forthcoming empirical chapters, no simple separation of these two ways of looking at the globalized world will be made. Instead, macro-level themes and micro-level conceptual tools will be blended together to provide analytical focus to the empirical material. In the final chapter of the book, Chapter 10, I will draw some overall conclusions related both to the macro-level themes and the micro-level conceptual tools, in the light of the evidence from the whole book. I turn now, however, to the first of the empirical chapters, the grist for the mill of the book.

Part 2
Changing Ways of Working

4
Shifting Identity

This is the first of the chapters that tackles a specific issue with respect to the role of IT in a changing world. The focus is shifting identities in the way that people see and construct themselves, with a particular emphasis on identity in the workplace. I have argued in Part 1 that information and communication technologies are strongly implicated in profound changes in the nature of work in contemporary society. The identity of individual workers, and their identification with particular occupational and professional groups, is affected by, and affects, the nature of work they carry out, and how they conceptualize themselves and their work role.

This chapter examines three case studies in some detail, representing a very small sample from the whole population of work categories, occupations, sectors and roles. However, the purpose of the chapter is to generalize some concepts, themes and insights from the case studies of potential relevance to other contexts. This is tackled in two ways. First, each of the case studies is self-contained and includes issues and implications derived directly from the field study in the particular case. Second, in the final section of the chapter, conclusions are developed for the topic of shifting identity as a whole, drawing on all the case material and using specific analytical themes and concepts derived from Part 1. In particular, this analytical summary will examine the questions:

- How are globalization processes implicated in shifting identity in the workplace?
- What is the role of information and communication technologies in these processes?

- How is identity linked to knowledge and shifting power–knowledge relations?

A brief outline of the three case studies is as follows. The first case study looks at the changing work and professional identity of computer hardware engineers in a UK division of a multinational company. The second case study examines work and identity issues of a group of computer systems administrators employed on a contract basis by a large manufacturing firm in the United States. The third case study addresses the work and identity of administrators and scientists involved with district-level administration in India, related to the attempted introduction of geographical information systems.

COMPUTER HARDWARE ENGINEERS IN COMCO

Comco is a multinational company, with origins and headquarters in the United States, that designs, manufactures and services electronic products and systems for measurement, computing and communication. It employed over 100 000 people internationally at the time of writing, and was one of the world's largest computer service and support companies with 35 response centres and support offices in about 120 countries.

The research on which this case study is based was carried out in the UK sales and support centre, which dealt with the service requirements of software and hardware products in the United Kingdom, and employed about 2500 people in 1999. The main activity in the centre was to respond to customer phone calls concerning software and hardware support. The aim was to solve the problem over the phone where possible, but if not an engineer had to visit the customer. The company's customers included the whole range from large organizations to individual computer users. Comco products and services were divided into high end and low end, with the former including networks and UNIX systems, and the latter including PCs, printers and plotters.

The field research was focused on the work of Comco's hardware engineers, and was carried out based at the headquarters of the organization in the south of England, and one of the regional offices in the north-west of England. The field study was conducted over eight months in the period 1998–1999, and included 28 in-depth interviews and 50 hours of participant observation. Full details of the case study may be found in Hayes and Walsham (1999) and Hayes (2000).

Changes in the Work of Hardware Engineers

The relationship between hardware engineers and the company changed significantly in the period from the mid-1980s onwards. The work of hardware and software engineers was split at that time, and in the early 90s one of Comco's business process re-engineering projects was aimed at shifting the work of engineers to being home-based rather than office-based. This was resisted by many Comco engineers at that time, but in 1996 a new role of 'agent' was created that effectively achieved the earlier objective.

An agent was an engineer who worked as a one-person company for Comco, with very limited rights but relatively tight control from Comco. The company's concept was that these agents would be relatively inexpensive compared with in-house engineers, would use their own resources such as cars and a home base, and would be paid in a commodity fashion by the number of jobs carried out. Only a small percentage of existing Comco engineers became agents, but many others were recruited from outside, some of whom had been previous Comco contractors. These were normally engineers with some technical skills, but without university degrees or extensive training. A new organizational structure was created whereby the agents were managed by a small internal department of eight people and five regional managers.

As part of the agent model, a new call dispatch and management system, called Dispatch System, was implemented in 1997. This was the vehicle through which phone calls were organized and distributed to the various agents, although the actual allocation was made by a dispatcher based on his or her knowledge of the individual agents and the geography of the area. The data from Dispatch System were transferred to the engineers via their mobile phones to Traveller, a palm-top computer. Engineers downloaded information on customers into their Traveller, and they transmitted information to headquarters on their estimated arrival time at a customer's site, as well as the time that they started and completed the job. At Comco headquarters, the data from the system were used for the payment of agents, but also for monitoring agents' performance, such as whether they were late on their estimated arrival time.

As part of the field work for the case study, Hayes spent a day with several of the hardware engineers, engaged in observation of their work processes during that day, and in conversation with the engineers between customer visits, usually in the engineer's car. Although the work content for the agents was broadly similar, individual 'stories' of how they conceptualized their work, and their workplace identity, differed greatly. Three such different accounts are given below, relating to engineers who will be called Gary, Keith and Neil.

Gary's Story

Gary was an ex-employee of Comco, and had a degree in electrical engineering. He had worked for Comco for 17 years in the United Kingdom and seven years abroad. He trained engineers in fixing plotters, and he was regarded as the UK expert in fixing hardware and software problems of design jet plotters. He used to live close to Comco headquarters, but after the implementation of the agent model he decided to move from the south to the north-west of England, which was the region where he was born. He wanted to be close to his son who was living in this area. Gary's son was an engineering student, who joined his father in customer site visits during his university vacations.

Gary believed that Comco outsourced plotters because they were not a major contributor to profit any more:

> When Comco decided to outsource plotters to agents a lot of engineers were surprised because they thought that plotters require high technical skills and they are very expensive pieces of equipment to be outsourced. But it seems like plotters are not a profitable product for Comco to retain.

The decision to leave a permanent job in Comco and to become an agent was difficult for Gary: 'Internally there was no other job I could or wanted to do. They offered me jobs internally but none of them had to do with plotters. I prefer this job now.'

Because of the shortage of plotter engineers, Gary had to cover a broad geographical area, and he estimated that he spent two-thirds of his time travelling or talking on the phone, and only one-third carrying out technical tasks. Gary thought that his work had been helped a great deal by the use of the remote Traveller system: 'Before that (the implementation of Traveller) we had to go in the morning to the office and be in a specific place. If it was not for Traveller, I would not have managed to come back to the north-west.'

However, because of the limited memory of Traveller, which restricted the data that could be held on it regarding past jobs, Gary kept his own manual log book with details of work done and other comments that he believed might be useful in the future.

Gary thought of himself as closely associated with Comco even though he was not an employee any more. His confidence came from his expertise, and he knew that Comco needed him to carry out good quality work on plotters and to train new engineers. His sense of being part of Comco was manifested in the meetings of agents with the regional manager. In some cases, where agents attacked Comco's policies, he took the side of Comco, and he was keen on recommending ways to improve work practices and reduce costs for Comco.

Gary regarded customer relations as a key part of his responsibility as a Comco agent. For example, rather than relying on Comco to supply the right parts for all repairs, he kept his own stock of commonly used spare parts in the boot of his car and at his home. If the wrong parts were sent to him, he was normally still able to carry out the repair and thus to satisfy the customer: 'If I had not got these spare parts I could not finish the job. I would need to visit the customer for the second time. I don't want to go for a second or third time, that is not professional and Comco would lose all of its customers if we didn't aim for a first time fix.'

Gary's intention was to continue to work as an agent for Comco and to train Comco engineers. He was trying at the time of the research to persuade his son to work for Comco, but his son did not like the way of working of an agent: 'I do not want this job. I want a real job, working with other people.' Gary however was content with his new way of living. He was buying a house in an area where he had always wanted to live, and he thought that he would be able to live there until his retirement.

Keith's Story

Keith was one of the first agents employed by Comco. When Keith was asked to talk about his work experience, he did not summarize his work to date, as most of the engineers did. He thought that, in addition to his work experience, he should talk about his childhood experiences, his social and ethnic origins, and the problems stemming from his background:

My dad was Irish and my mum was English and she died when I was eleven. After that, I was brought up in an orphanage in Liverpool. I dropped out from school when I was 14, and I have had many jobs since then. I worked in the market selling fish and at a baker's. I've been an industrial worker, worked in dry cleaners, and in the army. I was always interested in engineering and especially in radio and radio signals so I went to college and got a certificate on signals and radio equipment and worked for nine years at sea. After that I did basic programming and got interested in computers. I moved to London ... when I was working in London I used to put on a slight Irish accent to disguise my Liverpool accent so people wouldn't look down on me. The slight Irish accent made people think I was an educated Irishman.

Keith had realized early on that the IT industry was moving towards contract maintenance and outsourcing. He had set up his own company and he offered field engineers to other companies, but he had not found it easy to run a successful business. He started to work for Comco because he knew the regional manager, Tom, from a time when Keith was offering his independent services to the company for which Tom had worked previously. Keith said that Tom knew his ethos and credibility, and the job for Comco was what Keith wanted: 'I lived in the pockets of other people for a long time so I really like working for myself. The only downside is that since I started running my business from my house's two bedrooms, I have become more introvert.'

Keith had mixed views about the use of the Traveller-based system, and pointed out its advantages and disadvantages from his perspective:

The good thing is that it gives you the call and all the details that you need to close the call down. The bad thing was that at the beginning we were stuck with it, and we didn't know what to do with it. We thought they were trying to stop us from doing our work the way we know how ... If you are going to do it right (input your information on time etc.) you are going to be paid on time. But if you are controlled by technology with no feedback and you can not get through to the call centre when you need to, you get alienated.

Keith, like Gary, wrote his own private log book. He stressed that Traveller had limited history capabilities. Keith said that he normally set his times for his customer visits at 8 a.m. from his home. He then tried to be with the customer within a range of 15 minutes from his estimated time of arrival. He was worried because his estimated time of arrival was below average in terms of accuracy according to a recent Comco report.

Keith regarded customer relationships as an essential part of the job:

Although we are agents we are building up a relationship with the customer because we are permanent contract staff. This relationship allows the building of trust and understanding with the engineer. If customers do not like you they will be unhappy, and if they are unhappy they are going to complain and you are the one who is going to be blamed at the end of the day.

However, Keith had a dual motive in keeping the customers satisfied. Keith called on one particular customer who had had a bad experience with Comco customer service on a printer. Keith repaired the printer, and told the customer that if he had any future problems, Keith could fix them independently for 40% of the price that Comco was charging.

Keith said that 95% of his work was Comco visits at that time, but that this business had enabled him to survive as an independent company. In the future, he wanted to improve his performance as perceived by Comco, for example in terms of accurate estimated times of arrival at customer sites. However, his future intentions also included efforts to increase the number of his company's private customers, using Comco visits as an access method, but with the aim of diversifying away from his almost total reliance on Comco business in the future.

Neil's Story

Neil had worked as an agent for Comco for a year and a half at the time of the research. Before joining Comco, he had been a workshop engineer, and he had then been made redundant. He was recruited as an agent by Tom, the regional manager, who had been Neil's manager in his previous job. Neil was one of the few engineers who undertook 'technical escalations'. Escalations were engineering jobs that the majority of engineers were not able to fix. The regional manager chose engineers whose expertise could be trusted to re-visit the customer and fix the problem.

For Neil, fixing machines was his hobby as well as his job: 'My house is more like a workshop. I drive my wife mad. I spend all of my free time playing around with machines.'

Although Neil was skilful, he was not regarded as professional by many of his colleagues. The older engineers, in particular, did not like his unconventional looks for a field engineer. He had long hair tied back in a ponytail, and he normally wore a leather jacket and a tie with cartoon characters on it. He was regarded as antisocial by his fellow agents, for example in not saying good morning when he met them whilst collecting parts. Neil himself did not express particular concern about his colleagues' views of him: 'We are all too busy anyway, everyone is flying around in the car here and there. The only thing I really enjoy is to spend hours fixing machines.'

While driving to visit customers, Neil explained how he felt about the job as a field engineer: 'It is driving me mad to have to deal with people. I just want to do quick fix but the rest is a waste of time. They [the customers] are nothing but strangers to me, they are just stressing me out while I am doing my job.'

Neil explained that he was very satisfied with the money he was making from his job as a Comco agent:

> Some jobs are opportunities which are coming up once in a blue moon and this was the blue moon for me. I could not believe my luck when I first started working for Comco and got a feeling of how much money you can make by using Comco's name. It is worthwhile being a contractor for two to three months just to have the experience. I have enough by now. I just want to grow my business and have people work for me. I want to be the boss.

Neil thought that Traveller was not useful because of its connection problems and poor history facilities:

> Traveller is not of big use to us. Whatever I need to know I can e-mail Tom and he can authorize it. Comco does not like this way because it is not automated and they want to know what time you are going to the customer. It is not useful to us. It is a waste of money. We would be better off having lap-tops that we can use for other jobs as well.

During his visits to the customers, Neil was very quiet and he was very brief in answering any queries. Neil believed that talking to the customer was not a part of his job and that Comco was paying him solely to fix customer's machines and not to give additional advice: 'If they want to talk to me they have to pay me. It is consulting and I have a company which can provide this service.'

Customers' reactions to Neil varied. In one case, he fixed a problem in a computer training centre, where the customers had good computing knowledge, and they were satisfied that their machines were now working. However, in another case of a printer in a hospital, a member of staff asked him what could be done if the problem recurred. Neil's reply was that they should ring Comco, and the customer was not satisfied with his apparent lack of interest in explaining the problem to them and in providing practical advice.

Neil knew that dealing with customers was one of his weak points. He had recently created a new company with Colin, another Comco agent, undertaking non-Comco work. Colin was very sociable and was often sent to customers for 'human escalations', i.e. to calm down angry and dissatisfied customers. Colin, however, was not as good as Neil at technical issues. They planned to distribute their skills in their new company according to their expertise. They planned that Neil would eventually stop going on field visits, and they would employ a young engineer to visit customers. Neil would stay in the office fixing machines brought to him by Colin and their employee.

Learning from the Stories

What is immediately striking about these stories is the radically different conceptualizations of the nature of their job, their own identity, including their work identity, and the role and perceived value of IT systems in their work life. For example, with respect to their job role, Gary saw customer relations as integral to his responsibilities as a Comco agent. Keith also regarded customer relations as important, but partly in order to divert Comco customers to his own private business. Neil saw his role as fixing machines, and felt that customers should pay him for any additional professional contact, such as advice on future actions.

With respect to identity, an even wider diversity is visible, even from the short stories of the agents' lives recounted here. The complex and continuous process of identity formation involved personal histories before becoming Comco agents, current attitudes to their work, and the intricate enmeshing of work with home and personal life. Keith had continuously upgraded himself in work terms since his difficult childhood and saw the Comco agent role as a further stepping stone to his own successful private business. Neil also saw Comco as a stepping stone, but with a short-term financial bias, and as a means to move his interests to the technical parts of the job where he perceived his strength to lie. Gary, in contrast, was happy as a Comco agent. It had enabled him to move to an area where he had always wanted to live, and he planned to stay there until retirement.

What can we learn about the particular role and attributes of the IT system in this case? First, there were obvious technical limitations, commented on by all the agents, in terms of the Traveller's storage capacity. In appropriating the technology, Gary and Keith developed a way of working round this technical limitation, by keeping their own log books. Neil did not see customers as important in themselves, and therefore did not see any need to supplement the Traveller system in this way. The engineers also talked about connection problems, and again they devised their own ways of dealing with this issue. For example, Neil talked about using e-mail to Tom, the regional manager, if he needed authorization for something, rather than going through the Traveller system.

The IT system was deeply implicated in the surveillance and control that Comco used to manage its agents, and this was recognized and commented on by all the engineers, but in very different ways. Gary felt relatively confident in his relations with Comco and viewed Traveller positively. This relatively secure position can be attributed to Comco's perception of Gary's technical expertise with plotters and thus his value to them in fixing machines and training other engineers. Keith felt less certain about the value of his expertise as perceived by Comco, and thus he was worried that he needed to improve his performance on particular surveillance indicators, such as the difference between forecast and actual arrival time at customer sites. Neil clearly resented Comco's attempts to control him via the Traveller system, and he attempted to subvert this where possible. The fact that he was able to achieve this to some extent no doubt related to his expertise as perceived by Comco, for example on technical escalations. I will return to a more formal analysis of aspects of this case study in the final section of the chapter, following the two other case studies.

COMPUTER SYSTEMS ADMINISTRATORS IN US CO

The second case study draws on Schultze and Boland's (1997) description of the work of computer systems administrators, employed by a consulting company that they called ConsultCo, but hired on a contract basis to work for US Co, a large manufacturing firm with its headquarters in a mid-western state of the United States. The particular work for which they had been hired involved a knowledge management technology called KnowMor based on a platform of the groupware Lotus Notes. The responsibility of the system administrators was to set up and operate the system environment to ensure the smooth running of the application in US Co.

The field research was carried out by Schultze in an eight-month period of participant observation in US Co, between October 1995 and May 1996, working four days per week on site. She studied the work of two other groups, but we will focus here on the work of the three systems administrators, Ilana, Dan and Jon. Schultze (2000) provided some further details of the case study, including analysis of the work of the other groups, contrasted in an interesting way with a 'confessional account' of her own experiences as a field researcher. The purpose of this section is to reinterpret the findings on US Co contained in these papers, with a focus on themes and issues of identity, based on the reported perceptions, feelings and actions of the system administrators.

Searching for Objectivity

The position of contract workers such as Ilana, Dan and Jon can be thought of as precarious. The fact that they were hired in this way indicates that US Co felt that such work was not part of the company's core competence, and thus could be outsourced. Even though the system administrators referred to themselves as 'consultants', the permanent employees of US Co called them 'contractors' and labelled their work 'commodity'. The particular task for which they were employed was termed third-level support, which was the most lucrative form of contract work and dealt directly with the technical core of the system, i.e. the hardware, software and communications infrastructure. Work that dealt directly with end users was called first-level support. Second-level support lay somewhere between first- and third-level activities.

How did the system administrators try to present their work as of high quality and high value, and in so doing establish or maintain their own professional integrity and identity? The first way can be thought of as representing the 'objectivity' of their work. The third level is 'above' the specific, local and messy world of end users, maintaining a 'neutral' technical platform. However, this position had to be defended:

> I (Schultze) asked Ilana about the error on [a user's] machine; she said that there was really nothing she could do because 'we are not allowed to'. She said that [the user] would have to call the help desk. If it were up to her she would like to touch the machine and figure out what was going on. She added that she had received a 'note from Jon' reminding her that she should not be working directly on users' machines. She had received this note because she had helped a user who needed to print something out of Notes and there was no other way he could print it, and he needed it for a presentation. So she went over there and helped him.

A second way of trying to maintain an image of objectivity and distance was through written documentation. Jon was very conscientious about documentation. He was in his late forties and had been in the information systems profession for a long time. He had a contract with US Co for only 16 hours per week, whereas Dan's was for 24 hours per week and Ilana's for 40 hours per week. Jon therefore relied most on the documentation to get up to speed on what had happened during the days he was not there. In addition, documentation was a means of protecting the system administrators from attack. Blaming and finger-pointing were pervasive in a technological environment in which every breakdown had to be explained and traced to its root cause. Schultze and Boland provided a specific example of the use of documentation for protection:

> The Notes databases that [the SAP consulting company] used . . . had too many views, which was going to bring down the servers. Jon and Dan recognized this and told [an SAP project manager] who basically said 'I hear you but I am not going to do anything about it'. Eventually the servers were brought down . . . Dan proudly declared that 'we were totally covered' because they had all the documentation that went on between them . . . so that [the SAP project manager] stood there as the fool for not having listened to them in the first place (pp. 553–554).

However, although documentation offered protection, Dan and Ilana resented having to write it. They were much happier in their direct bodily engagement with the technology. Indeed, their method of working was precisely this, flicking through multiple screens in quick succession, and sometimes working on more than one machine at the same time. Writing, in contrast, involved extracting themselves out of the technology and constructing an account of it. Such an account is necessarily a partial, simplified and distanced rendering of the local, complex and subjective experience of working with the technology. Objectivity and subjectivity were intertwined in the carrying out of their work, and the subsequent reporting of it.

Placelessness and Mobility

There was no fixed 'place' for the contractors in US Co. They were part of a transient workforce, working in different locations, spending hours on the road every week, being allocated some space in each company, but always subject to impermanence and change. Ilana in US Co could be considered an exception, to some extent, in that she worked full time for US Co for one year in the 'integration lab'. Ilana was in her twenties and US Co was her first client site. Although she had a fixed location for this period, the space of the lab was not subject to specific ownership. Ilana had a cardboard box on her desk in which she stored some of the smaller artefacts she needed to do her work. She had not personalized her work space with pictures of loved ones or other keepsakes. One gets a sense of impermanence of place even here, despite Ilana being there for a year.

An interesting incident occurred following a rumour that US Co was going to build a new headquarters with no room at all for the computing contractors. A solution was dreamed up by two of the ConsultCo contractors, namely a large tractor-trailer truck with computers, satellite connections and bunks to sleep in. This would be driven to a client's site and plugged in to the organization in order to 'fix it'. Schultze and Boland used this fantasy to infer the consultants' attitudes to their ideal work situation:

> Their mobile home/office promised them complete independence from their client organizations. They would not constantly be reminded of their placelessness through lack of equipment, stationery and space. Instead, having their own equipment and a stable team of co-workers ... promised them a sense of being and belonging. However, this feeling of stability and security did not come at the price of confining and restricting boundedness typically associated with place. ... It took the best of both space and place, and it promised the contractors a sense of pause while they remained in motion. They could leave the messiness of their clients' day-to-day operations behind without relinquishing their sense of place (pp. 554–555).

Of course, one can make too much of a single fantasized incident. Nevertheless, the rootlessness of these contract workers is not an unreal dream. On reading the above account, I was struck by the parallels of the fantasy with the nomadic life of the Maasai in East Africa or the Romany people in Europe, who retain their sense of place and belonging through an established social organization in the moving place of their encampment or caravan. In contrast, the current nomadic life of contract workers such as Ilana, Dan and Jon lacks both the stable social organization and the moving enclosure.

The system administrators were very aware of the implications of mobility, not just in terms of their bodies, but in terms of the mobility of their minds or skills. They were not keen to develop in-depth knowledge in single limited domains, such as that of Lotus Notes, since such technologies are transient and expertise in them can become rapidly obsolete. The system administrators constantly scanned the market for new technologies, and focused on products with wide appeal and general applicability. They wished to protect their freedom to move on, both to new places and to new technical domains.

Struggling to Identify

Schultze and Boland summarized their account of the systems administrators' world of work, and their search for identity in it as follows: 'We depict these contractors as people struggling to "go on" in a world in which space and place, mind and body, logical and illogical explanations, clean and dirty work, physical and mental activity, and specialized and transcendent knowledge are posed as dualisms' (p. 556).

The argument here is that the system administrators felt the need to present their work as involving logical, clean, mental activity based on knowledge that transcends particular places. Such work is contrasted in a dualistic way with physical, local, specialized work, in which 'illogical' things happen and fixes and work-arounds are the norm. However, in practice, the work of Ilana, Dan and Jon involved both of these types of work, inextricably intermingled together. In terms of personal identity, they struggled between the self-disciplining needed to present their work as the former, whilst identifying with the latter. Ilana being reprimanded by Jon for getting involved with a user provides a clear example of these tensions. On the one hand, Ilana felt the need to help in a specific, local context, whereas she was required by ConsultCo to present herself as dispassionate and distanced from such localized activity.

I have hinted earlier at an explanation as to why such a representation of the self as the distanced, objective knowledge worker is deemed necessary by ConsultCo and its employees. The emphasis on core competencies in Western organizations, and the related outsourcing of many tasks previously carried out by permanent employees, has led to a legion of contract workers carrying out activities on a commodity basis. The representation of the work carried out by these people is a key element in determining the price of the commodity. In this case, Comco wished to reinforce the high-level status of their third-level workers, and present their employees as possessors of transcendent knowledge that is not locally specific and can be seamlessly transferred across space. The fact that this creates pressures in terms of the identity of the workers themselves, who must confront the realities of their work as well as its representation, has been the main theme of this section.

GIS SCIENTISTS AND DISTRICT-LEVEL ADMINISTRATORS IN INDIA

The third case study in this chapter concerns attempts to develop and use geographical information systems (GIS) to aid district-level administration in India. In particular, the focus is a set of GIS projects that took place under the umbrella of the Ministry of Environment and Forests (MOEF) of the government of India over the period 1991–96. The technical work to develop the systems was carried out by scientists in a range of institutions, including two remote sensing agencies, three research groups within universities, and three other scientific agencies concerned with forestry, space research and the study of science and technology in development. The systems were intended to be used by district-level administrators. Issues of identity of the administrators and scientists are the key themes of this section, related to the attempted introduction of the GIS technology.

The field data on which this case study is based were collected from five separate field trips to India over the period 1993–96. A total of 127 semi-structured interviews were carried out with 105 personnel at different hierarchical levels. In addition to the interviews, the researchers used other data sources including systems demonstrations put on by each of the GIS project sites, archival data in the form of reports and filed documents, and some informal contact with personnel outside the formal interviews. Further details of the case study may be found in Sahay and Walsham (1997) and Walsham and Sahay (1999).

Overview of the GIS Projects

A schematic of key events and phases of the case study is shown in Figure 4.1. The MOEF initiated 10 GIS projects in January 1991, in collaboration with the eight scientific institutions referred to above, with the aim of examining the potential for using GIS technology to aid wasteland development. Wastelands are categorized as degraded land that can be brought under vegetative cover with reasonable effort, and land that has deteriorated due to lack of appropriate water and soil management.

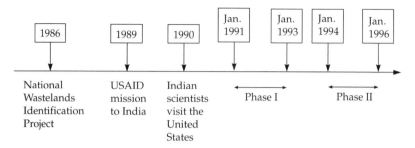

Figure 4.1   *Key events and phases in the GIS case study*

The initiation of the project in 1991 can be traced back to two earlier events. In 1986, the government of India started the National Wastelands Identification Project, involving the mapping of the distribution of wastelands across the various states of India. Detailed maps were produced on a 1:50 000 scale for 147 selected districts using remote sensing techniques. The existence of these maps provided a basis for considering how to develop and manage these wastelands. The stimulus for the possible application of GIS to this issue was provided by a chance meeting of some GIS experts from Ohio in the United States with Indian government officials, in the context of a general USAID mission to India in 1989. This was followed by a visit of an Indian expert team to see GIS installations in the United States in 1990, and then the eight scientific institutions in India were invited by the MOEF to test the efficacy of GIS in wasteland management, using specific districts as research sites. These districts were relatively close to their respective scientific centres in some cases, but in other cases they were as far away as 1000 miles.

The staff of the scientific institutions saw the objectives of the project to be primarily technological in Phase I, involving the production of working GIS systems based on real data from the field sites in their particular districts. The detailed models and systems developed by the institutions tended to reflect their view of themselves as scientific research and development centres. For example, there was a heavy reliance on data obtained by sophisticated remote-sensing techniques, reflecting the nature of the interests of the typical research scientist in these institutions. There was less emphasis on other socio-economic variables relevant to wastelands management, such as population and livestock data. In addition, and of crucial importance to later development of the project, many of the scientists involved in the project saw their institutional mandate to be limited to the development of technology rather than to its transfer to administrators at district level.

Although the Phase I projects were completed in early 1993, proposals for continuation were not submitted until about a year later, and then only by five of the original eight institutions. This period of transition from Phase I to Phase II was characterized by uncertainty about the objectives and nature of the continuation phase. The Project Director saw it as involving the transfer of the developed systems to the district level so that they could be used for real management applications. However, the project managers in the scientific institutions did not view their staff skills or resources to be adequate for this task in most cases. The institutions asked for further funding largely to provide more hardware and software, whereas the Project Director felt that the institutions should concentrate on using the existing equipment and on its transfer to the field.

Eventually, five institutions agreed to terms for Phase II and these continuation projects were authorized by the MOEF. Soon after this, the Project Director left the MOEF and transferred to another institution, and there was very limited further central direction of the Phase II projects right through to the end of the research period. Despite this lack of coordination from the centre, all of the five Phase II projects went ahead, in different ways and with different levels of success in terms of the stated project goals. At the end of the research period, some efforts had been made in some of the sites towards transferring the technology to district level, but there were no actual working systems receiving real use.

The Representation of Space

At one level, these projects can be thought of as yet another example of a failed technology transfer project, all too common in the history of aid agencies and their attempts to promote the use of Western technologies in Third World contexts. One could argue, for example, of the need for improved training and education, or institutional development. Whilst acknowledging that these may be relevant, more underlying reasons for repeated failures of the type described above can be linked to basic issues of culture and identity. As discussed in Chapter 3, information technologies such as GIS, developed in the Western countries, can be thought to reflect and embed Western values. These may not be compatible with deeply held beliefs and attitudes in other cultures. In this sub-section, I examine one aspect of this incompatibility, namely the representation of space.

India is not a map-based culture. Typical Indians will rarely, if ever, use maps in their daily life. Walsham and Sahay (1999) described their field visit to a GIS scientific institution, where they spent over an hour in the stifling heat of the middle of an Indian day trying to find the location of the institution. None of the Indian scientists, or the Indian researcher, had considered the use of a map for this purpose; instead, they asked local people by the side of the road. When I, the English researcher, queried the efficacy of this approach, I was firmly told that maps were not used for this purpose in India. If the GIS scientists, whose professional life was centred around the production of computer-based maps, made no use of them in daily life, it is perhaps unsurprising that GIS themselves are viewed as alien in an Indian context.

A GIS project leader in the National Informatics Centre (NIC), one of the other institutions in India trying to introduce GIS, said: 'The most difficult part of GIS introduction is getting people to think spatially. There is no simple strategy here. A first step would be to motivate NIC's own people. They must start thinking spatially first.' This remark is interesting, but surely misstates the core of the issue. It is not that Indians do not think spatially, but that they do not in general use external conceptualizations of space, namely maps, as key aids to spatial awareness. District-level administrators, for example those concerned with forestry management, are well aware of spatial distributions of trees in their areas. However, they do not in general conceptualize this in terms of maps, whether computer-generated or not.

Sahay (1998) linked Indians' conceptualization of space to fundamental aspects of their identity. He argued that Indians view space as basically 'in-here', subjective and inherent to the person, rather than 'out-there' as some objective identity. Space and place in Indian culture and religion are viewed as of greater personal significance than time. Recent political events in India, in which the fundamentalist Hindu political party gained advantage by stirring up passions about the location of a Moslem mosque, related to the notion of the sacredness of place. Sahay summarized the lack of fit between GIS technology and these aspects of Indian cultural identity as follows:

> The objective reality depicted in GIS software is interpreted to represent a disconnection of space from place, a relationship that allows interaction between absent others. In contrast, in Indian society, a strong relation is seen to exist between notions of space and place arising out of political, cosmological, religious and social considerations. These differences between subjective considerations and objective reality (of the GIS) seem to contribute to the discomfort which some Indians feel in relating to the notion of a GIS map (p. 181).

Sahay added that the purpose of a GIS reflects a sense of being able to control space and nature through technology. This need to dominate nature is also not a concept that comes naturally for many Indians, who typically see themselves as part of nature rather than standing outside of it.

Each to One's Own Role

Indian society has traditionally been stratified on functional lines with caste as the basic structural feature. Hinduism, the religion of the majority in India, emphasizes a social framework that embodies caste rituals, and these have governed the lives of most Indians for hundreds of years. The presence of caste is felt in virtually all aspects of Indian economic activity also; for example, modern entrepreneurs are still mainly drawn from the trading castes. One of the sacred Hindu texts, the Bhagavad Gita, says: 'And to thy duty, even if it be humble, rather than another's, even if it be great. To die in one's duty is life: to live in another's is death.'

Reincarnation as a higher form of life is believed to be dependent on accepting one's lot in the current life, and performing one's duty in that role. Naipaul (1964) is critical of the rigid functionality that he sees as deriving from these ideas:

The man who sweeps the dingy bed in the hotel room will be affronted if asked to sweep the gritty floor ... the clerk will not bring you a glass of water even if you faint ... study these four men washing down the steps of this unpalatable Bombay hotel. The first pours the water from a bucket, the second scratches the tiles with a twig broom, the third uses a rag to slop the dirty water down the steps into another bucket, which is held by the fourth.

The compartmentalism of role and activity was a clear feature of the GIS projects. Most of the GIS scientists viewed their goal as producing accurate scientific models for the GIS, which they then expected the district-level administrators to use. They saw little need for consultation in this process, as expressed by one of the scientists as follows:

There is no problem in getting technology out to the field because once people see the scientific basis on which the recommendations have been developed they will adopt the technology. The involvement of local people (district-level officials) is not really required in this process. We can specify the alternatives and give recommendations to the local people. They can take the suggestions.

A further explanation, in addition to functionality, for the rather extra-ordinarily blinkered nature of the above statement, is that social relations in India are highly hierarchical and status conscious. A scientist, such as the one quoted above, would see himself as 'above' the district-level officials, and would not be happy in engaging with them on any sort of equal footing. This was expressed by one GIS project leader as follows:

> Preparation of joint proposals [between scientists and district admin-istrators] is a very difficult job because some of the scientists may not feel very comfortable. In fact, they are saying 'Why are you attach-ing us to them, we have to depend on them, why should we not do independent projects like we have been doing.'

In addition to the gulf between most of the scientists and the district-level administrators, there are also issues of compartmentalization in the districts themselves, linked to conceptions of separateness of role and identity. The multi-layered nature of GIS systems, where data on different characteristics are brought together as overlays in the same map-based system, assumes that management issues will be addressed in a coordinated way. For example, the management of land resources in any country can be thought to involve a wide range of disciplinary specialities, including agriculture, forestry, wildlife management and many others. However, in India, these issues have typically been handled in relative isolation by the different agencies involved. Over 20 separate government agencies operate at district level in India, each dealing with a particular functional area, and reflecting the wider governmental fund-ing structures that are built around departmentally-based schemes. An employee in a non-governmental organization operating at the district level in India described this as follows:

> The main problem is the compartmentalism of activities. Different departments do not speak to each other. There is a problem of attitude, people do not want to do things. The crux of the problem is not technical but that of sustained coaxing. The dis-trict-level engineer says that he is interested only in dams, the agricultural scientist in soils, the forester in trees. Everyone says that I am fine and no one sits and talks with each other. There is extreme compartmentalization. There is a mental barrier among the people.'

Cultural Identity and GIS Technology

The above analysis of the links between the nature of cultural identity in India and the use of GIS technology is somewhat limited, in that I have addressed a small subset of possible conceptual linkages and in no great detail. Other issues that could be analysed in this context include the high status accorded to scientific knowledge in India, the form of Indian social relations as collectivist and personal in nature, and Indian conceptions of rationality and approaches to decision-making. The references cited earlier provide further material on such issues. Nevertheless, even with the limited analysis here, I have demonstrated that forms of appropriation or even rejection of GIS technology in India are linked to deep-seated issues of cultural and professional identity. One implication from this is that simple programmes of computer training, or models of GIS implementation drawn from other contexts, such as the Western countries, are unlikely to be effective in India.

Identity is not, however, static, neither at the level of the individual nor at higher levels of aggregation such as groups or societies, and this certainly applies to India. Indian society has complex long-standing historical roots, but change is visible as well as continuity. With respect to GIS technology, despite the above case study, there is a marked increase in the production and availability of maps in India, not least due to their importation by foreign companies and agencies. In addition, and with no small irony, Indian software houses in places like Bangalore and Delhi are supplying GIS services such as digitization of maps and software production to foreign clients, particularly the United States. Indians may not use maps much in their daily lives at present, but successful Indian businesses are being built around their production and use. It seems likely that this will have a significant impact in the medium and long term on Indians' use of maps and, more generally, their conceptualization of space, at least in the richer parts of Indian society.

ANALYSIS AND CONCLUSIONS

The case studies in this chapter have been presented in isolation from one another as a means of providing some richness and variety in investigating the topic of shifting identity. The cases have covered different sectors, countries, job roles and IT support systems. However, as outlined at the beginning of the chapter, a further objective

Table 4.1   *Globalization processes and shifting identity*

Globalization processes visible in the cases	• Commodification of work and outsourcing as responses to global markets • Spread of Western-origin IT such as GIS • But glocalization in the Indian case
Linked to shifting identity	• Individual life projects in reflexive modernity • Trajectory of the self
No homogenization of identity, but increased individualization	• Great variety in individual trajectories • But concerns of more individualized conception of self
Tensions of identity	• Gap between representation of work and its reality • Need for a consistent sense of place • Local imagination in conflict with global technologies
These theoretical issues are of practical concern	• Important to how individuals conceive of themselves; carry out their work; respond to new initiatives

is to generalize some concepts and insights of potential value in other contexts than those described here. To do this, the three specific questions given at the beginning of the chapter will be now be addressed directly, drawing selectively from the case studies, and linked to specific themes derived from Part 1. A summary of key points in this section is provided in Tables 4.1–4.3.

How are Globalization Processes Implicated in Shifting Identity in the Workplace?

Aspects of the broad globalization processes discussed in Chapter 2 are clearly visible in all three of these cases. The attempt to standardize work across the world is one response of the transnational corporations to the need to address global markets in a consistent way. A particular form that this takes is the outsourcing of work that is perceived to be a commodity, such as the work of the Comco agents and the ConsultCo administrators. The work is then monitored and measured through the use of IT. The spread of Western-origin information technologies, such as GIS, is another manifestation of globalization, although we also see an example of glocalization in the Indian case as the technology encountered the local features of Indian culture.

What of shifting identity though, the focus of this chapter? Writers such as Beck and Giddens talk of the individual life projects that need to be continuously constructed in the reflexive world of high modernity. This is well illustrated by the variety of the stories of Gary, Keith and Neil in the Comco case. Indeed, Hayes and Walsham (1999) drew on the specific concept of the 'trajectory of the self' (Giddens 1991) to theorize a link between the stories. Giddens argued that past experiences and events provide support, raise barriers or are sources of uncertainty in a person's life. Individuals appropriate these past experiences and events to move into an anticipated future. Giddens' thesis is that this orientation to the future is a particularly distinctive feature of contemporary society, at least in the Western world. These ideas were used in constructing the life histories of the Comco engineers through an investigation of their perceptions and feelings about their past experiences, current activities and anticipated futures.

At one level, therefore, fears of homogenization of identity voiced by opponents of globalism, as discussed in Chapter 2, appear to be exaggerated when one considers the diversity of perception, personality, culture and technology appropriation encountered in any serious study of organizational life in the contemporary world. Individual life projects imply variety. However, a more subtle point, made by Coombs, Knights and Willmott (1992), is that this may be leading to more individualized competitive conceptions of self and social relations. The homogeneity then, somewhat ironically, lies not in the individual's identity *per se*, but in the common striving for an individualized identity. India could be considered as an example where this is not yet happening to any great extent, although the typical Indian's more collectivist sense of self rarely goes beyond the person's own family, caste, kinship, linguistic and religious group (Sinha 1988).

According to some globalization writers such as Giddens, 'existential anxiety' is encountered by individuals in trying constantly to readjust themselves to the conditions of 'reflexive modernity'. The ConsultCo case certainly provided some evidence of what might be called tensions of identity, arising from conditions where old rules and conventions are less applicable, but have not been replaced by new certainties. For example, the systems administrators carried out their work in a hands-on subjective way, but were required to represent this work as distanced and objective through precise documentation.

A further tension for the ConsultCo workers was their sense of placelessness. On this issue of need for a coherent sense of place, the three Comco agents had achieved this in their new circumstances, no longer based around the workplace and their colleagues there, but largely centred around their homes. This was not without its problems, with Neil saying that 'he drove his wife mad' by turning his house into a workshop, and Keith saying that he had become more introvert as a consequence. The importance of place in traditional society was discussed in the Indian case, in potential conflict with the de-centred notion of space in technologies such as GIS. Thus, the 'imagination' of the Indian workers was not captured by the technology, using Appadurai's concept introduced in Chapter 2.

Issues such as shifting professional identity, more individualized conceptions of self, gaps between the realities of work and its representation, and the need for a sense of place are not merely interesting theoretical abstractions. They affect the way in which individuals in the workplace conceive of themselves, carry out their work, and respond to new initiatives. Organizations often approach change management through simple prescriptions such as increased training, but what is needed are more thoughtful approaches that address the deeper issues of worker identity and security in a more globalized world.

What is the Role of Information and Communication Technologies in These Processes?

The cases all provide support for the broad thesis of Castells regarding the information age, namely that IT-enabled information generation, processing and transmission is fundamental to organizational and societal change, although the gaps between information about work and actual work tend not to be discussed in such high-level theories. Coming down, therefore, to the more micro-level, are some of the conceptual tools of Chapter 3 useful for analysis? In discussing the role of IT in micro-studies, the concepts of actor-network theory (see Table 3.2) were argued to be of help in examining the intermeshing of technology, people and organizations. Walsham and Sahay (1999) used this theory explicitly to examine the Indian GIS case. They argued that GIS can be viewed as an actor (or actant), with inscribed interests from its developers, but that the creation of an actor-network of aligned interests including the technology was not achieved in any of the Indian districts studied. The interests embedded in the GIS technology, such as the representation of space through external maps, were not aligned with the interests of local administrators. Attempts to enrol the human agents through various incentives were successful for the

Table 4.2 *IT and shifting identity*

Broad support in the case studies for the concept of the 'information age'	• IT-enabled information generation, processing and transmission fundamental • Although gaps between information about work and actual work not addressed by high-level theories
Actor-network theory helpful to examine intermeshing of technology, people and organizations	• e.g. GIS as actant with inscribed interests, such as map-based conceptualization of space • Failure to achieve robust actor network of aligned interests in the Indian case
IT used to support order and control but not improvisation in the Western cases	• Can cause resentment and evasion • Dependent on individual conceptualizations of work and identity
Relationship between IT and shifting professional identity of strong practical interest	• Some studies in the literature, but underexplored • Linked to issues of knowledge and power

scientists, who saw benefits to their work and careers from engaging with the technology, but not for the local-level administrators. It was also argued in Chapter 3 that appropriation of Western IT was likely to be more difficult to achieve in non-Western contexts, due to different models and conceptions of reality, and the Indian case provides a good example of this.

In the Western cases of Comco and ConsultCo, the technologies of work representation were used by the workers, but with a variety of views as to the desirability and value of the technology. Referring again to the concepts of improvisation and appropriation in Chapter 3, the Traveller and Dispatch systems in the Comco case were used by the company to support order and control, but were not designed to support the more improvisational aspects of the situated practice of the engineers. This caused some resentment on the part of engineers such as Neil, and to some extent Keith, resulting in some deliberate manipulation and evasion of the system in the case of Neil. There was perhaps less scope for evasion in the ConsultCo case, with Ilana being reminded that she should not be doing 'unauthorized' work such as helping users. However, it is clear that individual workers in both these cases related to the control of their work through information technology dependent on their individual conceptualizations of their work practice and workplace identity.

Other writers have discussed the issue of the relationship between new IT and shifting professional identity in the workplace. Bloomfield and McLean (1996) presented a case study of the mental health sector in the United Kingdom. They described how new information systems were implicated in the 'empowerment' of health care workers, whereby their professional identity shifted from a group primarily involved in the direct care of patients, to one concerned with both direct health care and the management of information related to health care. Walsham (1998) explored the changing identities of particular professional groups, related to new information technologies, in the banking, insurance and pharmaceutical industries. Mclaughlin and Webster (1998) described shifting power–knowledge relations and professional identities of two groups of hospital workers, consultants and laboratory scientific officers, related to the introduction of a new laboratory IT system into a hospital.

Despite a few studies of the above type, the topic of shifting identity linked to information technology remains under-researched in my view. For example, whilst there is much hyperbole concerning the Internet and its potential to change the way that we work and who we are, substantial studies of this in practice are rare (an example is Turkle 1996). This is not a topic for researchers alone, since practitioners also need to take issues of shifting identity and new IT seriously. I have hinted above that the topic is related to power and knowledge, and this connection is now explored in more detail.

How is Identity Linked to Knowledge and Shifting Power–Knowledge Relations?

Following Foucault's ideas of power-knowledge inseparability, introduced in Chapter 3, Willmott (1993) argued that contemporary organizations provide a sense of security and identity for individuals within them, provided workers discipline themselves to conform to the key values that are promoted as central features of the culture. It was also argued in Chapter 3 that IT can make events, objects and people more visible, and thus one use of the technology is to discipline conformance. One can see elements of this in the systems administrators' presentation of themselves as carrying out third-level support, and in the Comco agents' self-discipline of their time through their links with Traveller. However, power–knowledge relations are complex and locally specific, and there is often considerable scope for personal resistance on the part

Table 4.3   *Identity, power and knowledge*

IT as a way of encouraging self-disciplining conformance	• Sense of security and identity if workers discipline themselves to conform to key organizational values
	• IT makes events, objects and people potentially visible, and can be used to encourage self-disciplined conformance
Cases support this to some extent, but local power—knowledge relations complex	• For example, Comco agents' self-discipline through links with Traveller
	• But relative immunity when having valued expertise
Different concepts of power in different cultures and complex international power—knowledge relations	• Spatial knowledge in India not map-based, and linked to Indian identity
	• Governments may accept technology due to external pressure, but much scope for local resistance

of individuals. We saw how, in different ways and for different reasons, both Gary and Neil felt relatively immune from the pressures of Traveller-based surveillance. Gary was able to draw on his deep knowledge of plotters to leverage power over Comco who placed high value on his expertise. Neil had expertise on 'technical escalations', and his ability to evade tight control was also related to his earlier links with the regional manager.

It can be argued, more generally, that people are very aware of existing power—knowledge relations, a point made by Wynne, and discussed in Chapter 2, related to a lay person's 'trust' in experts being related to their perceived dependency on them. However, it can also be argued that people are very adept at manoeuvring within the perceived constraints of existing power relations when seeing an opportunity to do so. Even in low-paid menial jobs, workers will attempt to influence their job role and resist simplistic and sometimes offensive categorizations of that role. Holmer-Nadesan (1996) provided a fascinating example of such resistance. She described how 'service workers' at a university hall of residence, involved in cleaning and other such maintenance functions, objected to their description as machine-like support workers. Instead, they developed and maintained their human identity in roles such as 'surrogate mothers' to the students in the halls.

In the Indian case, power—knowledge relations can also be used to theorize about the case. It was argued in Chapter 3 that there are different attitudes to the very nature of knowledge in different cultures, and knowledge of space in India provides an excellent example. It is not that Indians have little knowledge of space, but that spatial knowledge is generally not based on external map-based conceptualizations. The arrival of technologies such as GIS in India is strongly linked to global concerns for the environment, originating mainly in Western countries. Bodies such as the World Bank and Western aid agencies are pressing technologies on Third World governments, largely in an attempt to improve the monitoring and management of natural resources such as forests in those countries. However, although widely 'accepted' at the government level, due to the power exerted by the Western agencies, there is much scope for local-level resistance as exemplified by the Indian case. This is linked to deep issues of Indian identity, and cannot be addressed successfully by interventions based on naive notions of technology transfer.

5
Teaming Up

The focus of this chapter goes beyond the individual level of Chapter 4 to the collaborative work of groups or teams, and the ways in which this work might be supported by information and communication technologies, and in particular by groupware. As noted in Chapters 2 and 3, there is an increased emphasis in contemporary society on knowledge generation, knowledge-sharing and knowledge transfer. Allied to the trend towards 'virtual' working and collaboration at a distance, this created the conditions in the 1990s in which groupware technologies such as Lotus Notes were implemented by a wide variety of organizations, including many of the transnational corporations operating worldwide.

The extensive spread of groupware has spawned a rich academic literature, including many case studies, and a selection from this literature forms the basis of this chapter. Some of the cases described below relate to a very broad concept of 'team' working, being concerned with collaborative work across wide geographical regions, and sometimes across organizational boundaries. Other cases are focused on a narrower definition of team working, namely that of a relatively small group of people working together, perhaps within the same geographical location. A common theme of all these cases, however, is collaborative work. As with Chapter 4, the cases are treated initially in a self-contained way, drawing insights from them directly. The final section of the chapter provides a more formal analysis of all the case material, drawing where relevant on concepts and themes from earlier in the book, particularly from Part 1. The questions examined directly in this final section, and implicitly throughout the chapter, are:

- What are the links between groupware technologies and globalization processes?
- How effective are groupware technologies in supporting collaboration and knowledge sharing?
- How are groupware technologies implicated in power relations?

Three bodies of work are presented in the main part of the chapter. The first of these concerns a case study of the use of Lotus Notes to aid knowledge-sharing and teamwork in the UK sales division of a multinational pharmaceuticals company. Secondly, I will examine an interesting book of case studies of the application of groupware systems in a range of large organizations operating in increasingly globalized contexts. The final two case studies concern the implementation of groupware technology to support collaboration in distributed organizations. One of these involved enterprises based in Norway, whereas the other dealt with a company operating more globally, but with a Norwegian host company.

LOTUS NOTES IN COMPOUND UK

Compound UK is the selling division of a multinational pharmaceuticals company. It is concerned primarily with selling products to hospitals and general medical practices in the United Kingdom, and also undertaking clinical trials of new drugs with participating doctors. The context within which the company operates, namely the UK health sector, was subject to a series of major reforms in the late 1980s and early 1990s. The UK National Health Service (NHS) had been reorganized to mirror market principles through the introduction of an internal market-place. This led, amongst other things, to a rethink of the criteria for the purchasing of pharmaceutical products, no longer concentrating solely on their efficacy, but also on their cost and efficiency.

The introduction of these market reforms also split the health care sector between primary care, namely general medical practices, and specialist care in hospitals. Many primary care doctors became fund-holders, having budgetary responsibilities for drugs, hospital referrals and staff costs. Similarly, hospitals became more autonomous, responsible for their own budgets, and specialist care doctors became part of a larger group of decision-makers in hospitals, including managers and accountants. From the point of view of Compound UK, this made sales situations more complex, with a wider range of actors involved in purchasing decisions in addition to the changes in purchasing criteria.

As part of its response to these shifts in the market, Compound UK was reorganized in 1993 into eight regions. The aim of this restructuring was to provide each region with considerable autonomy in planning and responding to its own locality, and thus to make the organization more responsive to the new market-place. The key focus here was the commercial department, involved in the actual selling of products. This consisted by 1996 of a director, eight regional managers, 12 area managers, and about 150 sales representatives (reps). All members of the commercial function, apart from the director, worked from their own homes, while employees working in other departments were located at the head office, Compound Square.

Senior management also felt that the organization could become more competitive by encouraging employees to draw on the information and knowledge in the company across functional and geographic boundaries. Thus, in 1994, the company implemented Lotus Notes (Notes), the leading groupware technology at that time, to enable improved sharing of information and teamworking. There were four main uses of Notes after its introduction in Compound UK. First, it provided a company-wide e-mail facility. Second, it was used to create a database to support the cooperative activities involved in 'strategic selling'. This database allowed employees to input information and their views onto strategic selling sheets in a structured way, with the aim of bringing together employees' knowledge to complete a successful sale. A third use of Notes was the provision of a wide variety of discussion databases that focused on issues, products or a particular functional role. The fourth use of Notes was the contact-recording database, providing a shared resource for employees to record details of customer contacts. This is a widely used practice in selling companies, and had been present in various paper and electronic forms in Compound UK from the early 1970s.

The research on which this case study is based took place in two phases. The first phase was from October 1995 to February 1996, during which 33 in-depth semi-structured interviews were undertaken, lasting between one and two hours. In addition, considerable informal interaction took place between the primary researcher and company personnel. Prior to the first phase, this researcher had carried out an earlier piece of action research in the company, which provided background knowledge of the context. The second phase was from February to May 1997, during which 21 follow-up interviews were conducted to assess the perceptions of the groupware system at a later stage. Full details of the case study may be found in Hayes (1998) and Hayes and Walsham (2000a, 2000b).

Competing Discourses of Empowerment and Control

The contact-recording database provided a focus for competing discourses in Compound UK. On the one hand, some senior managers suggested that Notes should be viewed as empowering, and that members of the field force should only input contacts that they deemed relevant to future sales situations. Other senior managers suggested that reps should input a significant enough number of contacts to prove that they were working hard. Some of the managers, including the commercial director, stressed both polar discourses at different times. He was reported by one of the reps as saying, 'You are going to keep on using the system', but also as saying, 'You are not judged solely on your contact rates.'

The contradictory rhetoric of empowerment and control was seen by some employees to be associated with the company's changing economic conditions. When sales figures were high, there was little mention of the number of contacts recorded by a rep. When sales figures dropped, or when a new product was launched, the commercial director wanted 'proof' that the reps had been visiting enough doctors. This switching left the sales force feeling bemused and unclear as to the key purpose of the contact-recording database. The human resource director noted this as follows

> For three years reps' targets were set around levels of activity [contacts]. They [senior managers] wanted to measure them [reps] against activity targets. This has been eradicated and the emphasis now is on trust, though people are aware that contact recording on Notes allows the ability to survey contacts. This has led them to be unsure as to how they should use it.

Many area managers, who were closer to the actual activities of the sales reps, were reluctant to enforce the use of Notes for complete contact recording when they knew that their reps were working hard and performing well. However, they were aware that senior management looked at the contact rates and drew inferences from them. One area manager mentioned how one rep in his area completed large numbers of contact records that: 'were of no use to anyone and generated very little business. But the general manager noticed the number of contacts that were recorded and thinks [the rep] is brilliant; this has pissed a lot of the better salesmen off.'

Members of the field force were confronted with a choice here. Some reps stressed the language of empowerment, saying that they were undertaking longer and more detailed visits aimed to develop relationships with doctors, rather than maximizing their calling rates. However, other reps felt that senior management attitudes would never change from the old philosophy of control by number of contacts. Interestingly, the bulk of the members of the sales force hedged their bets by completing a similar number of contact records as prior to the restructuring, but also completing them and the strategic selling database in greater detail. This produced, however, some resentment on their part due to the additional workload involved in doing this.

Employees undertaking the new decentralized sales activities, working from their own homes in different geographical regions, would have been difficult to monitor without the use of a technology such as Notes. A rep in South Wales felt that the new system was mainly designed to enable central management to feel in control, rather than to empower him and other reps in their local selling:

It is the people based in headquarters who feel isolated. This is why they use technology so they can monitor what people in the field are up to. The computer allows them a handle on what to do. How would they have known that I was sat in a hotel meeting with you [the researcher] before they introduced Notes? Now I will put it into my contact-recording database. I have already called [the area manager] to tell him where I would be this afternoon, when in years gone by I would not have bothered.

However, although reps conformed to some extent, various devices were used to pay 'lip service' to perceived senior management requirements. As one rep noted:

There is a product being launched soon and we will be expected to see everyone on our territory within a certain time frame. There is no way I will be using strategic selling or contact recording to any effect at this stage. I will just pay lip service and put in the bare minimum that is expected of me.

Some reps refused to input any contacts that they felt were not directly beneficial to their work, and others recorded a single line or even a full stop. This would then register as a new contact.

The area managers, as noted above, had the difficult task of providing a buffer between the sales force and senior management. One area manager said: 'It is hard to motivate the lads [*sic*—the reps]. I cannot sell the benefits of using Notes to them, and really I have stopped bothering, as long as no one from head office gets on to me.'

Field-force management walked a fine line between trying to manage and motivate the reps by a sense of what was important to them, and the need to be seen to be compliant with senior management's wishes. A middle course of action was to emphasize the value of Notes in domains where the reps might feel it to be useful, and to downplay it in areas where the reps felt it was a waste of their time. An area manager in the Midlands of England explained his approach to counselling his reps on the use of the Notes' databases as follows:

> In primary care it is not complex, and all products are old and have been in place for a while. We tell them [the reps] just to keep the contacts and strategic selling sheets ticking over so they are not noticed by head office. Why should they waste their time on the computer, when they should be out selling things? In specialist care we do encourage them to have a few more strategic selling sheets, as it is more useful in hospitals.

Careers and Politics in the Notes Arena

Within the reps themselves, a spectrum of positions could be detected concerning the use of Notes, and in particular its political implications. Some reps harnessed the visibility of contact recording for their own purposes, by registering a large number of contacts to put them in a high position in the 'league tables'. These tables were developed centrally, under the direction of the commercial director, to record the number of contacts and strategic selling sheets for each sales representative. The behaviour of ambitious reps in striving for a high position in the tables was resented by some of the other reps. This was particularly true in the context of primary care where, as noted above, strategic selling sheets were often of limited value. One rep commented sarcastically on his ambitious colleagues: 'There are not that many complex sales situations in my area, and I only need to keep active a few strategic selling sheets at a time, unlike some of the shining stars!'

A further component of Notes that was used as a political resource by some employees was the e-mail facility. Senior managers received many messages informing them of something relatively mundane that had been completed by employees at lower levels in the hierarchy. These were described by some senior managers, and their personal assistants, as pointless. A senior medical liaison manager noted this as follows:

There are a lot of highly career-orientated and cut throat people in Compound UK, and they have taken every chance to portray themselves to the senior managers in a good light. There are a lot of yes men, and this is encouraged in Compound UK by one manager in particular. If you look at the use of the technology, it mirrors their ambitions.

The discussion databases with a national and cross-functional audience were used at times with similar intentions. Politically orientated employees were aware that the national databases were reviewed and contributed to by many senior managers, including the commercial director and the general manager. Thus, ambitious reps and some lower-level employees at the head office in Compound Square saw them as a vehicle for career development. A particular rep commented as follows:

There is a political element definitely. People hijack databases to make political statements. They want to be seen and heard. The national discussion databases are where the political animals are to be found. The regional databases are not the same. They are about local and regional issues, and are more concerned with sharing than anything else.

Many employees felt less uneasy when sharing their views on regional-specific or function-specific databases, which were used to express and share views and comments between colleagues in the same region or function. For example, the 10 medical liaison managers developed a discussion database to review and contribute to specific medical issues on a regular basis. However, the medical director asked if he could take part in the discussions. Soon after he had access, the use of the database declined. One of the liaison managers commented:

The medical liaison database was really well used but has petered out now. This happened soon after our boss, the medical director, asked if he could be included in it because he had heard how successful it was. No one felt they could comfortably share views in the knowledge that he was reviewing the database.

Lessons from the Case Study

Positive rhetoric surrounding groupware often concerns its role in supporting teamwork in a more democratic or egalitarian way. E-mail, for example, can be sent by the lowliest employee to the CEO. If nothing else, the Compound UK case demonstrates the naivety or insincerity of this position. Sending an e-mail to the CEO is a highly political act. Groupware is not inherently democratic. It can be used for a variety of purposes, and the nature of the communication that takes place over the medium needs to be analysed in its specific historical, cultural and political context.

Hayes and Walsham (2000a) make a distinction between 'political' and 'safe' enclaves in the use of groupware systems in Compound UK. The former refer to arenas such as the national discussion databases where, as we have seen, much deliberately political activity took place. The latter refer to regional and functional databases where employees felt less uneasy in sharing information and opinions with colleagues. These settings were more conducive to serious discussion and reflection on ongoing activities and events. However, safe enclaves are political in so far as they are shared social spaces. The distinction between the types of enclaves refers primarily to employee feelings about them, and the nature of communication that took place in them.

So, how well did the groupware support teamworking in Compound UK? It is certainly the case that extensive use was made of e-mail, contact recording, strategic selling sheets and discussion databases. But Hayes and Walsham raise some concerns about the nature and value of some of this communication, using a conceptual distinction between perspective-making and perspective-taking (Boland and Tenkasi 1995). The former refers to a process whereby a community of practice (Lave and Wenger 1991), such as the reps in a particular region, develops and strengthens its own knowledge domain and practices by communication with others in their community. Perspective-taking refers to the process of collaboration between different communities working across functional boundaries, in order to appreciate the viewpoints of the other communities, and thus to synergistically utilize each community's distinctive knowledge.

With respect to perspective-making in the Compound UK case, it can be argued that the regional and functional databases fulfilled a useful function. They enabled the relatively 'safe' presentation of information and discussion within specific geographic or functional communities. However, it is worth noting that some ambitious reps excluded themselves from these enclaves, since they saw no individual benefit to themselves by joining in. The case of the medical liaison database falling into disuse when the boss was admitted to the enclave suggested that perspective-making, at least in the specific circumstances of Compound UK, was best pursued in enclaves with higher hierarchical members excluded.

Less success in perspective-taking can be read into the Compound UK experience. The national databases were ostensibly concerned with this purpose, being open to a wide set of communities, but the political nature of these enclaves restricted their value in sharing perspectives across the communities. Many reps, for example, excluded themselves anyway, and those who participated were normally keen to be seen to agree with senior management, restricting any diversity of view and the potential for learning from others. However, in the safe enclaves of community-specific databases, those that had experience of working with other functions would sometimes provide advice to members of their own community on how best to interact with members of other functions.

Moving on to the strategic selling databases, there is evidence that these were effective in some circumstances in bringing together the views of different communities within Compound UK in order to address a complex sale situation in the specialist care sector. There was rather more scepticism, at least among the reps, concerning the value of strategic selling sheets for primary care, with the inference being that reps in this area who made much use of them were normally doing so for political purposes connected with the central league tables.

Did the surveillance of reps through contact recording achieve its purposes? This depends on what one views that purpose as being. If the goal was to encourage good salespeople, then there is little evidence that those reps who scored well on the league tables were necessarily those who were doing the best job at selling the company's products. However, it could be argued that the climate created by the constant fear of surveillance, the panopticon effect discussed in Chapter 3, might have resulted in an average increase in the work rate of reps and thus higher sales. It is impossible to be certain on this, and hard to see how to create a base line against which to measure this effect, in such a changing context. One thing that can be argued with rather greater certainty is that the rhetoric of empowerment can be considered as a sham, since the reps in general did not feel empowered, and they felt that the old control philosophy was always there, above or beneath the surface.

A final comment on this case here concerns the role of the field force management as 'piggy in the middle'. They were caught between the need to appear to comply with senior management directives, such as contact recording, and the need to provide credible leadership to the reps through an understanding of the value of particular activities to the aim of actually selling products. This dilemma resulted in a range of coping behaviours, such as advising the reps in what areas to concentrate their contact recording activity through to having 'stopped bothering' as long as no one from head office intervened. It is not obvious that this was beneficial to Compound UK's economic success. This observation relates to an interesting case study of an air traffic services organization by Hallier and James (1997). Senior management of this organization imposed more exacting performance demands and controls on front line employees. However, middle managers responded by disguising lower level employees' disaffection with this treatment, largely to protect their own interests in areas such as personal promotion. This resulted in isolating senior managers from the reality of employee relations, and in middle managers only putting in effort in areas where they felt that they would be directly rewarded by senior management. Hallier and James concluded that the end product of the imposition of the stringent controls was higher interpersonal rivalry, lower standards of employee treatment and the subversion of corporate aims. Whilst Compound UK is not directly analogous, there are clear parallels in the dilemmas felt by the middle managers in the two cases regarding controls imposed by senior management being of doubtful value in motivating front line staff.

GROUPWARE AND TEAMWORK: AID OR HINDRANCE?

This section draws on a range of studies of groupware in major international companies reported in a book edited by Ciborra (1996b). Seven different cases are described in the book, all of which are of considerable interest to the topic of this chapter. However, in view of space constraints, three cases have been selected for further discussion here. The reader interested in additional detail on any of the cases is advised to consult the book itself, in addition to various other source documents referenced there. The purpose here is more personal and specific, namely to make a particular selection from the material in the cases as a contribution to various themes on groupware and teamwork that are germane to this chapter.

Before going on to this selection, it is worth noting a key conclusion from the book as a whole. Ciborra, in the first summary chapter, argued that the development and use of groupware technology in large, complex organizations is variable, context-specific and drifts over time. Thus, the question mark in the book's title as to whether the technology is an aid or hindrance to teamwork remained at the end of the study, since there is no general answer to the question. The very definition of groupware depends on how an organization moulds it to the specific context: ' "What groupware is" can only be ascertained *in situ*, when the matching between plasticity of the artefact and the multiform practices of the actors involved takes place' (p. 9).

In terms of methodology for the studies, multiple interviews were conducted with various actors involved in the application of groupware in the organizations studied. In each organization a variety of other data-collection techniques were used including observation, archival review and technology use. Each of the case studies was then written up by the researchers who specialized in that case, and I move on now to my pick-and-mix collection of results from these studies.

Tracking Customer Support Services—Orlikowski (1996a)

This case is a relatively optimistic assessment of the use of Lotus Notes technology in supporting workers in a customer support department of a software company, called Zeta, with headquarters in the Midwest of the United States. The department's responsibility was to provide technical support via a telephone hotline to all users of Zeta's products, including clients, consultants, value-added resellers and Zeta client service representatives in the field. Technical support was a complex activity, since the products involved advanced networking and database technologies that allowed users to build their own applications. Customer calls were rarely resolved with a brief response, but typically involved several hours of research, including searches of reference material, attempts to replicate the problem and a review of program source code.

Notes was acquired in 1992 and an incident tracking support system (ITSS) was developed. After a successful pilot, the system was implemented across the whole of the customer support department. Orlikowski carried out a follow-up study on its usage in 1994, following an earlier piece of research on the system in 1992. She records a whole set of organizational changes resulting from the ITSS implementation.

For example, the nature of the support specialists' work changed, with an increasing emphasis on documenting work process and searching of the established knowledge base thus created. This was seen to have a number of advantages: helping an individual specialist to keep track of a particular problem and attempts at its solution; sharing of such knowledge with others so that a wider group could contribute to problem solving; and creating a database of such incidents to aid the solution of similar customer problems in the future.

Orlikowski also discussed changes in the nature of the work of the managers of the customer support specialists. One aspect of this was that the written trace in the ITSS provided the managers with direct data for performance monitoring and evaluation. Whilst Orlikowski mentioned that there was fear of this electronic surveillance on the part of some support specialists, she stated that there was considerable acceptance by most specialists that work monitoring was a natural aspect of their job. Orlikowski argued that this acceptance was, in part, attributable to the customer services department's cooperative culture, and also to the use to which management put the data. On the latter point, she quoted an employee as follows:

> Management uses the numbers to justify more personnel, to bring back problems to developers to alert them to what's been happening with a new product. They're your advocate. Numbers have become more a positive for us rather than being used against us (p. 38).

Orlikowski identified other organizational changes associated with ITSS use as including a changed distribution of work involving support partners for more junior staff, new forms of proactive collaboration, and the use of the knowledge base as a training tool. She made a useful distinction, from a practical management perspective, between different types of changes:

> I want to distinguish three types of changes: *anticipated* changes— changes that are planned ahead of time and occur as intended; *emergent* changes—changes that arise spontaneously out of local innovation which are not originally anticipated or intended; and *opportunistic* changes—changes that are not anticipated ahead of time but are introduced purposefully and intentionally during the change process in response to an unexpected opportunity, event or outcome (p. 56).

Orlikowski provided examples from the Zeta case study of changes in each of these categories. A more detailed analysis is given in Orlikowski (1996b). The categories provide general concepts for thinking about the management of change in any groupware implementation.

Although Zeta is an international company, with sales and client service field offices around the world, the focus of the Zeta case is the US customer support operation. However, there is an intriguing reference in the case to difficulties in trying to extend the ITSS technology to the three main overseas support offices in the United Kingdom, Europe (country not specified), and Australia. After implementation in 1994, all four support offices had access to each other's ITSS databases, although the US one was much larger. Global collaboration was not, however, plain sailing, as illustrated by a quote from a US specialist:

> If we ask for details on a certain piece of it (a problem) or ask them to clarify a certain point, it may be days, sometimes it's weeks, before a response will come through ... It's just very frustrating because here you are working with somebody, you work for the same company, you're on the same team (p. 44).

Orlikowski noted that the US customer services department managers had been in touch with their overseas counterparts to 'try to promote a more common and collaborative view of global support'. No interviews were conducted with staff from the overseas offices, but one suspects that they would have had a different story to tell. The case as presented implies that the fault lay with the overseas offices, whereas a reasonable hypothesis is that we are dealing here with major organizational and cultural differences between the support offices in the different countries, and that the 'same team' mentality is not something that arises naturally from being members of the same company in different countries. This theme is addressed more fully in the next case study.

New Product Development—Ciborra and Patriotta (1996)

This case concerns a particular use of Lotus Notes in Unilever, one of the largest consumer businesses in the world, with over a thousand successful brands worldwide. The application was aimed at supporting innovation centres, which were responsible for the global coordination of specific product categories. In particular, the groupware was designed as a medium over which ideas for new products could be developed by cross-functional and transnational teams through a process of electronic interaction. This was part of the 'innovation funnel', a method for structuring a new product development from initial ideas to actual product in the market-place. The idea is that the overall development process requires a broad range of inputs initially, these are gradually refined and selections are made, and then a small number of development projects are pushed through to rapid completion and market introduction.

An innovation process management (IPM) system, based on Notes, had been developed and introduced over a two-year period as a way of keeping relevant people around the world informed about particular innovation projects. The number of users was about one thousand. The system included two levels of access: above-the-line and below-the-line. Below-the-line information represented the day-to-day work carried out by a specific project team. It contained a series of activities, not yet well-defined or 'publishable'. When the team made progress, information was posted above-the-line for everyone on the system to read. Team members could not write above-the-line, except for the project leader. A gatekeeper read above-the-line information, and could approve a project by clicking on an approval button, but could not access the internal documents of the project team.

The research on the case was carried out in 1995 on the basis of the work of a specific innovation centre, concerned with the dental product category. The lead centre in this group was based in Milan, with five regional innovation centres in Arabia, Brazil, India, Indonesia and the United States. The use of IPM was quite advanced in this category at the time of the research, with all pending projects represented on it. The above-the-line information was complete and up-to-date but, according to the case writers, was not fully exploited. I will now examine their analysis of the use and limitations of this system.

Ciborra and Patriotta argued that the introduction of a new philosophy of product development based on the innovation funnel and the Notes-based IPM system modified the patterns of exchange between the centre and the periphery. A shift took place from a local strategy in product development to a global one, with decisions needing worldwide consensus and the agreement of the core innovation centre in Milan. This slowed down the decision-making process. In addition, there was less commitment to the innovation funnel on the part of people in countries farther from the epicentre. There were also misunderstandings and breakdowns in communication that could be attributed to the introduction of an international environment linking *de facto* different cultures. Ciborra and Patriotta use the following quote to illustrate this:

This morning when I arrived in my office I found an e-mail from one of our colleagues who manages IT and innovation in ... The message said that people from another foreign innovation centre had done things that she [the manager] had never imagined they could do; in a few words, they had moved a project in the funnel assuming they could do so; in the US they did not think in the same way and this led to a long exchange of information (p. 133).

A second area where the new system had serious limitations was in the support of the actual work process, particularly below-the-line. Alternative media here were e-mail, pieces of paper, telephones, faxes, and meeting reports, all of which were perceived as more agile and more secure than the IPM system. Ciborra and Patriotta report that the system was largely used to formalize and make explicit decisions and events that had already occurred, rather than to support informal work practices concerned with the development of innovative new projects. Even above-the-line, substitute media were often used, such as project briefs, project planning tools and conventional fax, telephone or e-mail.

The transparency of the system was viewed as a problem and a 'bit scary', to quote one of the users. Ciborra and Patriotta say that, for example, a French employee might feel interested in comparing ideas on a problem with some Italian colleagues in the innovation centre, but might not 'be so thrilled' about informing other German or English colleagues. However, the need to show to some and hide from others was not part of the philosophy of IPM, except for the above- and below-the-line distinctions, which were themselves introduced at a later stage in response to fears about the totally transparent system in the first version of IPM.

Ciborra and Patriotta conclude that, at Unilever, there was a teamwork culture, but that there were difficulties in extending this to a global community culture. They argue that this situation is typical of large business organizations who are trying to resolve the tension between the need for openness and transparency, facilitated by technologies such as groupware, with their current hierarchical 'formative context':

While the new socio-technical systems [including groupware] ... emphasize the 'public good' nature of task and product knowledge, the hierarchical formative context into which these innovations are embedded supports a different class of behaviours, such as the pursuit of individual objectives, opportunism, knowledge hoarding and hiding ... As a result of such a tension, groupware and teamwork drift, since they are amended, modified and diluted in order to make their innovative concept and structure compatible to the pre-existing context (p. 141).

In order to host a genuinely 'public good' attitude using transparent technologies such as groupware, Ciborra and Patriotta argue that there has to be a radical change of attitude in organizations to traditional concepts of hierarchy.

Group Decision Support Systems at the World Bank—Bikson (1996)

The organization in this third case study that I have selected from the Ciborra book is the World Bank, a non-profit agency 'owned' by its member countries, and concerned with alleviating poverty by providing economic, technical and financial assistance to the poorer countries of the world. At the time of the research in 1995, the Bank had a multinational workforce of approximately 10 000 people, with 90% of them located in Washington DC, in the United States. The Bank also had about 70 field offices, and a typical headquarters staff member spent up to 120 days per year travelling in the countries with which they worked.

The particular groupware application described in the case is a form of group decision support system called GroupSystems, a software system designed to support same-time same-place interactions among many-person groups. Meetings occupied a large amount of time at the Bank, and there were concerns that they prevented staff from getting on with the 'real' work, that they had unclear outcomes, that follow-up actions were not well specified, and that they often resulted in yet another meeting. GroupSystems provided a range of facilities designed to support more efficient and effective meetings, including anonymous concurrent brainstorming, group structuring of meeting comments, assessment of decision alternatives by ranking or voting, and real-time feedback using visual displays.

The system was piloted in the Bank in 1993, using a dedicated room with 14 linked workstations. It had been in use for two years at the time of the research, and Bikson concluded that the use of the software had been generally successful. Participants gave the computer-mediated meetings higher scores than conventional meetings in areas such as improved learning and participation. Two qualifications need to be noted, however. First, there is always the possibility of a 'Hawthorne effect', whereby the novelty of the meetings produced by itself a positive response, although Bikson argued against this in view of factors such as repeat business. A second qualification is perhaps more significant, namely that the computer-based meetings were particularly well planned, and facilitated by a neutral third party. A number of interviewees believed that if the same amount of advance preparation and skilled staffing had been used in traditional meetings, many of the same improvements would have been experienced.

It is interesting to see the types of meetings that were thought to be best enabled by the technology. Bikson used the interview data to argue that meetings involving divergent thinking—the generation of ideas, alternatives, plans, explanations, proposals—were well supported by the GroupSystems software. In contrast, convergent cognitive tasks—making decisions, resolving conflicts, allocating scarce resources—were less well supported. There is a certain irony that this group *decision* support system (GDSS) seemed poorly suited to facilitating decision-making, but rather better suited to group discussion. Perhaps the term GDSS should stand for group discussion support system? The simplest explanation for this result is surely that of power and politics, key features of the convergent cognitive tasks referred to above. Bikson largely supported this hypothesis when reporting interviewees' explanations for the relative failure of the system in these areas. These included: 'not all groups that meet are empowered to make decisions'; 'different experts are not sure that all participants should have an equal voice'; and that the pace of decision-making in a computer-facilitated meeting 'may violate the norms and ethics of decision-making'.

In meetings to support divergent thinking, where the technology was felt to be particularly valuable, specific advantages of anonymous meeting participation included 'saying the unsayable'. For example, people may feel constrained in normal meetings to say that a bad idea is bad, whereas it is easier to do so anonymously. A second specific advantage concerned the making of shared meanings. The technology was heavily used by focus groups in the post-pilot phase, and Bikson argued that this probably reflected the value of the technology in enabling the development of shared values and meanings within such professional groups. Bikson also noted some potentially negative aspects of anonymous meeting participation. These included a case where 'honestly critical feedback' from a sizeable proportion of participants 'angered the program managers'.

Bikson reported that, at the end of the research period in 1995, the Bank had started to consider the portability of the software, so that meetings could be facilitated in other parts of the world, between headquarters staff, field staff and representatives from the recipient countries in which the Bank was involved. The GroupSystems coordinator in the Bank expressed some concern regarding the limited market focus of US group-ware vendors:

> Given the broad range of needs for improved interaction and problem-solving between [developing countries'] representatives and donor country decision-makers, groupware developers have very limited vision when they aim their wares only at white middle America (p. 178).

However, portability is not just a matter of technical provision or vendor attitude but also, as briefly noted by Bikson, of cultural port-ability. Bikson reported the view of one interviewee as 'the less open the culture, the more the benefit from the technology. It should work well in other countries'. This seems the most simplistic form of technical deter-minism, arguing that the technology will in itself 'open out' a closed culture. In a more perceptive response, a second interviewee expressed the view that 'the system would be less well received in countries that are more tolerant of openly critical in-person discussion than the United States'. This seems a plausible hypothesis but nothing more than that. It is clear that the World Bank in 1995, despite its global mission, was still in an early learning phase with respect to the cross-cultural applicability of groupware technology.

COLLABORATION IN DISTRIBUTED ORGANIZATIONS

Further empirical material on groupware implementation, with a specific focus on the earlier phases of technology adoption and adaptation, is provided by Munkvold (1998, 1999). He carried out six case studies of the use of groupware technology to support collaboration in distributed organizations, defined as consisting of two or more organizational units in dispersed geographical locations. The organizational units were teams, departments or whole organizations. Three of the case studies involved enterprises based in Norway, and the other three dealt with companies operating more globally, but with a Norwegian base company. One of each of these categories has been selected for presentation and analysis here. The research method used by Munkvold for the cases was largely based on interviews, supplemented by his attendance at various meet-ings, the use of documents, and e-mail contact in the second case below.

Supporting Tendering in Offcom

This case study concerned the implementation of Lotus Notes to support the tendering process in a network of six Norwegian telecommunications companies, called Offcom. The network was established in 1993, and data for the case study were collected for a period of 16 months in 1995–96. The companies in the network were all small enterprises with the number of employees ranging from three to 30. All the companies were located in the Oslo area with a travel time of one and a half hours between those furthest apart. One of the companies was located in the same building as the Offcom administrative office.

The initiation of the network resulted from a report by the marketing director of one of the companies, followed by an invitation to the other companies to join in. The companies were all involved in selling to the Norwegian offshore industry, their products were complementary, and they had collaborated in the past. However, they had only acted as single systems suppliers for major projects, and the companies hoped to use the Offcom network to compete on major contracts with large international companies in the tendering process. Their explicit goal was to gain one major contract in Norway, and at least one major contract in the UK market.

Notes was chosen by Offcom as a supporting infrastructure for the network, initially using a third-party vendor. However, the document management system in Notes was developed by the R&D department of Telenor, the Norwegian telecommunications supplier, as part of a 'virtual corporations' research project. Development and testing of the system took around two years, partly due to various organizational issues in Telenor, including its restructuring in 1995. The Offcom network did not succeed in getting major contracts as hoped, and the network was terminated in 1996. The document management system never came into regular use, but some interesting analysis is given by Munkvold of the adoption and adaptation phases in the two years of project development.

With respect to adoption, the effort and engagement put into the collaborative arrangement by the different actors varied significantly, which led one of the interviewees to characterize the network as consisting of the 'A and B teams'. People in the B team organizations often did not attend the board meetings, did not read their e-mail, and did not volunteer to take on tasks for the network. Three reasons are given by Munkvold for this lack of enthusiasm. First, one of the organizations became part of an international technology group and had to move towards this group's standard policies. Second, another organization became concerned that its previous customers, large system vendors, would regard it as a competitor through its participation in Offcom. Finally, the market situation was slow during the first part of the collaborative project, leading several companies to give priority to their own individual projects.

Other reasons for limited enthusiasm on the part of network companies related to perceived variable benefits, depending on geographical location. The company at the most distant location from the Offcom office saw clear benefits in electronic document transmission, whereas the company in the same building as this office expected little benefit from the technology: 'From our point of view, we have not come any further from today's solution of delivering a floppy disk to the Offcom administration. We also have document templates today, and we can use "cut and paste"' (Munkvold 1998, p. 133).

Several of the organizations also expressed concern that the technology represented additional overhead on top of their existing systems.

Munkvold defined the adaptation phase of IT systems (following Cooper and Zmud 1990) as involving the development, installation and maintenance of the application, the development of new organizational procedures, and the training of users. Some difficulties arose in these areas in the Offcom project. First, there were unclear responsibilities among the many actors in the project, not least as to the precise duties for project management between Telenor R&D and Offcom. A second difficulty was the large geographical distance of 2500 kilometres between Telenor R&D in Tromsø, and Offcom users in Oslo, making detailed project discussions rather difficult. There is a certain irony that a virtual corporations project, sponsored by a major telecommunications supplier, should itself be handicapped by the limitations of electronic communication at-a-distance. Munkvold identified a number of additional problems during the adaptation phase, including membership instability in the network, varying IT competence, and the vendor's limited experience with similar IT implementation projects. The project was eventually stopped due to the termination of the Offcom network itself, but even if this had not happened, it is by no means obvious that the Notes-based collaboration among these organizations would have succeeded.

A Global Area Network in Kværner

The focus of this second case study, taken from Munkvold (1998), is the implementation of a global area network called Kigan (Kværner internal global area network). Kværner is a multinational engineering group, originating in Norway which, at the time of the research study in 1996, consisted of more than 430 companies and branch offices in 45 countries. Following the take-over of Trafalgar House, a large British engineering group, in 1996 Kværner was the largest Norwegian company, and the biggest engineering company outside the United States.

The Kigan project was started in June 1995 using Telenor as the vendor partner. The contract included the establishment of telecommunications services for voice, e-mail and data worldwide in the Kværner group. The objectives from the perspective of Kværner were to facilitate more effective collaboration between companies in the group, to enable access to 'centres of competence' in the network, and to increase coordination between companies in the group in areas such as global purchasing and service contracts. Kigan was based on wide area network (WAN) technology providing permanent virtual circuits for transmission of e-mail and attached documents. It was also used as the basis for an intranet service, offering different types of company information through Internet technology, such as world wide web (WWW) browsers.

The implementation of Kigan was contracted out to a small team of four people in Kværner Engineering in Oslo. In addition, four regional centres were established in Houston, London, Singapore and Sydney. The decision to adopt the system or not was fully decentralized, in that each of the companies in the Kværner group was free to decide whether to become part of the network. The original plan was to have all the companies linked in Kigan by the end of summer 1996. The process was slower than expected but, by February 1997, all the large and central companies in the group were connected, except for South America. The statistics for net traffic showed a rapid increase in the use of the network by this time, and the Kigan project coordinator characterized the technology as 'mission critical'.

Munkvold collected data on the project in the period from February 1996 to February 1997. His access was relatively limited, but nevertheless there are some interesting points in his description of the adoption and adaptation phases. With respect to adoption, this proved to be slow and complex, and one of the key reasons was the decentralized decision structure in the Kværner group. Some companies thought that the technology was too expensive. More fundamentally, perhaps, Munkvold argued that the basic thrust of the Kigan project was increased coordination and collaboration among the companies in the group, and that this new way of working was resisted in some cases. Other issues that worked against the take-up of the technology included collaborating with local non-Kværner partners rather than with distant companies in the group, and waiting for critical mass before joining in.

In the adaptation phase, technological issues were important in that the network represented an inflexible solution. Munkvold reported that the project coordinator considered it a 'serious mistake' that a particular technology was chosen for the whole project, rather than building a network architecture that could serve the needs of all the different companies. For example, the Kigan network was incompatible with the existing technology being used in some of the companies. The implementation team was relatively small, and senior management did not give any 'explicit signals' regarding the benefits of the Kigan network.

The project coordinator also believed that cultural differences were of increasing importance to Kværner as it became more global. Munkvold (1997), in describing results from four of his case studies including Kværner, stated these as including language barriers, and different practices for solving problems and decision-making. The Kigan project coordinator did not think it possible to develop a 'common culture' in a distributed organization like Kværner, pointing to the fact that each Kværner company had been acquired, often without any change in management. Further details of this intriguing area are not provided in the case materials as presented by Munkvold. At the end of the research period in 1997, the Kigan project can be viewed, however, as at least a partial success, but the goal of worldwide collaboration in a complex, diverse and decentralized group such as Kværner remains hard to achieve.

ANALYSIS AND CONCLUSIONS

A summary of the cases discussed in this chapter is given in Table 5.1. Lotus Notes was used in the majority of cases, reflecting its dominant position in groupware technology in the 1990s. However, the range of applications of Notes and the other technologies, even in this limited set of cases, is very wide in at least two senses. First, the technologies were used to support particular functions in a company, inter-functional knowledge-sharing, collaboration between companies in a group, and networking between independent companies. Second, the specific activities and sectors that were supported by the technology were very varied including incident tracking systems in a software company, tendering in the engineering industry, through to meeting support in the World Bank. There were also great differences in the reported success of the technology use, reinforcing the view of Ciborra, cited earlier, that

Table 5.1 *Summary of groupware cases*

Case	Author(s)	Location	Technology	Purpose	Key points
Compound UK	Hayes/ Walsham	UK	Lotus Notes	Knowledge sharing across functional and geographical boundaries	• Competing discourse of empowerment and control • Safe and political enclaves • Field force management as 'piggy in the middle'
Zeta	Orlikowski	US (mainly)	Lotus Notes	Incident tracking support system	• Improved work process • Surveillance not a major threat • Anticipated, emergent and opportunistic changes
Unilever	Ciborra/ Patriotta	Italy plus worldwide	Lotus Notes	Supporting the innovation funnel for new products	• Above-the-line and below-the-line • Problems with support of work process and transparency • No global community culture
World Bank	Bikson	US	Group Decision Support System	More efficient and effective meetings	• Valuable for interaction, e.g. focus groups • Limited largely to discussion, not decision • No knowledge of usefulness in developing country environments
Offcom	Munkvold	Norway	Lotus Notes	Improved collaboration on tendering	• A and B teams • Variable perceived benefits • Major problems in adaptation phase
Kværner	Munkvold	Norway plus worldwide	Global Area Network	Collaboration between companies in group	• Decentralized adoption process slow • But ended up as 'mission critical' • Not possible to develop 'common culture'

groupware outcomes result from the matching between the plasticity of the technology and the practices of the actors in a specific context.

Only a small subset of the literature on groupware has been discussed here, and other cases provide further variety of purpose and outcomes. For example, Karsten (1995) described her research on the use of Notes in a small Finnish computer consulting company, called CCC. It is worth mentioning here for two reasons. First, it provides an example of an attempt to support internal collaboration within a small company, a type of case missing from the ones reported so far in the chapter. Second, in a later publication (Karsten 1999), the author provided a valuable longitudinal perspective on the change process in this company linked to the use of Notes:

> At the end of the three-year study period, the form of organization had become more integrated, more consensual, and there was more collaboration in projects. The consultants had modified their roles, as their discourse about the firm became more visible ... as their participation increased in volume ... and as their work became more visible. All these were much influenced by the use of Notes, some as planned, but others opportunely and as unexpected consequences of Notes use (p. 243).

Karsten (1999) summarized the results of 17 different applications of Notes reported in the literature, including CCC above, and the Zeta and Unilever cases reported earlier in this chapter. She categorized the applications into three usage types: exploratory or conservative, expanding, and extensive. She placed Unilever in the first of the categories, and Zeta and CCC in the last. She concluded, in line with the view expressed in this chapter, that there is no 'collaboration-inducing' inherent model in Lotus Notes. The outcomes from a specific application depend on such issues as the 'care' needed in bringing about desired changes, the management of the emergent and drifting nature of the change process, and the gradual translations needed from changing work practices to broader organizational practices.

Whilst accepting this broad view of the specific nature of any particular groupware project, I would argue that it is possible to draw some broad 'generalizations' from the case study evidence in this chapter. In particular, some general answers can be provided to the questions raised at the start of the chapter, and these questions are now addressed directly. Linkages are made between the case material of the chapter

Table 5.2 *Groupware technologies and globalization*

Groupware technologies seem to offer good support to collaboration in global contexts	• Enable time–space distanciation and zoning • Pervasive and standardized networking through social structure
But local 'formative context' of the application is crucial	• Difficulties include non-supportive cultural environment and variable perceived benefits • Technology as one actant only in complex actor networks
Limited evidence of cross-cultural working supports strong glocal effects	• Global community culture in TNCs not feasible • Different styles of group interaction, attitudes to decision-making, view of knowledge

and earlier concepts and themes from Part 1 of the book. A summary of key points in the remainder of this section is provided in Tables 5.2–5.4.

What are the Links Between Groupware Technologies and Globalization Processes?

As discussed briefly at the start of this chapter, groupware technologies seem to offer high potential value for knowledge-sharing in the increasingly virtual forms of co-working that are common in the contemporary world. Expressing this more formally in the language of the social thinkers discussed in Chapter 2, such technologies enable time–space distanciation and zoning as discussed by writers such as Giddens and Robertson. Castells argued that IT supports the pervasive expansion of networking throughout the social structure, and groupware technologies provide a good illustration of this, with the promise of standardized approaches to knowledge-sharing in organizations such as the transnational corporations.

However, the case study evidence in this chapter cautions against a simple standardization hypothesis. The formative context within which the groupware technology is being utilized is crucial to the collaborative processes enabled by the technology. In the Zeta case, the acceptance of the groupware system by the customer support specialists was attributed to the customer services department's cooperative culture. In contrast, the culture in Compound UK was characterized by competing discourses of empowerment and control which made the reps feel highly uncertain of the rationale for, and utilization of, certain elements of the system such as the 'open' discussion databases. Networks of independent organizations, as described in the Offcom case, can be thought of as particularly difficult contexts in which to enable effective collaboration. The widely different motives of the organizations may lead to differential levels of commitment to the use of collaborative technologies, as exemplified by the A and B teams in the Offcom network. The lack of effective use of the group decision support systems in the World Bank in supporting decision-making, as distinct from discussion, can be put down to the highly politicized context within which decisions on research allocation, for example, are taken.

In the language of actor-network theory, discussed in Chapter 3, the groupware technology can be considered as only one actant in complex actor-networks of people and technology. A successful application implies the alignment of interests of all the actants, and the formative context can be thought of as one of these. If the collaborative message inscribed in the technology is not aligned with the culture of the formative context, then the actor network is likely to fragment. Orlikowski (1993) provided a further example of a relatively difficult formative context for the introduction of groupware, using a case study of a large consulting company called Alpha. The attempt to use the Notes technology to support shared effort and cooperation clashed with the organization's individualistic and competitive culture and rigid hierarchy. The reward system did not emphasize collaboration, and the competitive culture was continuously reinforced by an 'up or out' approach to the retention of individual consultants.

The multicultural formative contexts for groupware systems in transnational organizations creates further difficulties in terms of standardization, as reported in all the case studies in this chapter where systems were not restricted to a single country. In Zeta, global collaboration on the incident tracking system proved problematic from the perspective of the US employees. In the Unilever case, it was reported that there were misunderstandings due to the introduction of an international environment linking different cultures. In the World Bank, there was little knowledge at the time of writing of the case with respect to the possible applicability of the groupware system in developing countries. At Kværner, doubt was expressed about being able to develop a common global culture, citing language barriers and different decision-making approaches in the different countries within the group. As noted in Chapter 3, the very concept of knowledge itself may be perceived differently in different cultural environments, and so may attitudes to appropriate group interaction and knowledge sharing.

Thus the global thrust of the technology introduction encounters the features of the local culture and the emergent forms of collaborative working differ in different places, the glocalization effect discussed by Robertson. Although all cases above hinted at these effects, in-depth analysis was not presented. Indeed, substantive cross-cultural studies of groupware implementation in radically different cultural contexts were not readily available at the time of writing. However, in Part 3 of the book, I will address the influence of culture on the appropriation of IT in detail using examples of other information technologies and systems.

How Effective are Groupware Technologies in Supporting Collaboration and Knowledge-Sharing?

The previous sub-section tended to emphasize the difficulties of implementing effective groupware systems, for example in different cultural contexts, but it would be wrong to imply from this that such systems are invariably ineffective. In terms of the cases in the chapter, the Notes system in Zeta had many benefits associated with it, as reported by Orlikowski, related to documenting the work process in ways that aided problem-tracking and knowledge-sharing between specialists, and creating a knowledge base to support training. GroupSystems in the World Bank provided valuable support for interaction and discussion according to Bikson. Even in the Compound UK case, where Notes was regarded as problematic in some application areas, its use in others such as the regional and functional discussion databases was generally regarded as successful.

When discussing knowledge-sharing in Chapter 3, it was argued that some forms of tacit knowledge may be difficult or impossible to

Table 5.3 *Effectiveness of groupware in supporting collaboration*

Groupware can provide support for collaboration and knowledge-sharing in supportive formative context	• Documenting work process, establishing knowledge base • Supporting interaction and discussion of focused groups
But may be more difficult to support local situated work practice	• Tacit knowledge hard to capture, encode, disseminate • Role of local community in situated work practice
Need for continuous management of process	• Anticipated, emergent and opportunistic • Drifting of groupware technology • Fundamental nature of improvisation

'capture', and thus to encode and disseminate. Authors such as Suchman emphasized the importance of local, situated work practice, drawing on tacit knowledge to take appropriate local action. Are groupware systems supportive of this? The innovation process management system in Unilever provided an illustration, according to Ciborra and Patriotta, where the system was largely used to document what had occurred rather than to support the informal work practice of developing innovative new projects. It is perhaps no coincidence that the systems that best supported local practice, such as those in Zeta, were developed and implemented locally, rather than being imposed from outside or top-down. This would support Star's view, noted in Chapter 3, of the importance of the 'web' of local community in situated work practice. It is difficult, if not impossible, to create a feeling of local community in people who are supposed to collaborate at-a-distance. Munkvold argued this in the Offcom case when discussing the problems of collaboration between two groups situated 2500 kilometres distant, despite their access to leading-edge telecommunications.

Assuming a positive formative context, and a sensitivity to local community and situated work practice, there is still a need for the continuous management of process in the introduction of groupware systems to aid collaborative working. In Zeta, where the groupware system and its use evolved over a period of years, the different approaches to change were labelled by Orlikowski as anticipated, emergent and opportunistic. The first and last of these are a key focus for management action, and the emergent changes, arising spontaneously out of local innovation, need to be monitored and supported. Ciborra (1996b) talked about the 'drifting' nature of groupware technology in practice, and by implication the need to support and manage this process. As discussed in Chapter 3, Ciborra sees improvisation as fundamental to work practice, with routine being derived and de-rooted from this. Thus, the challenge is to design and manage information systems in general, and groupware systems in particular, primarily to support improvisation rather than routine. I would not go this far myself, since routine activities are valuable and need support, but a focus on improvisation provides a valuable counterpoint to an emphasis on management as being solely about control.

How are Groupware Technologies Implicated in Power Relations?

Groupware systems, as with many other computer-based systems, tend to make visible processes and views that were more hidden previously,

Table 5.4   *Groupware and power relations*

Perceptions of surveillance and control through groupware systems specific to local contexts	• May be perceived as largely non-threatening in supportive environments • However, less supportive environments may lead to defensive action • Need to create below-the-line or 'safe' enclaves
Reward systems may support non-collaborative behaviour	• Individual objectives, knowledge-hoarding • Fears of openness in above-the-line contexts
Intranets offer new opportunities but share many issues with groupware	• Ubiquity and low cost of access • But formative context and other socio-technical groupware issues still relevant

as noted in the discussion of Zuboff's concept of 'informate' in Chapter 3. This can, of course, have major advantages in terms of sharing knowledge and other forms of collaborative working. However, the existence of new visible data may be perceived as a threat in some cases, for example in leading to increased surveillance by management and tighter control. This control may be perceived as relatively benign, as reported by Orlikowski in the Zeta case. However, in the example of the contact records in Compound UK, many reps felt that the use of numbers of sales contacts as a form of surveillance was inappropriate. As noted also in Chapter 3, surveillance can produce multiple forms of resistance, and the Compound case provided a nice example of some reps recording a single line or even a full stop in order to register a contact record.

Even in supportive formative contexts, none of us wishes to have all our written thoughts and views made visible to the whole world. This is particularly the case where those viewing the material are perceived to have some power over the individual concerned, such as in a traditional hierarchical organization. Some degree of freedom from surveillance and visibility may be seen to be necessary to enable communication and knowledge-sharing to take place in a relatively unconstrained way. For example, in the Unilever case it was necessary to create a below-the-line form of communication accessible only to a specific project team. This is similar to the description of 'safe enclaves' in the Compound UK case, where pharmaceutical reps felt able to share views on the selling process outside the gaze of higher levels of the hierarchy.

Although this was not discussed directly in the earlier case descriptions, financial reward systems are an aspect of power relations in organizations that can be considered to play a significant part in stimulating or constraining collaborative behaviour. Where individuals see little in the way of reward for knowledge-sharing, or indeed where they are rewarded solely for their own individual contribution, it is not surprising that knowledge-hoarding is likely to take place. The reps in the Compound UK case were largely rewarded in the short term by their sales figures, reducing the incentive for them to collaborate. In the longer term, reward could take the form of promotion to head office, explaining more fully the conformist behaviour of ambitious reps in above-the-line contexts, where they were visible to senior management.

Finally, in this chapter on collaborative technologies such as groupware, what about intranets as a new, ubiquitous and cheaper means of collaborative support? Brown (1998b) argued, based on work in Xerox, that organizations should be seen as 'communities of communities', and that new technologies such as intranets are well suited to provide support to the development of communication within and between communities. He discussed the need to design organizations and their technological systems to support this perspective:

> Any design of organizational architecture and the ways communities are linked to each other should enhance the healthy autonomy of communities, while simultaneously building an interconnectedness through which to disseminate the results of separate communities' experiments. In some form or another the stories that support learning-in-working and innovation should be allowed to circulate. The technological potential is available to support this distribution (e-mail, bulletin boards, home pages, etc. are capable of supporting narrative exchange) (Brown 1998b, p. 232).

The technological potential to support collaboration may be available, but the problematic socio-technical groupware issues discussed in this chapter apply equally well to intranets. In order to use intranets to support collaborative working, it is still necessary to provide a supportive formative context, attention to issues of situated local practice, appropriate approaches to surveillance and control, and reward systems that encourage knowledge-sharing and openness. The experience of groupware systems in the 1990s should be used to inform more thoughtful approaches to the IT-enabled support of collaborative working, including the use of intranets, in the coming decade.

6
Reorganizing the Enterprise

The previous two chapters considered the relationship between IT and work at the individual and group levels. The focus of this chapter is company-wide information systems, related to major programmes of change in an organization as a whole. These have been touched on already, since many IT initiatives at the individual or team level form part of a broader change agenda. For example, the case study of computer hardware engineers in Comco in Chapter 4 was part of a wider business process re-engineering (BPR) programme in that company.

Company-wide initiatives related to new computer-based information systems are not a new phenomenon. For example, material requirements planning (MRP) systems have been used for many years in a wide range of manufacturing companies, and these systems aim to provide data to support all functional areas of the organization and their integration. However, although such company-wide systems have been present for a long time, the 1990s saw a major increase in the application of comprehensive organizational change initiatives, with IT seen as the driving force or, at least, as a major part of the initiative. Three key questions concerning the reasons for this phenomenon and its effects are addressed in this chapter:

- Why have company-wide IT-based initiatives been increasingly used as the vehicle for organizational transformation?
- What effects have major organizational initiatives had on work and worker identity?
- How well have company-wide initiatives coped with organizational variety and cultural specificity?

These questions will be explicitly addressed in the final section of the chapter. The next three sections present an empirical base for such an analysis by describing some detailed case material on company-wide IT-based change initiatives. The first of these concerns a new computerized decision support system that was central to a major change in the corporate lending process of a large UK bank. The second case study provides an example of a BPR initiative aimed at re-engineering the back office sites of a medium-sized UK bank. The third case study relates to the application of enterprise systems, or enterprise resource planning (ERP) systems, to give them their fuller name. It concerns the implementation of such a system in a diversified transnational company with Norwegian origins.

CORPORATE LENDING IN UK BANK

This case study concerns a major clearing bank, known for confidentiality as UK Bank, which was the first bank to attempt to introduce a computer-based decision support system (DSS) into its middle market corporate lending process in the UK retail banking sector. The system chosen by UK Bank, called Lending Adviser (LA), represented a leading-edge technology, and as such evoked considerable interest in the sector as a whole. Other major retail banks have since developed similar computer-based DSSs for their UK credit risk management divisions.

Although the LA project started as an initiative led by a functional line, concerned with corporate lending to SMEs, other functional lines started to recognize opportunities presented by LA, and to structure changes around it. The project became part of a company-wide change initiative, and was used in an extensive public relations initiative aimed at the Bank's shareholders. The project was heralded as the Bank's response to the need for more effective risk management, highlighted by serious losses that the Bank had incurred during the UK recession of the late 1980s and early 1990s.

The case study is based on a longitudinal research project conducted between 1993 and 1996 in UK Bank. The research started when LA was in its pilot stage, and followed the implementation of the system through to 'business as usual' status. The primary method for gathering data was extensive in-depth interviews with project stakeholders, and 140 formal interviews were carried out. Full details of the case study and extensive analysis may be found in Scott (1998, 2000) and Scott and Walsham (1998).

The LA Project

The UK banking industry was a deeply traditional sector in the United Kingdom for many years, but the 1970s and 1980s saw a major change take place, with increasing deregulation and competition. UK Bank was subject to these changes along with everyone else, but its losses in the economic recession referred to above were perhaps the most dramatic amongst the UK retail banks. A major problem was that the £40 billion lending portfolio generated by UK Bank was difficult to monitor and manage. The recession revealed UK Bank's overdependence on property as security for loans in an overheated market.

In response to this situation, senior management decided to appoint a managing director to review the risk process. The managing director formed a team that focused on some fundamental questions: What is the basis of our lending expertise? What are the best practices in lending? What is a quality portfolio? When the project team asked UK Bank loan managers to define 'quality' lending practices, they were often told that this could not be done, since lending was part art as well as science. However, the eventual conclusion of the project team was that a quality portfolio could be achieved by 'rules' that guide the loan assessment process.

During the course of their work, the project team went to the United States, where the financial services industry had already begun to try to harness the data on their mainframe computers in decision support systems. The team decided that the LA technology, seen on their visit to the United States, fitted with their strategy of formalizing the lending process, and was the means they wished to use to achieve what they regarded as necessary change within UK Bank.

The concept behind LA was that it provided lenders with an analysis of a borrower's capacity to repay debt out of future cash flows. The loans manager entered data gathered from an interview with the customer, and historic management records, into the relevant fields of up to 52 LA screens which were laid out like business forms. LA calculated the probability of a loan defaulting, drawing on data profiles of companies who had defaulted or not defaulted in the past. The parameters of these calculations were weighted to reflect data gathered by knowledge engineers who had attempted to elicit 'best practice' from selected 'good' loan managers. The assessments from the LA system were shown graphically as gauges called 'meters'. If the initial LA assessment regarding a particular loan application was negative, then the loans manager could reject the application, pursue additional data that might influence the meter, or 'override' the meter reading by writing a 'footnote' explaining why.

Implementation of LA and the Change Programme

The concept of LA was introduced to the loan managers in a political campaign of acceptance led by change leaders carefully selected by the LA project director. Survival rhetoric abounded, with managers being told that UK Bank had no choice but to implement LA. Referring to the aftermath of the severe losses incurred during the recession, the project director said: 'I had a burning platform to work with—always a great ally to a change agent.'

There was considerable concern among the loan managers as they faced the prospect of using computers in their job for the first time. The study of users revealed a number of positive aspects of the LA system: a computer-based organizational memory; central access to organizational data; what-if analysis capability; and electronic transmission of applications. However, it also revealed negative aspects from the perspective of the loan managers, including the constraints imposed by the use of LA on work practices, and heightened anxiety regarding job security due to extensive reorganization.

Loan managers' concerns with respect to working practices centred on loss of autonomy, longer working hours, and the way in which their job was disembedded from its traditional social context. For example, where loan managers could write a paper-based assessment at a customer site, or at home after their family had retired for the night, they were now effectively chained to their desks by their computer, as the release of lap-tops was considerably delayed. This loss of flexibility was compounded by the length of time that it took to 'load' a business case on to LA. The loan managers had been told that this should take them up to one hour, but in practice this turned out to involve four or five hours for a straightforward case, and 15 hours or more for complex cases. The managers found themselves working long hours under considerable stress to meet unrealistic targets in terms of numbers of cases to be loaded in a given time. This had a serious impact on users' home lives, particularly if they also had to commute long distances to work, as they did in the London region. One loan manager commented: 'My wife has put her foot down since our first child was born ... Now she is saying that I have to go in at 8 a.m. and be out by 6 p.m. I am not supposed to work weekends either—however, I haven't managed to keep to this yet.'

Despite the hardships associated with the new system, managers were reluctant to indulge in overt resistance to the introduction of LA. A typical response is as follows: 'To date it has been negative, but that is because it took so much time during loading that should have been spent doing other things, developing business. In the medium term, I am ambivalent. I am not hugely positive, but not really negative either.'

Scott (2000) attributes this attitude as owing much to the conditions of dependency in which the loan managers found themselves. Senior management had seized upon the opportunity presented by LA implementation to introduce a series of extensive organizational changes, including compulsory redundancies. The title of 'local branch manager' was abolished and newly named 'corporate managers' were brought together in cluster teams whereby each manager serviced an area or business sector rather than a particular community. Management grades were reduced from eight to three, sweeping away the historical credit risk career path. Regional and local head offices, the bastions of the previous banking tradition, were rationalized and dissolved into business areas.

The aggregate effect of the organizational changes and the introduction of the LA-based approach to loan assessment resulted in a relatively radical shift to UK Bank's loans portfolio. The new focus was on 'safer' parts of the market; small businesses at the riskier end of the credit spectrum were placed on immediate 'exit policy' as criteria for creditworthiness shifted from the individual loan manager's judgement and expertise to the more quantitative and standardized LA measures. Loan managers tended to see many of their clients as unique cases, and often had problems adjusting to the concept of standard categories and the rigid industry codes used in LA. One manager articulated this scepticism as follows: 'The [UK Bank industry code] is such a blunt tool. I am troubled by that. At the moment, the classifications are running to catch up with the business ... There should be a health warning on these classifications.'

The use of LA industry codes, combined with the increasing hurdles put before companies seeking credit loans, concerned all the managers in the study in terms of its impact on the overall UK Bank portfolio. For example, one manager expressed this forcefully as follows:

The current changes are squeezing the bottom of the portfolio ... Lending Adviser has made it hard for [medium sized] businesses to get a loan, but so bloody difficult if you are a small business. It is an information driven system and provides an entry barrier for small businesses.

The Changing World of the Loan Managers

If we focus first at the level of the individual loan managers, this case study provides a striking example of shifting identity linked to new IT systems and work processes, as discussed earlier in Chapter 4. The shift in the case of these managers can be considered as quite dramatic. They used to be 'pillars of the local community', with a high degree of autonomy in their loan activities, operating in a relatively calm world and with what was perceived as a job for life. Following the introduction of LA, they were expected to become dispassionate loan workers, subject to much closer surveillance, and where loan judgements were seen as adhering to global standards rather than local contingencies.

These changed conditions created tensions of identity in the loan managers. Many of them still identified with clients at the local level, but found that their new role conflicted with this earlier conception of what it meant to be a bank manager. The title of their job changed in line with these new expectations, with the traditional label of branch manager being replaced by corporate manager. It is, of course, relatively easy to change the label, but less easy for individuals to adapt their self-identity to conform to the new labels. Scott (2000) points out a further identity issue that surfaced in the field interviews. The most persistent and emotive issue raised by middle managers was the need for them to do their own typing under the new conditions. Most managers, all of whom were male in the sample studied, associated keyboard work with clerical status and regarded it as the domain of the 'girls in the back office'. Scott argues that the change appeared to threaten some managers' sense of their own masculinity.

Issues of professional identity and tensions associated with their new expected role were undoubtedly exacerbated by the climate of attrition within which the managers were operating. Redundancies were common, and a significant demographic shift took place within UK Bank. For example, all the loan managers over 50 years of age interviewed in the research study took early retirement. Younger staff were given opportunities and responsibilities previously reserved for long-serving loan managers. However, they had to face these new roles with less training and experience, and less pay than their predecessors.

There was little room for significant resistance to all of these changes on the part of the managers, as mentioned earlier. However, there was a variety of response to the changes, with some individuals coping much better than others. In addition, there was some limited scope for trying to manipulate LA, as described by one of the local LA application managers:

> Some have seen it almost as an arcade game, seeing if they can move the meters up by playing with the figures ... There have been cases where if a manager gets an alert [negative warning], he will manipulate

the figures until it is back in the acceptable zone, rather than having to go through the process of explaining it to head office ... We are trying to manage this response to the system.

However, the more common response was to go along with the 'guidance' offered by LA, and I turn now to the question of whether this was a 'good thing' for UK Bank, and more broadly for its activities within the country as a whole.

Broader Organizational and Societal Effects

Was the aggregate effect of the changes to UK Bank's approach to the lending process, mediated through the actions of the individual loan managers and their use of LA, beneficial to the efficiency, effectiveness and profitability of UK Bank as a whole? There is no clear-cut answer to this question. On the one hand, it could be argued that the new approach and the use of LA ensured that more informed decisions were taken on loans, that highly risky sectors of the market were largely eliminated, and that 'bad' loan managers could be identified and either retrained or retired. Not surprisingly, this optimistic picture of the changes tended to be the one favoured by senior managers in UK Bank and those charged with LA implementation. On the other hand, it could be argued that much long-standing loan expertise was lost to the Bank through retirement and retrenchment, that the retained managers were on average less knowledgeable, and that the 'conservative' behaviour induced by LA might in the long run have negative effects for the Bank's loan portfolio. On this latter point there were concerns, at least on the part of some loan managers, that the relatively blunt instrument of the standard categories and the rigid industry codes might provide a worse basis for good loan decisions than the earlier methods based on local management's judgement. In some sense, the question of the overall value of the new LA-based approach for UK Bank is still an open one, and the next economic recession may provide some harder evidence of the quality of the Bank's loans portfolio.

One clear effect, widely acknowledged at all levels of the Bank, was the squeezing out of the small business sector, an area which UK Bank had spent much time and effort in building up during the 1970s and 1980s. This was a part of the portfolio that had previously engaged much of the loan manager's time, and had been an expression of their judgement and expertise. The question as to whether the severe reduction in loans in this area was good for UK Bank is part of the contentious issue discussed above, and there is no clear answer. A related and broader question, however, is: Is this good for the UK economy as a whole? More generally: What are the societal effects of the use of LA-type systems by most of the large banks in the UK?

The use of quantitative models based on standard categories affects the profile of companies who can and cannot get loans in a given society. At a lower level, for example, the extensive use of credit scoring systems for loans to individuals means that it is more difficult to get a loan if one comes from a 'bad' area as defined in a rather rigid way by one's postcode. Similarly, LA-type systems advantage some business sectors and disadvantage others, and the overall societal effect of this is highly unclear, and not normally debated. Scott (2000) calls this a 'revolution under the cloak of normality', whereby 'technical' decisions taken at the level of individual banks have profound societal effects, with no democratic process to debate the merits or demerits of this. Scott relates these concerns to the changing nature of the 'risk society' as described by Beck and discussed briefly in Chapter 2, and she argues the need for a wider debate on the effect of new approaches to risk estimation, including the use of LA-type systems.

BUSINESS PROCESS RE-ENGINEERING (BPR)

The most common label for organization-wide change initiatives for most of the decade of the 1990s, at least in large Western organizations, was business process re-engineering (BPR). BPR was popularized by such writings as those of Hammer (1990), Hammer and Champy (1993) and Davenport (1993). However, its widespread application was facilitated by the management consultancies who seized the opportunity presented by BPR to gain large and lucrative contracts. Indeed, many consultancies re-engineered themselves to re-present their expertise in terms of BPR, and the bandwagon effect of organizations following one another led to an important overall phenomenon.

Despite the clear BPR label and its widespread rhetorical use, an examination of the writings of its exponents shows that there was little substantive agreement on the precise meaning of the term, and the detailed change programme that it implied. Jones (1994) pointed out that there were different opinions in at least five areas, including the scope of change envisaged, the scale of change as incremental or radical, the means of achieving change, the intellectual source being drawn on to underpin the change, and the role of IT. Certainly, there were core concepts that were widely agreed upon, such as the notion that BPR involved re-engineering processes along the whole value chain so that they were interconnected, rather than being independent silos. This, in theory, resulted in a better-integrated organization with a closer custo-mer-oriented focus. How this was to be achieved was, however, much less clear. Michael Hammer, in his notable and some would say notor-ious 1990 paper in the *Harvard Business Review*, used the word 'obliter-ate' as underlying BPR, arguing against incremental change from the current systems and ways of working towards a radical green field site approach. Later criticism of this centred on the unrealistic and unde-sirable approach of 'eliminating the past', and many BPR approaches in practice did not adopt Hammer's extreme position. Another debatable issue with respect to BPR, and one of direct relevance to our interests here, concerned the role of IT. Was IT the key driver of BPR, as seen by Davenport (1993) for example, or merely an important component of the re-engineering process? Indeed, some organizations embarked on BPR programmes which did not involve significant change to the computer-based information systems at all.

After the first wave of BPR in the early 1990s, with the writings being almost exclusively from unqualified supporters, a reactive but much smaller set of articles started to appear, written largely by academics, which adopted a hostile stance to BPR. For example, Willmott (1994) criticized the rhetoric which argued that BPR empowered the individual. In contrast, Willmott saw BPR as a vehicle for tighter management con-trol, and a cloak for widespread job losses and the intensification of work: 'It (BPR) . . . promotes the continuing contraction of employment as orga-nizations (continuously) re-engineer their processes. Those who remain are obliged to work at an ever-quickening intensity and pace' (p. 40).

In a similar vein, Grey and Mitev (1995) questioned whether employ-ees who suffer the negative effects of a top-down BPR initiative are ever likely to commit themselves to it: 'So the basic contradiction of BPR consists of the fact that a hierarchically imposed vision of change in the interests of profitability is intended to secure the commitment of those who will ultimately suffer as a result' (p. 13).

This critical literature supplied a healthy antidote to the unreservedly positive rhetoric of the BPR proponents. However, in keeping with the approach in this book, BPR is not viewed as either inevitably good or bad. I will argue here that BPR, like other organization-wide change initiatives such as that in UK Bank discussed above, has complex effects that are related to the history and context of its implementation, and the specific way in which the change programme is designed, implemented and appropriated by the organizational workers. In order to illustrate this position, the rest of this section will concentrate on a specific reported case study of a BPR programme in a bank in the United Kingdom. This case was chosen since it is particularly rich in its description and breadth of analysis. However, a variety of BPR experiences and outcomes can be seen from in-depth case studies dealing with organizations in other countries, including the United States (Gallivan 1996) and Australia (Sayer 1998).

BPR in Probank

The description in this sub-section is based on two papers by Knights and McCabe (1998a, 1998b), presenting a case study of BPR in a medium-sized bank which they call Probank. Their research was conducted over a six-month period during the mid-1990s, and was largely focused on the two 'back office' sites of the bank. One of these sites, employing 600 staff who were mostly female processing staff, is reported on in detail. Both papers describe aspects of the experience of BPR in this back office site, but the first paper also includes elements of the history of earlier re-engineering projects. The case study is based on about 40 recorded interviews with staff at various levels, attendance at about 15 team- or customer-oriented meetings, and additional documentary evidence.

In the late 1980s and early 1990s, Probank used telecommunications and on-line customer database technology to restructure and centralize its operations. This resulted in a substantial reduction in branch staff through voluntary redundancy, and a rapid expansion in back office staff concerned with administrative processing. Although this was not called BPR then, the Head of Re-engineering at the time of the case study viewed this as the early stages of BPR, since it focused on identifying and re-engineering the bank's two key processes of administration and selling. By the end of 1992, the term BPR was being used explicitly for the change process.

Branch staff and management reacted to the restructuring in a largely negative way, displaying animosity towards individuals implementing the changes and towards staff in the rapidly expanding back office. Branch employees were, of course, concerned with job losses, but their worries also related to customer service quality. They expressed a concern that customers would not get as good a service through an impersonal and distant back office as they would through their local branch bank. Whilst there was no overt resistance, covert resistance and considerable tension occurred between the branch and back office staff.

In 1992 a switch was implemented towards 'armchair banking' for the customer, by re-routing branch mail and telephone calls from customers to the back office. Many customers resented having to contact the back office instead of their local branches. Both branch staff and customers can be seen to have been opposed to the change partly because it denied the importance of personal customer knowledge held by staff in the local branch. Customer service problems were increasingly apparent under the new arrangements, with 40% of calls 'lost' in the system, due to customers being 'cut off' or transferred, or being unable to get through in the first place due to the telephone lines being busy. The armchair banking staff were often unable to cope with the volume of calls, and some staff from branches were drafted in to assist. The branch staff resented this, particularly when they had to sit next to people who were effectively taking over their work.

The next phase of BPR involved an attempt to address some of these back office problems by redefining the job scope of the back office staff. In 1993/1994, multi-skilled teams were introduced, whereby staff would spend some of their time answering customer phone calls, and some of their time carrying out routine processing work on customer accounts. Reactions from staff to this change were mixed, depending on their previous job role. For example, a former processing member of staff commented: 'At the moment work is all phone oriented. So you cannot sit and get on with processing ... In your own job you really can't get your teeth into it ... You're being pulled off to do the phones.'

It is interesting to note that the staff member still regarded her earlier job as the 'real work' and the new phone responsibility as a distraction from this. In contrast, another worker who had previously worked for seven hours a day on the phones commented favourably on the changes: 'It's got better recently because you're not on the phones all day. You do halfy, halfy really. It's a lot better, a lot less stress.'

Although some staff responded favourably to the new multi-skilled role, relatively high levels of stress were still present, since staffing levels were clearly being closely monitored by management to keep costs down. Operation staff were said to begin 'screaming and running about' when 'the phone goes wild' in the sense of a call backlog building up. In addition, there were tensions between the multi-skilled teams, with some having high processing productivity levels, whereas others answered incoming calls quickly but at the expense of their processing work.

In a climate with relatively high stress and tension levels, there are always 'spaces for escape' from management monitoring and control. A relatively amusing example from the case study was that of staff pretending to talk to a customer over the telephone by moving their mouths, whereas in fact they were having a rest or doing processing work. Rather more subtly, staff could perform their work in a variety of ways, ranging from enthusiasm through to detachment or indifference. For example, in terms of answering a customer call over the telephone, the staff member could be pleasant, cool or disdainful. A telephone could be answered immediately, after a few rings, or it could be ignored. Productivity measurement can also be evaded. A nice example is provided in the case study, concerning answering a request for a customer balance by stating that the customer is £3 in credit, without giving the further information that an unpaid cheque exceeding the balance was being returned. Such action would end a call quickly, and therefore contribute to productivity targets, but is unlikely to be beneficial to customer service. The withholding of the additional information is also a way for staff to control their own stress levels, as explained by a staff member: 'You can make a problem ... if you tell them that you are returning a cheque today for £20 then he may hit the roof and try to give an explanation as to why, and you are lengthening the call that way.'

In addition to problems in the back office itself, the case study reported that in 1995, at the end of the research period, there continued to be tensions between branch and back office staff. Attempts were made by Probank to tackle these issues, including providing contact names and numbers for branches to back office staff in case of difficulties. However, a member of the service expressly designed to improve relations between the branches and the back office said:

> I think there is a lot of resentment within the branches definitely ... there's no doubt about it ... [being directed] ... at the back office staff who work here ... a lot of the branches have the attitude that 'well they took all this away from the branches, let them get on with it, let them sort it out'.

Re-engineering in Practice

Authors such as Willmott, referenced earlier, saw BPR as being concerned with job losses, intensification of work, and tighter management control. What does this case say about these issues? Well, certainly there were widespread job losses, particularly in the branches. In terms of intensification of work, there appears to have been a rather more nuanced position, with at least some back office staff feeling that the multi-skilled teams were a less stressful environment than their previous seven-hour telephone day. Management attempted to tighten control, but there was some evidence of 'spaces for resistance' in various forms, some of them quite subtle in terms of staff response to customers.

What of empowerment, that buzz word of the BPR gurus? For branch staff, whose jobs were threatened or removed, the word appears ludicrous. The position for the back office staff was more complex. The multi-skilled teams did not produce 'empowered' staff of themselves, which contradicts the simplistic assumption, as Knights and McCabe (1998a) point out, that multi-skilling necessarily leads to more rewarding work. Nevertheless, some back office staff seemed happier with the new arrangements. However, even for these people, the form of empowerment did not encompass increased autonomy, but rather a release from the previous burden of a single pressured task such as taking customer phone calls.

A key objective of BPR is supposed to be a more customer-focused organization. The evidence from this case study is at best mixed, and on balance there appears to have been a worsening of customer service, at least as perceived by customers who preferred the familiarity and personal service of their local branch. The back office service was clearly of highly variable quality. Conditions of excessive stress, as were sometimes encountered when the 'phones went wild', are of course likely to be disadvantageous to customer service. However, Knights and McCabe (1998a) argue that an even greater concern for BPR advocates, based on this case study, is that before such a situation is reached, in order to reduce their stress levels employees may decide to cut customers off, or adopt other subtler stress management methods that damage customer service.

One aspect of Hammer's original advocacy of BPR, mentioned earlier, was the use of the word 'obliterate' to describe the recommended approach to organizational change. Of all the conclusions derived from the case study, this appears to be the most clear-cut. It is not feasible to obliterate the past, when it is retained in the minds and attitudes of the staff members. After several years of BPR, branch staff still retained a view of 'their jobs' which had been 'taken away' by the back office staff. The only form of 'obliteration' that would appear possible would be to start again, using completely new staff, an approach which has of course been followed by new organizations in some sectors, such as the direct insurers' challenge to established insurance companies.

Knights and McCabe (1998a) argue, interestingly, that resistance to new ways of working in change programmes such as BPR in Probank is not solely concerned with organizational politics, centred on workers' resistance to management or one group trying to achieve advantage over another. Although both of these are important, organizational politics also needs to be thought of in terms of identity relations, or how individuals seek, through political manoeuvring, to further or secure their individual careers and identities in an uncertain world. The resentment felt by branch staff in Probank cannot be solely attributed to loss of power and fear of unemployment, but also to the threat to their professional pride and self-identity, associated with their earlier role.

Knights and McCabe (1998b) ask why branch back office resentment and conflict was not directed more at senior management, who were instrumental in creating the new conditions, rather than at fellow workers. They cite a team leader in the back office who pointed out how staff, in the face of redundancy, fought individually against one another to curry favours with management and thereby secure jobs. They conclude that job insecurity can have an individualizing effect on organizational power relations. I would attribute such a response in part to their awareness of dependency and limited room for manoeuvre, namely that individual staff members feel that they cannot influence the broad organizational agenda, but that they can influence perceptions of their local standing. This does not imply support for senior management agendas, but a recognition of relative powerlessness to affect them. In addition, as discussed earlier in Chapter 4, a further reason for worker conformity is that individuals may gain a sense of identity and security by disciplining themselves to conform to key values promoted as central features of organizational culture.

ENTERPRISE SYSTEMS

BPR was fashionable in the earlier part of the 1990s, but in the later part of the decade many large organizations turned to the promise of enterprise systems. These company-wide integrated systems offer the potential to facilitate a smooth flow of data between different functions of the business, and to get away once and for all from the situation of different and incompatible information systems supporting areas of the business that ought to be closely linked. Modules of the system, based on a common central database, can be developed to support financial applications, manufacturing operations, sales and marketing, human resources, and links to suppliers and customers.

In a sense, enterprise systems can be thought of as one approach to BPR. The enterprise is re-engineered to fit the computer system. It is true that modules of the systems can be tailored to some extent to a particular organization, using variable parameters available in 'configuration tables'. However, as noted by Davenport (1998), options are limited by the structure of the basic system. He provides an example of a company with a long practice of giving preferential treatment to its most important customers by occasionally shipping them products that had already been allocated to other accounts. The company found that its new enterprise system did not allow it the flexibility to deal with orders in this way.

There was an enormous growth in the sales of enterprise systems in the 1990s, with the market leader being SAP, followed by companies such as Baan, Oracle and PeopleSoft. Davenport (1998) quoted estimates of US$10 billion per year being spent on enterprise systems at the time of writing in 1997/8, which he argued could probably be doubled if consulting expenditures were added. As with BPR, the consultancies have been very much part of the driving force for enterprise systems, having developed significant expertise in implementing them that can be profitably re-used with new clients.

Davenport (1998) provided a valuable counter to the view that enterprise systems can solve an organization's information system's problems in an unproblematic way. Although rather thin on detail, he describes 'success stories' at various companies such as Elf Atochem. However, he also outlines 'horror stories' at Mobil Europe, Dell Computers and Dow Chemicals amongst others. It is worth summarizing some of the allure of enterprise systems, according to Davenport, but also the problems that he saw by investigating specific case experiences.

With respect to the allure, we have already mentioned the promise of improved communication between different parts of the business and its customers. In addition, the maintenance of large numbers of separate legacy systems for different areas of the business is expensive, and the single-solution integrated enterprise system offers the opportunity for a lower cost base. A further potential benefit of these systems is direct access to real-time management information, and management may see this as a promise of better control. Indeed, some companies see enterprise systems as the vehicle for centralization of control. Davenport quotes an executive at a semiconductor company as saying: 'We plan to use SAP as a battering ram to make our culture less autonomous.'

With respect to problems, the first of these arises directly from the above quote, namely: Is this use of computer-based information systems to centralize control good for the business? Writers such as Zuboff (1988, 1996) have argued that this is a misuse of the power of computers, since it does not liberate and utilize the productive and innovative capability of employees, but instead stifles their potential and thus harms themselves and their organization.

Other problems with enterprise systems noted by Davenport include lack of flexibility, despite contingency tables and the possibility of omitting some modules if they seem too restrictive. The software can be considered to drive business practice, rather than the other way round, and the question is whether that is a good thing. For example, if everybody in a particular market sector is using the same enterprise system, where does an individual organization's competitive advantage come from? Finally, Davenport noted that companies had encountered difficulties in trying to implement the same enterprise system in different regions and countries.

Davenport concluded his article with a useful set of questions for the management of any company who is contemplating going ahead with an enterprise system:

> How might an enterpise system strengthen our competitive advantages? How might it erode them? What will be the system's effect on our organization and culture? Do we need to extend the system across all our functions, or should we implement only certain modules? Would it be better to roll the system out globally or to restrict it to certain regional units? Are there other alternatives for information management that might actually suit us better than an enterprise system? (p. 131).

Although Davenport mentioned stories of success and failure, his case descriptions are too short to gain a good feel for the above issues in a particular organizational context. Indeed, rather like the early days of BPR, it is difficult at the time of writing to find in-depth case studies of enterprise system implementation, written from a critical academic stance rather than a vendor sales pitch or for public relations purposes. However, some research work of this type is in progress (see, for example, Truex and Ngwenyama 2000) and in the next section, a specific case study is presented, although the case detail in this short paper is rather less than would be ideally desirable to inform a deeper look at the issues raised above.

SAP in Norsk Hydro

Hanseth and Braa (1998) described a case study of an SAP implementation in Norsk Hydro, a diversified company with Norwegian origins, whose business is centred on the production of fertilizers, light metals, oil and gas. In particular, the authors looked at the most ambitious SAP project in the company, carried out in Hydro Agri Europe (HAE). No details of the research methodology are provided in this version of the case study. However, a later book chapter (Ciborra *et al.* 2000—Chapter 8) reports more broadly on the Norsk Hydro case study, and indicates that the case was based on 30 face-to-face semi-structured interviews of one and a half to four hours in length, some shorter meetings and phone conversations, internal documents and newsletters, and the work of some masters degree students.

At the time of writing of the case study, HAE had 19 production locations and a total of 72 sites throughout Europe. Some of these were fertilizer companies that had been bought out during the 1980s and, in line with traditional Hydro management policy, they were run in a 'hands off' way. However, in 1992, fertilizer prices were very low and the whole division was in crisis. The division management responded by launching an ambitious re-engineering project aimed at integrating the independent national companies into one operational unit. However, with a culture of separate working, and a focus on caring for their own territories, little change took place.

With respect to IT, the company had a highly heterogeneous collection of systems, with each company having its own portfolio of applications. Computers, operating systems, database management systems and communications networks were varied and normally obtained from different vendors. In January 1994, in line with the broad goals of the earlier re-engineering initiative, HAE launched a new IT strategy project, based on an enterprise system for the whole division, and SAP was the chosen vendor. This initiative to create one common system and set of applications across all units was approved by senior management later that year, and the SAP project started in early 1995. The project completion date was planned to be mid-1999, and it was split into three phases: developing and implementing a pilot; validating the pilot and developing the 'final' version; and implementing that version in the whole division.

The validation phase involved five regional project teams. The Scandinavian team had more than 100 members and they raised more than 1000 'issues' requiring changes in the system. As a consequence of the need for this tailoring, the phase took much more time than expected, and the 'final' version was delayed. The authors described the SAP project as having been 'permanently close to collapse' but, despite this, they considered that SAP had been a more effective vehicle for organizational change than the prior re-engineering project. Indeed the re-engineering project was subsumed into the SAP project, but the goal was retained, expressed as 'one single integrated European learning organization'.

The case study discussed the interface between the new SAP system and the previously existing communications infrastructure. For example, SAP processing was centralized in the United Kingdom under the new arrangements, which was viewed by the individual companies as a mixed blessing. Whilst it provided an integrated central processing service, local support was problematic. The global service provider was organized in relatively independent national subsidiaries, and seemed unable to coordinate itself effectively across national boundaries. In addition, the use of English by central support staff created a barrier with those countries where this was not the local language or widely spoken.

Despite difficulties such as these, Hanseth and Braa identified some significant benefits from the SAP project in terms of integration across the division and mutual learning:

> Through the project, people all around Europe have become acquainted with each other, learning about each others' ways of working and doing business; 'best practices' are identified and tried and then transferred to other locations. Through this process, the different units get ideas about how to improve their own work far beyond what is addressed by the SAP project and they discover new areas where cooperation and integration would be beneficial (p. 193).

However, the SAP system itself cannot be regarded as a single integrated system. The SAP user groups were charged with identifying local requirements, but with the aim of transferring local practice to common division practice where possible. There was a serious problem with this in cases where the differences were beyond the control of the company. These included differences in national legislation concerning accounting, taxes, and environmental issues, and different transport systems. In addition, there were differences in business cultures and market structures in different regions or nations served by the division as a whole. The SAP solution was customized for each site. These variants had much in common, however, and they were linked together. Hanseth and Braa argued that the SAP in HAE was not 'one coherent common system' but 'a complex heterogeneous infrastructure'.

Does this variety matter? In other words, it could be argued that the goals of integration were achieved to a large extent with what could be considered appropriate local variation where necessary. Some case study respondents did not, however, see the picture as quite so rosy. For example, the variety between different local variants makes it difficult to implement further company-wide changes: 'We have made things difficult for ourselves. We have customized it [the SAP system] too much.'

Hanseth and Braa used the theoretical basis of actor-network theory, as outlined in Chapter 3, to view the SAP infrastructure as an 'actor' with properties of irreversibility, making it hard to control. This is nicely illustrated by a quote from a member of the oil division: 'SAP is like concrete—it's very flexible until it sets. Then there is nothing you can do to change it.'

Learning from the Case Study

Hanseth and Braa ended their case study on a rather polemical note, following the above analysis of the relative inflexibility of the SAP system once it had been installed. They described it as 'everybody's enemy by resisting all organizational change', and use the startling title for their paper of 'technology as traitor' to emphasize this point. This author, without of course the first-hand field experience of the case study, would nevertheless argue a more nuanced position by trying to answer some of Davenport's questions on enterprise systems with the hindsight knowledge of this case study.

Did the SAP system strengthen or weaken competitive advantage for HAE? On the one hand, it was argued that the SAP project has facilitated mutual learning about 'best practice' across the company, surely to the benefit of competitive advantage. The cost base of the new system may also be lower, although this is not clear from the case study. On the other hand, the system may have reduced the flexibility of the individual national and regional units to respond effectively to their own business cultures and markets.

Was it a good idea to implement the system across the whole organization and across all functions? It seems clear that the way in which this was handled in the HAE case allowed much local diversity in the SAP solution. This handled the problem of variety, and enabled the roll-out across the whole company and across a wide range of functions, but the system diversity thus created can be seen as a problem in terms of a 'concrete-like' infrastructure resisting future company-wide change. It could be argued, and indeed was by one of the quoted respondents, that too much local variety was permitted. In a different unpublished case, known to myself through the company's SAP project leader, one of the conclusions drawn from having also implemented an SAP solution

across a Europe-wide company was 'do not leave room for local variation on the template'.

Finally, was an enterprise system such as SAP the right solution for
HAE, or were there better alternatives for their information management? It seems reasonable to argue that some approach was needed to
try to integrate systems across this company, bearing in mind the
heterogeneous systems in place previously, and the need to share data
and experience across the enterprise as a whole. Whether SAP, or an
enterprise system in general, was the right way to do this is more
problematic. The SAP infrastructure was created with more time and
effort, and doubtless money, than had been anticipated. Will it provide
a flexible infrastructure for the company's future competitive stance in an
ever-changing market? There must be serious doubts about this.

ANALYSIS AND CONCLUSIONS

The cases of Lending Adviser (LA) in UK Bank, of BPR in Probank, and
of enterprise systems in Norsk Hydro, show much diversity in terms of
the consequences of new approaches to the use of information technology and associated organizational change. However, they can all be
viewed as part of a broad trend in the 1990s, at least in large organizations, towards company-wide initiatives for organizational transformation, with computer-based information and communication systems as
key elements. I will now examine the questions posed at the start of this
chapter as to why this trend has occurred, and what its effects have been,
drawing on concepts and themes from earlier chapters where appropriate. A summary of key points is provided in Tables 6.1–6.3.

Why Have Company-Wide IT-Based Initiatives Been Increasingly Used as the Vehicle for Organizational Transformation?

The pressures of contemporary society discussed in Chapter 2, implying
the need for global initiatives, are felt by managers of all enterprises trying
to function in world markets. However, even where an enterprise
addresses its national market only, an awareness of fashionable worldwide
approaches to change such as BPR is a prerequisite to a manager's survival, an aspect of globality as discussed in Chapter 2. An obvious response
to this on the part of those concerned with information technology is to
try to develop computerized information systems that are perceived as
state of the art in global terms, and which enable connectivity across the

Table 6.1 *Reasons for trend to IT-based company-wide initiatives*

Pressures for global best-practice standards in information systems to enable integrated knowledge-sharing	• By the TNCs operating globally • But also in national markets in view of globality • Reinforced by the international consulting companies
However, standardization on software is easier than standardizing on IS to support key business processes	• Legacy systems grew organically to support business processes • New systems may not support situated work practice or may 'impose' new practices
Major initiatives offer the promise to management of lower cost base and, crucially, tighter control	• Can be argued that this is the role of senior management • But need to balance innovation/autonomy with order/control

whole organization and integrated knowledge-sharing. This view is reinforced by the activities of the international consultancies, who have a vested interest in supporting large-scale global change initiatives where they can earn large revenues. From a Foucauldian perspective, as outlined in Chapter 3, the consultancy companies are happy to subscribe to a 'regime of truth' in which their knowledge of BPR or ERP systems is inextricably linked to their powerful position as primary suppliers of such knowledge.

This desire for global best-practice standards in IT and related information systems can be of great commercial benefit to a company that taps into it. The dominance of Microsoft in operating systems and associated application software, at the time of writing of this book, provides a good example. Standardizing on systems software is, however, an easier task than standardizing on information systems to support the key processes of the business. Legacy systems grew organically to support business processes and related situated work practices, whereas new systems may not support these practices or may 'impose' new practices, as was seen in all the case studies in this chapter.

Senior managers of organizations who have implemented major change initiatives through BPR or the use of ERP systems would probably agree with the above analysis of major changes in work practices related to new information systems, but they may argue that the changed work practices were desirable or even essential. Such initiatives offer the promise of a lower cost base through reduced numbers of personnel, for example, but crucially they also offer to senior management the promise of tighter control.

The argument that control is a fundamental key to understanding the attraction of the company-wide change programmes discussed in this chapter can be supported from the case study evidence presented here. The LA system can be thought of as enabling the senior management of UK Bank to improve their control of the lending activities of the bank, by reducing the semi-autonomy of the branch bank managers through the discipline of the computer system. The centralization of the back office activities in Probank can also be seen as increasing management control. HAE can be viewed as trying to use the SAP system to integrate and control their widely scattered and disparate Europe-wide operations. More widely than the specific case material presented here, the promise of improved central control can be seen to underpin the whole BPR phenomenon. 'Obliteration' offers a fresh start, and the potential for a newly designed controlled organization. Similarly, enterprise systems have an integrated controlled feel about them, in contrast to the relatively anarchic sense of disparate systems.

What is wrong with this desire for close central control? It could be argued that the role of the senior management of an organization is exactly that, namely to create efficient, controlled enterprises. But, as discussed in Chapter 3 in the work of Weick, organizations need to be concerned with innovation and autonomy as well as with order and control, otherwise the sources of growth and change are blocked. Major change initiatives, aimed at standardizing procedures across organizations, run the risk of exactly this. The reference to ERP systems in the Norsk Hydro case as 'electronic concrete' provides a sharp metaphor for this danger. It was also noted in Chapter 3 that attempts at tight control tend to induce multiple forms of resistance, and such effects could be seen in all the case studies in this chapter.

What Effects Have Major Organizational Initiatives Had on Work and Worker Identity?

In addition to concerns as to whether the major organizational change initiatives discussed in this chapter have resulted in better organizations from an economic perspective, are the broader social consequences on the individual worker and society at large acceptable? As argued in Chapter 4, the role of work in the process of changing self-identity is a relatively neglected issue. People work for material reward, of course, but their sense of identity and self-worth is also strongly connected to their identification, or lack of identification, with their work role and practice. If their role and practice is affected in a significant manner, as it invariably is

Table 6.2   *Effects of organization-wide initiatives on work and self-identity*

Individual sense of identity and self-worth linked to identification with work role and practice	• Consequences of major change programmes may not be beneficial • Case material supports mixed outcomes at best
Should management worry about this?	• Yes, since it will influence the result of company-wide change initiatives • May even be a cause of major failure
There is also a need for a wider agenda in this area	• We are all part of the society made up in part by business organizations • We should be concerned with issues of stress, loss of work-identity, work intensification, reduced autonomy and unemployment

in major organizational change initiatives, then there may be unforeseen and not necessarily beneficial consequences, for the individual, but also for the organization and, in aggregate, for the wider society.

In the UK Bank case, retirement and re-training did not achieve the goal of creating a cadre of corporate managers with unambiguous commitment to their new work role. Most of them continued to feel ambivalent about the LA system and the work practices associated with it. Whether this resulted in better loan practice for the bank as a whole, or UK society, is open to debate. Again, we saw compliance on the part of retained workers in the Probank case, and even some limited enthusiasm for the new work arrangements in the centralized back office on the part of some staff. But this was not shared by branch staff, and it could be argued that customer service suffered as a consequence of the new arrangements and work roles. There was little detail on individual responses to changed roles and practices in the SAP case, but it is reasonable to hypothesize that major concerns will have been felt by staff when asked to tailor their work to the new system rather than the other way round. Problems of this nature are hinted at in Davenport's 'horror stories' of enterprise system implementation.

So, should management worry about changing work roles and self-identity of their workforce? The answer to this is clearly yes, even if one takes a narrow instrumental view of an organization's goals. Problems of staff identification with their work, and crises of work identity, will affect the outcome of company-wide change initiatives, and may at worst be a cause of major failure. But managers, and the rest of us in society, should also be concerned with the wider agenda in this area. We work in contemporary organizations, we are customers or clients of them, and we live in the society of which they form an integral and important part. We should all be concerned with issues of individual stress, loss of work identity, intensification of work, reduced autonomy and unemployment. They affect us all, directly or indirectly. In Chapter 2, I described Giddens' concept of existential anxiety in rapidly changing circumstances, and Castells' analysis of those excluded from society, or seeking their identity in resistance movements. Our business organizations should not be centres of alienation, but should try to offer work roles and practices with which people can readily identify in a positive way.

How Well Have Company-Wide Initiatives Coped with Organizational Variety and Cultural Specificity?

A further reason why company-wide change initiatives have diverse and sometimes unpredictable consequences relates to the wider issue of organizational variety. This arises partly from the individuals who work for the organization, discussed above, with their varied backgrounds and identities, needs and goals, fears and aspirations. However, organizations also have a variety of different routines and procedures, context and histories, even if they are operating in the same sector. Anyone who has studied or worked for more than one organization in a particular sector will be aware that a similarity of product or market does not result in a similar organization in any strong sense.

These statements may be obvious to many people, but the rhetoric of some of the main BPR proponents ignored them. Obliteration of the existing organization implies getting rid of the messy world of organizational variety, including its existing history, systems, people and

Table 6.3   *Change, organizational variety and cultural specificity*

Organizations have different routines and procedures, context and histories	• Rhetoric of 'obliteration' ignores this • Doubts as to whether fitting the organization to the new system is feasible or desirable • Creation of irreversible infrastructures
Gradualism may be a better approach to change	• Empirical data often support this • Metaphor of continuous care rather than invasive surgery
Serious problems of standardization when systems span major cultural boundaries	• Local variety at odds with the concept of close central control • Can hypothesize that these issues are even more complex in non-Western cultures

procedures. Initiatives can be taken, and programmes developed, to try to change all of these, but existing and past states need to be taken into account and dealt with directly, or the consequence is likely to be a change programme based on an idealized idea of the way that the world should be, rather than grounded in the way that it currently is. Many of those who were responsible for BPR initiatives were doubtless aware of this. However, one wonders how many of the failure stories which are widely reported as happening relate to management emphasizing the goal of some future nirvana, without giving adequate consideration to the necessary steps on the way there.

ERP vendors do acknowledge organizational variety, as we have seen, and provide configuration tables or modular design as ways to implement this. However, the emphasis is on fitting the organization to the system rather than the other way round, so that the organizational variety which is being emphasized relates to the future more than the past. In a similarity with BPR, the past is assumed to be something that one wishes to eliminate. Questions need to be raised about the feasibility and desirability of this. In addition, even if the organization succeeds in creating a new world based on the ERP system, will its concrete-like structure constrain future adaptation and variety? Borrowing from the language of actor-network theory, information infrastructures are being created that have strong properties of irreversibility.

Although written before the time of the major take-off of ERP systems, and thus containing no illustrations of these, a special edition of the journal *Information Systems Research* (1996, Volume 7, No. 1) described a diverse set of empirically based papers on the theme of IT and organizational transformation. They can be thought of as complementary to the case studies presented in this chapter, also being concerned with company-wide change initiatives, heavily reliant on IT. The work of the authors in the special issue supports the theme of organizational variety that we have emphasized in this sub-section, but an additional emphasis is that change should often be viewed as gradual rather than dramatic or rapid. Yates and van Maanen (1996) summarize this in their editorial introduction to the issue:

These papers illustrate a fascinating array of organizational transformations (and, in one case, a failure of transformation). A common theme running through these pieces is that organizational transformations involving information technology are going on all the time but, when examined in detail, they may not appear as dramatic nor as rapid nor as technologically-determined as is often assumed. The

particular methodological approaches taken by these papers highlight a gradualism often overlooked in studies of organizational
transformation (p. 4).

This quote implies a need for continuous management and adaptation,
and an attention to detail, which contrasts strikingly with the rhetoric of
big-bang change initiatives to re-engineer the organization or to carry
out a one-off implementation of a new enterprise system. The metaphor
of continuous care for the patient might be more appropriate than one-
off invasive surgery.

A particular issue of variety with respect to company-wide change
initiatives concerns the case where the new system is designed to cross
major cultural boundaries. Special problems associated with this could be
seen in the Norsk Hydro case in their attempt to introduce an enterprise
system across 19 different countries in Europe. As we saw earlier, this
was approached by allowing much variety of local system, tuning the
variant in a particular organization to the cultural, market and legislative
specificity of the country in which it was operating. This local variety
can, however, be seen as at odds with the concept of close control
from the centre. In particular, it becomes very difficult to initiate top-
down change from the centre when this would necessitate specific and
normally different changes in each of the local systems and organizations. The conclusion from this is either to argue against allowing
local variety, creating problems of lack of fit to local procedures and
markets, or to argue that close central control is neither desirable
nor feasible, and that local subsidiaries should be permitted substantial
autonomy, provided that they remain broadly connected. This is a
crucial issue that needs to be addressed in all situations of cross-cultural
systems.

I have not, in this chapter, referred to any case studies of non-Western
countries, such as those of the Third World, or the rich countries of Asia
such as Japan and Singapore. It is very difficult to find published literature which relates to major IT-related change initiatives in these countries, such as those associated with BPR or enterprise systems. A brief
reference to an enterprise system in a consumer products company in
India was given by Bhatnagar (2000), but little detail on implementation
and consequences was provided. However, we can hypothesize, in line
with the arguments in Chapters 2 and 3 on cultures, that the issues of
self-identity, organizational variety and cultural specificity become even
more complex when considering implementing change programmes in
such contexts. The argument here is not necessarily that enterprise

systems, for example, are inappropriate in Third World countries, but merely that we have no collective experience of how such Western-origin technologies will fit in a radically different cultural context. As we saw in the case of GIS in India in Chapter 4, additional issues arise when attempting such a matching process. Further analysis of this area will be given in Part 3 of this book.

Finally, what of the Internet in enabling company-wide change initiatives based on IT? Is the Internet the solution for the management of an integrated IT-based information system, transparent to the centre? It seems highly unlikely to be realizable in any total sense. The Internet does permit relatively seamless electronic integration across physical borders, but this does not imply seamless human communication, whether between people, groups, organizations or across cultures. This important theme will be addressed in more detail in the next chapter.

7
Trust in Networks

There has been much emphasis in recent years on the partnering of organizations, and their interconnection in networks. These initiatives are designed, for example, to exploit synergies between partnering organizations, or to improve links with suppliers and customers. They are related to issues of global reach, and the striving for increased efficiency and speed of response in rapidly changing markets. Inter-organizational information systems (IOS) are often a fundamental part of partnering processes, or the connection of organizations in networks. These systems are increasingly carried over the medium of the Internet, as its scope, familiarity and ease of use increases.

Although inter-organizational links and networks offer significant opportunities, major human and organizational issues need to be addressed. For example, linking organizations together electronically does not of itself generate or support good trust relations between the partners, and may affect power relations in a way that is perceived as negative by one or more of the organizations. In addition, the international nature of many of the electronic linkages raises issues of cross-cultural communication. Three key questions addressed in this chapter are:

- How are inter-organizational trust relations affected by electronically mediated interaction?
- How is power implicated in network relationships?
- What human and organizational issues arise from the spread of global networking technologies, particularly the Internet?

I will provide a formal response to these questions in the final synthesis section of the chapter. The following three sections present some detailed empirical material on the use of information and communication technologies to support inter-organizational networks. First, a specific case example of electronic trading in the network of the London Insurance Market is described and analysed. Secondly, I discuss IOS and electronic data interchange (EDI) more generally, including a published case study of the use of IOS in Japan Airlines. Thirdly, the topic of electronic commerce (e-commerce) is explored, addressing business opportunities and risks, e-commerce in diverse cultures, and ethical issues with respect to the Internet.

ELECTRONIC TRADING IN THE LONDON INSURANCE MARKET

The London Insurance Market is an important part of the UK general insurance industry, built up around Lloyd's of London. It is a network of hundreds of semi-autonomous players, including underwriting groups, brokerage firms and Market managers. In the late 1980s and early 1990s, the Market suffered huge insurance losses due to a combination of circumstances. These included a bad run of natural disasters and increased damages awards by the legal system. In addition, the London Market faced increasing global competition in the large commercial and wholesale insurance business, and it was perceived as having a relatively high operating cost base compared with its competitors, normally attributed to slow change in its working practices.

As part of its response in the early 1990s to the disastrous financial results, and to the tough competitive climate, the Market sought to develop and use IT to lower costs by streamlining business processes, and to increase service quality and inter-organizational efficiency in the Market. A particular focus for this was to use EDI standards and messages to facilitate inter-organizational communication, and a joint venture called the London Insurance Market Network (LIMNET) was created to develop and manage appropriate systems. LIMNET made significant progress in a number of work areas, including systems for claims management and settlement, and accounting systems. However, the development and use of electronic systems to support the critical area of the negotiation and agreement of insurance business between underwriters and brokers, known as placement, was less successful. A system called LIMNET EPS (electronic placing system) was developed in the early 1990s, but low levels of adoption and use were still being experienced several years later. An examination of the reasons for this, and the controversies surrounding the system, will be the focus of the rest of this section.

The case study below is based on longitudinal research carried out over the period 1993–96. The study included 94 semi-structured interviews with Market participants, including brokers and underwriters, IT directors and staff, and senior Market management. These were supplemented by the extensive use of documentary sources, and a significant amount of time was spent in observing the work practices of insurance risk placement. Full details of the case study are given in Barrett (1996, 1999) and Barrett and Walsham (1999).

Risk Placement in the London Market

Clients throughout the world who require insurance or reinsurance coverage through the London Market contact an insurance broker, who investigates the details of the risk and collects any supporting information. The broker then negotiates with a 'lead' underwriter, who ultimately sets the financial terms of the insurance, such as the rates of premium to be paid, and adds any special conditions under which the risk will be insured. The risks placed in this 'subscription' market are often large and complex. It is therefore often necessary for the broker to ask a number of 'following' underwriters in the London Market to subscribe to the risk under the same terms and conditions set by the lead underwriter. This process is continued across the Market and, if necessary, across other global insurance markets, until 100% of the risk has been insured. The deal is then finalized between client, broker and underwriters. Each participating underwriter accepts a proportion of the risk, the client pays the premiums, and the brokerage firm receives its commission.

The traditional placement of risk, which continued even after the introduction of the electronic placement system, involved the manual transaction of insurance activities on paper. 'Placing' brokers carried a paper 'slip' containing the details of the risk, and upon which subsequent negotiations between underwriters and brokers related to the risk were recorded. The negotiations between brokers and underwriters took place face to face in a physical market-place, normally the underwriter's office. Brokers spent a lot of time queuing to visit lead and following underwriters in their offices.

The new EPS system was designed to replace the face-to-face and paper approach to the placing of insurance risk with the electronic passing of risk packages between brokers and underwriters. Brokers would be responsible for inputting an electronic record of the risk, called the common core record, at the start of the placement process. The concept was that the risk details would then be available to all participants involved in the risk at different stages of its life cycle. Placing brokers would electronically submit the risk to a lead underwriter, and then later transmit it across the network to a number of following underwriters. After successful placement of the risk, the electronic record could then be used to drive the final closing process, automatically feeding the transaction details to the accounting applications for example. At a later date, the same electronic record could be used to process claims in a timely manner through the electronic claims system.

As stated earlier, the LIMNET EPS system was not widely adopted in the Market, even by 1996, several years after its launch. A number of issues can be considered as contributing to this state of affairs. The system had certain technical limitations, and there were inadequate subsidies to support widespread diffusion. However, there was broad agreement across the Market that the major contributory factors were human and social issues concerned with the transformation of the nature of the work across the Market. In particular, many brokers and underwriters were sceptical about the effectiveness of the EPS system to support the placement process as espoused by its Market champions. It is worth noting that, unlike the situation of a single organization such as many of those described in the earlier chapters, it is not easy for senior management to enforce the use of a particular information system in a network of semi-autonomous organizations. It is necessary to gain majority consensus at least, and this was not achieved for the EPS system in the London Market. I will explore reasons for resistance and slow adoption in the rest of this section.

Work Transformation Through Electronic Placement

The traditional approach to risk placement in the London Market was based on the primacy of 'place', specific locations such as the underwriter's office, where trust was established and maintained through face-to-face personal relations. The full use of the EPS system would have broken this localized form of interaction, and replaced it by one based on interaction across both time and space. The potential advantages in efficiency, speed and cost were the stated reasons for EPS introduction. However, many underwriters and brokers saw significant disadvantages in the new approach. The importance of face-to-face negotiations was deemed critical by brokers in order to negotiate effectively in the best interests of their clients. A broker explained this as follows:

> The business is based largely on relationships and trust. This is why it is so vital to carry out business in a face-to-face manner . . . You are

negotiating the business. It is important how well you put across the case ... You use a lot of different skills in negotiating. You emphasize and de-emphasize certain aspects, handle objections ... It is a sales situation.

Many underwriters echoed this sentiment, and argued that negotiating through personal interaction enabled them to access the full range of cues from the other party, such as body language and tone of voice, to help them determine whether a risk should be accepted and, if so, at what price. Without face-to-face interaction, both brokers and underwriters feared that their ability to conduct the delicate negotiations of complex risk assessment would be seriously impaired. Supporters of electronic placing, however, felt that this concern was exaggerated. An IT director in the Market expressed this viewpoint: 'There is an unfounded fear of having no face-to-face communication as they [the brokers] feel they have to see the whites of their eyes and to see if their hands are trembling when they [the underwriters] sign the slip [accept the risk].'

A further objection to the EPS system was that it undermined the Lloyd's rule of Utmost Good Faith. This rule essentially states that a broker must display all known relevant information about the client and the insurance risk to underwriters upon presentation of the risk to them. A key issue concerned the difficulty of the broker inputting all relevant information about the risk into the EPS system, due to various system limitations. This was exacerbated in that the EDI messages on which the EPS system was based were unable to transmit supporting documenta-tion needed for risk evaluation, such as images and spreadsheets. The new technology threatened to disrupt existing forms of trust relations, without offering a satisfactory alternative.

It could be argued that these latter objections could be overcome in time by improved versions of the technology. However, a more fundamental objection to electronic risk placement in any form was the widely expressed view that it might erode the London Market's existing source of com-petitive advantage in the global market-place. A key advantage of this unique market structure was that innovative insurance products could be developed in a short period of time through face-to-face interaction between brokers and underwriters in a tightly focused geographical area.

Professional Identity in the Workplace

The work practices of the underwriters and brokers in the London Market can be considered as having changed very little over many years until the events being described here. The original face-to-face insurance negotiations took place in the Lloyd's coffee house over 300 years ago, and set the style for the London Market. Market participants had a clear professional role and identity linked to these stable market practices, but these certainties are being undermined. The EPS system was seen as a catalyst for major change in work practices and professional identities on the part of all parties concerned although, as we have seen, there was disagreement as to its desirability. A senior broker and EPS champion in one of the large brokerage firms summarized broker attitudes as: 'The attitude of individual brokers is that there is a loss of humanity to electronic wizardry . . . they can't see the balance, it is purely computer or old style. They have to see it as a tool to be used in our business.'

However, there was much fear about worsening employment conditions and job satisfaction. In an electronic trading environment, brokers feared that the social nature of their work would become less interesting and would involve longer hours at reduced commission rates. A senior underwriter summarized related concerns on the part of underwriters: 'There is a great deal of inertia with respect to the use of EPS by underwriters . . . they don't want to be typing into keyboards all day.'

Furthermore, for underwriters and brokers alike, the use of the EPS system, involving asynchronous communication, was perceived largely to eliminate the spontaneity and excitement of the face-to-face negotiation process. An underwriter expressed this as follows: 'The actual bargaining is the reason most of us like to do underwriting . . . the EPS system is seen to drive out the mystique often associated with financial services jobs in the City of London.'

Shifting power relations between underwriters and brokers were also a subject of concern to both parties. On the one hand, the EPS system could facilitate simultaneous risk transmission, giving the broker the opportunity to 'flood' the market by sending the risk to a large number of underwriters at the same time, rather than queuing outside an individual underwriter's office. The underwriters feared a drastic change in trading conditions, from a leisurely but measured discussion of the terms of the risk, to a situation where the risk was eventually placed with only those participants who responded quickly and at the lowest price.

However, it is by no means obvious that the underwriter would be the loser in the longer term from electronic risk transmission. It can be argued that the broker could be eliminated from the insurance chain altogether, this disintermediation permitting insurance clients to deal directly with underwriters. A chief operating officer of a large brokerage firm explained:

The accepted view in the broking industry is that in the long run there will not be sufficient profit in the chain for the broker and underwriter. This has set up competition in the chain between underwriters and brokers. Fewer brokers and underwriters will likely be able to survive.

Despite the widespread and profound concerns about the impact of electronic trading on their professional role activities, on the part of both underwriters and brokers, some individuals did view the EPS in a positive light. One senior broker remarked: 'EPS widens horizons. Some people see it making their job a dead end one, but it will allow me to work faster if everybody plays.'

Another broker commented on his increased productivity as follows:

I can work when I am not usually working ... I can conduct normal broking in the morning outside the core underwriting hours ... which is between 11.15–1 and 2.30–4.15 ... with more time available, I can serve more clients and customers and be more productive.

In addition to facilitating greater speed and productivity, some brokers saw the increase in their IT knowledge as a valuable consequence of their involvement with the EPS project.

Although positive effects such as these were articulated, the dominant view of Market participants was negative on balance, as reflected in the very slow adoption of the EPS system. A major sense of personal anxiety in a rapidly changing professional world was felt by many, and the EPS system provided a focal arena for debate about these concerns.

Implications

A key implication from the case study is that the London Insurance Market needs to confront the issue of adaptation to global market pressures, including technological change, whilst retaining aspects of its unique culture and market identity that have enabled it to be at the forefront of innovation in the insurance market for centuries. It is not obvious that full electronic trading is the solution to this dilemma. The way forward was perhaps hinted at in the earlier quote on the 'balance' between computer and old style. Electronic trading offers some opportunities for speed, efficiency and the bridging of time and space. At the same time, complex insurance risks need delicate and sophisticated negotiation, and asynchronous electronic media are not necessarily well suited to many aspects of this. An appropriate strategy may involve mixed modes and a thoughtful blend of the benefits of electronic and face-to-face interaction.

Trust comes out as a crucial element that must be successfully created and maintained throughout the negotiation process in the insurance chain. Trust in the London Market has relied on personal relations since its inception. The replacement of the face-to-face negotiation process by electronic alternatives, or hybrids of the two, must confront the issue of how new forms of trust relations can be developed and sustained. The technical weaknesses of the EPS system, which limited the transmission of data and breached aspects of the Utmost Good Faith principle, provided a clear illustration of an undermining of the basis of trust, and produced vigorous and justifiable resistance on the part of Market participants. However, even with technical improvements, trust relations involve more than data transparency, and the Market needs to be convinced that electronic systems do not undermine the solidity of trust on which the Market is based.

A further implication from the case study concerns the need for all Market participants to come to terms with the concerns and anxieties related to their shifting professional activities and identity in a changing global market-place. As discussed at length in Chapter 4, shifting professional identity linked to the introduction of new information technology is an important, widespread but relatively neglected phenomenon. The London Market case provides a further illustration of this. Barrett and Walsham (1999) suggest the need for the substantial retraining of brokers and underwriters to cope with their changing world. However, they argue that such training needs to be much broader than the traditional view of technical training. There is a need to raise the level of debate in the market as to how brokers and underwriters will be able to function effectively in a new electronically-supported environment. Little serious consideration was given to this at the time when the technology was first introduced.

INTER-ORGANIZATIONAL SYSTEMS (IOS)

The case study of the London Insurance Market is one example of an IOS. In this section I will examine the topic of IOS more generally. As noted at the start of the chapter, IOS have become a common feature of organizational activity in the 1990s, and it is highly likely that this trend will continue. Indeed, the growth of the Internet is a further factor in favour of IOS, offering a generally accessible medium over which such systems can be carried. The use of the Net for electronic business will be the focus of the next section of this chapter. This section will mainly describe IOS carried on other media.

Before looking in detail at some of the literature on IOS, it is worth distinguishing between IOS and the narrower topic of EDI. Hart and Saunders (1997) provide a helpful definition of this distinction:

> Inter-organizational computer networks support the exchange of computer-stored information across organizational boundaries. These linkages have been referred to as inter-organizational systems (IOS) ... Electronic Data Interchange (EDI) is a sub-set of IOS and refers to the exchange of business documents between organizations in a computer readable, structured and standard format (pp. 24–25).

Thus, the EPS system in the London Insurance Market case was an EDI case study, but also an example of IOS. Some systems are, however, examples of IOS but not EDI.

The literature contains quite a wide range of case examples of IOS. For example, Holland (1995) described a case study of the use of IOS in a textile supply chain in the United Kingdom, focusing on the interactions between a large textile retailing organization, called Chain Store, a textile manufacturer called Textiles, and other smaller members of the supply chain. IOS were used, in the form of EDI-based systems, to support areas such as logistics management, giving members of the supply chain access to current stock positions and the ability to place on-line orders. Computer-aided design (CAD) systems in Textiles were extended to include access by Chain Store. A system was developed to exchange dye information between Textiles, other garment manufacturers and a company manufacturing dyes. Holland argued that the advantages of the IOS were in quicker response to market changes in the supply chain as a whole, both for product replenishment and launches of new garment styles. In addition, quality of finished product was enhanced by better planning and monitoring across the vertically-integrated supply chain, but without common ownership of the companies in the chain. Finally, Holland hypothesized that competition in the future, in IOS-mediated supply chains, would tend to occur between product-market supply chains rather than between individual organizational units.

Choudhury (1997) identified various types of IOS, such as electronic monopoly, where for example a supplier is locked into a specific buyer, an electronic dyad with two or more supplier links, and multilateral IOS where there is a more open IOS-mediated market between buyers and suppliers. He described IOS of these various types for parts supply in the aircraft industry in the United States. In particular he described a large, commercial airline which used sole source contracts for some of the items it purchased, typically high volume hardware items, a small list of preferred suppliers for parts not under exclusive contract, and a much wider search for suppliers in the case of a grounded aircraft, where speed and availability are crucial. All of these purchases were mediated through different IOS. Choudhury hypothesized a relationship between the choice of various types of IOS, such as electronic monopoly, and characteristics such as degree of demand uncertainty and market variability.

Papers such as those by Holland and Choudhury provide valuable illustrative examples of IOS in practice, indicating considerable variety in their form and application. In addition, the hypothesized relationships between IOS and market types or style of competition are interesting, if not altogether convincing. The papers described above are based on case study data in the United Kingdom and the United States, respectively, but illustrative papers are also available from other cultural contexts. For example, Teo, Tan and Wei (1997) described the use of an EDI-based system in Singapore, called Tradenet, used to improve the efficiency of the international trading system in that country. However, there is a major dimension missing in this type of illustrative study, namely that the reader learns nothing about the deeper human relationships between the various organizations and the individuals in them. IOS come across as some abstract mechanistic phenomena that enable positive inter-organizational cooperation without the need for human interaction. In contrast, Hart and Saunders (1997) argued that power and trust are crucial factors in the adoption and use of EDI. In the next sub-section, a case study of IOS-enabled organizational change in Japan Airlines is examined in some detail, including issues of power and trust.

IOS in Japan Airlines

The description in this sub-section is drawn from an article by Chatfield and Bjørn-Andersen (1997), which was based on their research on IOS in Japan Airlines (JAL) carried out in 1994–95. They conducted 14 detailed interviews with managers from JAL, and a further seven interviews with managers from the JAL Group of firms, a group that included over 130 companies with which JAL collaborated, and in which JAL directly or indirectly owned an average equity interest of around 20%. The research interviews were supplemented by the analysis of financial and performance data, and the study of over 60 external reports on JAL or the JAL Group published in Japanese in trade journals, newspapers and magazines.

The case study described aspects of JAL's response to the increasing competition and globalization of markets that has taken place in the airline industry as a whole. In particular, two IOS were identified as of crucial importance, namely the use of EDI for value chain logistics coordination and the development of a computerized reservation system. On the first of these, the authors argued that EDI provided JAL and the companies in its value chain with timely and accurate information on such topics as flight schedules, purchase orders, cost structures and maintenance records. This enabled both cost reduction and improved speed and effectiveness of operation in areas such as fuel procurement and the provision of spare parts for maintenance.

Much of the above is similar in broad style to the EDI-based case studies described earlier in this section. However, the second strategic IOS was not EDI-based, but concerned the development of an advanced computer reservation system called AXESS. AXESS was an on-line, main-frame-based, integrated travel information and reservations system that was linked with hotel chains worldwide, as well as with foreign carriers' reservation systems. Specific features of AXESS that gave it advantages over competitor systems were its integration with other strategic information systems, including some of the EDI-based systems. In addition, it had certain innovative features such as being the first Japanese-language database in the airline industry, allowing information retrieval in either Japanese or English displayed in colour and in split windows.

Whilst recognizing the difficulty of isolating and assessing the impact of JAL's IOS-based transformations of the value chain on business outcomes, since other initiatives were also taking place over the same period, Chatfield and Bjørn-Andersen suggested that business growth and improved competition were enabled by the IOS. By the mid-1990s, at the end of the research study, JAL had become the world's third largest airline based on revenues, and was also showing a healthy profit increase. The consensus among the managers interviewed in the research study was that IOS had played a major role in this, and the authors quoted the president of the company at that time as saying: 'AXESS has already had an immense impact on our operations in Japan and overseas.'

As with the authors cited earlier in this section, the case material presented by Chatfield and Bjørn-Andersen is interesting and illuminating. The Japanese dimension contrasts nicely with the Anglo-Saxon domination of so much of the English language literature, and AXESS provides a good example of non-EDI-based IOS. However, two reservations can be put forward. First, we only hear about the unqualified success of the IOS. Were there no problems or failures with some of the systems developed, or at least some limitations or qualifications to the picture of total success? Of course, the methodology of interviewing managers may not have yielded these insights, but did the 60 articles from the Trade Press not offer some more nuanced interpretation?

A second reservation with respect to the published paper concerns the issue of the human aspects of organizational cooperation, such as power and trust. Now, the reader is in fact alerted to these issues in the paper. The JAL Group is described as a *keiretsu*-based value chain for JAL. Keiretsu in Japan is a group of individual firms viewed together because they are affiliated with a large local firm. With respect to the power of the dominant firm, JAL, over the others in the JAL-based keiretsu, Chatfield and Bjørn-Andersen argued that IOS adoption was not successfully promoted in the group by JAL's market power:

> ... IOS embeddedness is central to the transformation of JAL's value chains. Such embeddedness requires the active commitment and collaboration of network members, rather than mere compliance. Without such commitment and collaboration, members would not have accepted the importance of sharing information and knowledge reciprocally across the network partners. This acceptance was fostered by JAL successfully promoting IOS adoption *without using its market power* (p. 31—italics added).

Whilst welcoming the explicit attempt to address power relations, I would like to challenge the final implication. JAL must have had enormous influence over the acceptance of IOS, related to its market power over the keiretsu, even if that was not made explicit. Indeed, the most effective exercise of power over others often arises when it is implicitly 'accepted' by both parties.

Chatfield and Bjørn-Andersen also address the related issue of trust. They argue that the old-style keiretsu-based collaboration in Japanese organizations such as the JAL Group, based on mutual trust, needs to be augmented with IOS-enabled value chains for non-hierarchical communication across network members:

> One of the key findings is the impact of IOS on the transformation of the traditional top-down, hierarchical, keiretsu-based collaboration ... While this lacks flexibility, it has been the basis of competitive

advantage for Japanese industries because it is governed by mutual trust. However, even though this type of collaboration was effective in the past, today, in a time-based competitive world, it is not enough to rely exclusively on that organizational form of collaboration. Instead, keiretsu-based interfirm collaboration has to be *augmented* with IOS-enabled virtual value chains to facilitate flexible, *non-hierarchical* communication across network members (p. 37—italics added).

'Augmenting' the older approach implies retaining some elements of the old, but adding some elements of the new. It is assumed that trust will still be retained, but what are the new forms of trust in the new hybrid organizational form? Surely the communication across the IOS-enabled network is not non-hierarchical since JAL still retains its powerful place in the network.

Power, Trust and Risk

The article by Chatfield and Bjørn-Andersen goes further than many of its genre by raising issues such as power and trust in IOS-enabled networks of organizations. However, they give these issues fairly limited attention, and I turn now to some work that addresses such issues more directly. An early paper by Knights, Murray and Willmott (1993) recognized the importance of power and trust in networks mediated by IOS. Although extensive details are not provided, they illustrated their ideas using an inter-organizational network between 20 of the largest UK life insurance companies, designed to displace paper-based methods of trading between these companies and their distributors. However, implementation was not straightforward, since many of the companies remained unconvinced of its merits for their particular business. The paper quotes the Managing Director of the organization created to facilitate the IOS as criticizing the industry for getting involved in 'small, petty rivalries and silly arguments'.

However, from the viewpoint of the individual manager, becoming a 'network person' rather than an 'organization person' is not a trivial issue. Knights *et al.* discuss the difficulties felt by such individuals in 'committing themselves to collaborative agreements in a climate of increasing competition'. Those charged with managing the boundary between a specific organization of which they are a member, and the inter-organizational network which they are asked to facilitate, have a particularly ambiguous role. They must strive to bring 'their' company along into the network, whilst reassuring their senior managers that the company's interests are being looked after. Knights *et al.* describe this as a 'delicate, risky and time-consuming type of knowledge work'. They note that the outcomes of these activities, and the whole process of evolution of an IOS-based network, is often unpredictable: 'If our case is typical, this suggests that the process of network evolution may be far less coherent, controlled and rational than conventional wisdom in this field contends' (p. 979).

Kumar and Dissel (1996) focused on the potential for conflict in IOS. They divided IOS into three types, concerned with the pooling of information resources, value/supply chain IOS, and networked systems with reciprocal interdependencies. The insurance example above comes into the third category, and Kumar and Dissel argued that the potential for conflict in this category is high, since the exchanges and related transaction risks are varied and complex. They hypothesize that transactions in such networks are usually formed dynamically and often will not have a history of stable structures. Thus, the structure emerges incrementally, echoing the unpredictability argument alluded to above. Kumar and Dissel try to produce some prescriptions for risk management in each of their IOS categories, but they note the limitations of IT-based approaches here, arguing that: 'However, the sheer variety of reciprocal relationships would require the use of human agents ... to identify, assess, and manage the dynamically occurring risks in this situation' (p. 294).

Hart and Saunders (1997) identified power as an important influence on EDI adoption, such as that exerted by a large buyer on smaller suppliers. Their article includes a brief case study of power relations in a large office supply retail firm in the United States, and its introduction of EDI with its suppliers. The retail firm is described as having created an initial group of EDI-based suppliers through putting 'more pressure on suppliers over which it had relatively more power'. An incremental approach then added more suppliers to the network, but a number of firms formed a final non-EDI adoption group. 'Eventually the firm told the non-EDI suppliers that if they were not EDI operational by a specified date, their status as suppliers would be "reevaluated"' (p. 37). The retail firm accompanied this coercive use of power over partners with a 'hearts and minds' campaign to persuade the suppliers of the value of EDI.

Hart and Saunders linked this latter type of persuasive effort, if effectively carried out, with the development of trust relations. For example, the retail firm did not attempt to impose proprietary standards on its suppliers, but instead used industry approved standards. According to the authors, this provided a demonstration of concern for the supplier's goals on the part of the large retail firm by enabling relatively easy EDI exchange with other customers in addition to itself. It thus contributed to building trust between the large firm and its EDI suppliers.

E-COMMERCE

IOS, such as those discussed in the section above, are increasingly carried over the Internet, and come under the label of e-commerce which is the focus of this section. The Net, and associated technologies such as the world wide web, are a major new phenomenon of great importance to business activity, and indeed the world at large. The Net offers significantly lower transaction costs, is increasingly widely available, and can support a wide range of personal and commercial services. It is worth noting at the outset, however, that electronic communication does not always achieve the goal of effective human communication, as illustrated in a number of the case studies in the book to date. Thus, the Net does not suddenly replace the need for trust, for example, although it may be implicated in new forms of trust relations.

The phenomena associated with the Internet are changing rapidly, and the relative newness of them means that little digested experience is available at this time. In this section, some information and insights are offered on this early stage. I start with some definitions and current statistics of e-commerce in 1999. This is followed by a discussion of business opportunities and risks. An article on e-commerce in Spanish-speaking Latin America is then outlined, as a counterweight to the preponderance of North American and European experience reported in the literature. Finally, some ethical issues with respect to the Net are considered.

Definitions and Statistics

The label of e-commerce is problematic in itself, with the term e-business also being widely used. I prefer the latter, since it clearly includes both business-to-business and business-to-consumer applications, whereas the former has a more direct customer-focused feel. Nevertheless, e-commerce is the more common term at the time of writing, and thus will be used here. A second definitional issue is whether e-commerce has to be carried over the Internet, or whether it refers to the use of any telecommunications media for business purposes, but this latter would include many mundane activities such as the use of the telephone. As a compromise, PriceWaterhouseCoopers (PWC, 1999) define it as follows:

'The application of information technology to facilitate the buying and selling of products, services and information over public standards-based networks.'

Statistics on the scope and extent of e-commerce are also somewhat contentious, but some broad-brush estimates have been made. The foundation of Net usage for e-commerce purposes comes from its user base, and PWC (1999) estimated this as 140 million Net users in 1999, with 44% of those users in North America, taken to include the United States, Canada and Mexico. However, business use was skewed further towards the United States, with OECD (1999) estimating that it accounted for about 80% of global e-commerce. The total revenues for e-commerce in 1998 were estimated as US$50 billion (PWC, 1999), with at least 80% of this activity being business-to-business, and less than 20% business-to-consumer (OECD, 1999). Forecasts for future years were highly variable, but PWC (1999) suggested a forecast of US$1.3 trillion in e-commerce revenues in 2003, of which only some US$180 billion might be business-to-consumer.

OECD (1999) noted that, even if the figure of US$1 trillion were achieved sometime in the period 2003 to 2005, it would still be less than the 1999 sales in the United States alone using conventional means such as mail, telephone and newspapers. However, the importance of the e-commerce phenomenon cannot be measured solely on such metrics. Its impact is profound in the sense that all businesses across the globe are likely to be affected in a significant way by the e-commerce activities of themselves and their competitors, and thus it will be an item of high importance in any business agenda over the next few years.

Business Opportunities and Risks

So how should management assess the business opportunities and risks arising from e-commerce, particularly over the medium of the Internet? PWC (1999) argued that it offers four broad business opportunities. First, it can provide a faster, cheaper and more accurate link to suppliers. Second, that it can facilitate new internal business processes, for example through the development of intranets. Third, it may be the medium for new forms of relationship with supply chain partners. Finally, focused on business-to-consumer, it may provide a new direct, low-cost channel to customers. OECD (1999) noted similar points, but also pointed to changing product-market structures, impacts on labour markets through major changes in jobs and skills, and broader implications for society at large.

There are an increasing number of examples in the literature of e-commerce 'success stories', particularly in the high profile business-to-consumer end, despite its relatively small size in proportion to e-commerce generally. Companies such as `amazon.com` and `etrade.com` are given as successful early examples of direct selling over the Net, initially in the book and stock trading businesses, respectively. Newer companies such as `ebay.com` provide a more innovative product, in this case the facilitation of consumer-to-consumer auctions. Ghosh (1998) provides a further range of examples, including 'industry magnets' which target specific sectors, and companies such as `yahoo.com` that provide information services about the Internet itself.

With respect to successful business-to-business applications, we can use the earlier JAL case study in this chapter as one example. The company used e-commerce, in the form of both EDI systems and computerized reservations systems, to change the nature of their relationship with their suppliers and partners, and to create fast, cheap and efficient interactions with them. A further example was given by Magretta (1998), who described Dell's success in creating a US$12 billion company in just 13 years, emphasizing what had been achieved through e-commerce. For example, Dell bypassed the dealer channel to deal directly with customers, and established faster and cheaper links with suppliers. However, they also changed the relationships with suppliers, focusing on areas such as inventory being supplied on demand, and sharing design databases and methodologies with selected suppliers.

It is interesting to note that Magretta (1998) suggested to Michael Dell that his company's coordination with customers was made possible through technology, but 'there's still a good measure of old-fashioned, face-to-face human contact'. Michael Dell replied 'Yes, that's right.' Although there are companies which have succeeded in establishing themselves as solely e-commerce businesses, the more typical situation is where a company needs to blend e-commerce activities with older, more conventional approaches. Similarly, JAL created a blend of the old and the new, with the e-commerce activities being only one part of the picture.

What about the risks involved in e-commerce? First, it could be argued that the biggest risk is to do nothing, or not to formulate any e-commerce strategy, since the company's competitors and new direct entrants may take away their customers. However, even if a company has a clear e-commerce strategy, it is not guaranteed to succeed. We can cite evidence from some earlier case studies in the book to demonstrate this. For example, the London Insurance Market was successful in its EDI applications for areas such as claims settlement and accounting, but was unsuccessful in terms of the electronic placing system, for the reasons discussed earlier, involving shifting trust relations between brokers and underwriters for example. Similarly, groupware systems such as Lotus Notes are increasingly carried on the Internet, but the existence of such electronic channels does not necessarily produce effective teamwork, as we saw in the Compound UK case study in Chapter 5. Finally, the enterprise systems discussed in Chapter 6 are often integrated with the communication capabilities of the Internet, but this does not eliminate the need to consider the human processes of communication and knowledge-sharing.

The danger of the hyperbole surrounding the Internet is that individuals and organizations are overwhelmed by the promise and opportunities that it offers, without taking due account of the possible risk of failure. Woolgar and Ingram (1999) summarize their concern in this area, with particular reference to small businesses in the United Kingdom, but their cautionary comments are relevant more widely:

> The challenge especially for small businesses is to distinguish the real commercial opportunities from the much hyped potential. Amongst small businesses we observe a high failure rate at present. The risk is not only considerable but massively unpredictable. The hottest Internet companies are not expected to show a profit for many years, while old companies (like AOL) are now doing well after a shaky start.

The Case of Spanish-Speaking Latin America

E-commerce is being driven strongly from the United States at the time of writing but, in keeping with the global agenda of this book, we need to ask about other regions of the world. Davis (1999) provided a valuable summary of the situation in Spanish-speaking Latin America, and I will use his analysis in this section as an exemplar. This should not be taken to imply that this region is 'typical' of the world outside, only that it provides some insight into the effect of local contingencies on the global e-commerce phenomenon. The contingencies will be different in other regions, and my argument is that e-commerce will not develop in a uniform way across all regions of the world with the US-model as the eventual goal, but that it will be appropriated in ways that relate and develop from existing cultural norms and other historical features.

Davis quoted estimates that only 0.5% of the world's Internet hosts were in Spanish-speaking Latin America in 1998. The proportion of the population who were Internet users varied from a low of 0.01% in Paraguay to 6% in Costa Rica. This compared with the range of 22–27% of the population being Net users in the United States at that time. However, the rate of growth in the Latin American region was amongst the highest in the world. For example, the number of registered Internet sites in Mexico increased by 350% in one year between October 1996 and October 1997.

In terms of the nature of e-commerce applications in Latin America in the period up to 1998, Internet technologies were primarily being used by large corporates for the purposes of marketing and internal communication. However, there were also a significant number of examples of business-to-business applications, such as supply-chain management arrangements in Disco Supermarkets in Argentina and in Cifra, a large Mexican retailer. Business-to-consumer e-commerce was still a relative novelty, and in some cases users could purchase services more cheaply with a better range of choice from on-line providers in North America than from local retailers or agents.

Davis discussed some of the problems and challenges faced by Spanish-speaking Latin America in making effective use of the Internet and, in particular, e-commerce. Payment on-line is a problem for consumers since it is mostly insecure or requires a signature off-line. In addition, Davis argued that there is in general no strong service orientation from companies in the region, so that consumers are often suspicious of on-line goods or services from these organizations. The telecommunications infrastructure throughout the region is relatively poor in terms of low quality, narrow bandwidth and high connection and calling costs. A further barrier to Internet usage is the low proportion of web pages in Spanish, this being estimated at less than 2% of the world's sites at the time of writing.

Davis argued that initiatives were needed in Latin America to stimulate further interest, knowledge and use of the Internet and e-commerce. These suggestions ranged from the need for government policies with respect to Net usage, to improved educational facilities. Whilst not disagreeing with Davis about the need for such initiatives, there is an implicit principle underlying them, namely that e-commerce is a good thing, and this needs some qualification. In a similar way to the earlier discussion of the relevance of e-commerce to a specific business organization, it is reasonable to argue that no national government should adopt an ignorant or hands-off policy to the Net. However, it is not obvious that Net take-up and usage should be encouraged on identical lines to a different context such as the United States. Social, cultural, economic and language differences need to be taken into account in formulating appropriate policies in a given country or organization in Latin America. A similar comment applies for other regions of the non-Western world such as Asia and Africa.

Ethics and the Net

The Internet crosses national boundaries and permits forms of communication that did not previously exist. There are many positive features to this, including wider and easier access to goods and services, to the views of others, and in principle to the world at large. However, there is a dark side to this breaking down of boundaries, with ethical concerns about issues such as pornography, racism and privacy. Some of these topics relate to the Net in general, rather than e-commerce in particular. However, they are important issues that warrant some discussion here, and they often have a strong commercial dimension, such as the selling of pornographic images over the Net.

It can be argued that the most important single ethical issue with respect to the Internet is whether it will act in a way that further exacerbates the differences between the 'haves' and the 'have-nots' in our societies. Readers of this text, and the author, are all in the former category of course. The twentieth century has seen a widening gap between rich and poor people in the world, and between different countries and regions. Indeed, despite world wars and other negative aspects of the previous century, it could be argued that increased inequality is its worst legacy. Will the Net serve to increase this inequity, providing the privileged people, countries and regions of the world with a further resource to enable them to enjoy the benefits of improved access to people, ideas and goods and services, whilst relegating the disadvantaged to the role of outsider? There is no technological inevitability about this conclusion, but action is needed on a worldwide scale to counter these trends. There is an important role here for individuals, organizations, governments and transgovernmental agencies.

In terms of more specific issues, pornography has been mentioned already. The Net has provided a relatively non-regulated medium over which pornographic materials can be transmitted easily, and to a worldwide audience. Although some would dispute the need to censor and restrict this activity altogether, most of us believe that some form of regulation is needed, particularly in areas such as child pornography. However, the technical and legal issues involved are not easy. For example, Catudal (1999) argued that the Child Pornography Prevention Act (CPPA) of 1996 in the United States, whilst no doubt well-intentioned, showed a misunderstanding of the way in which prurient material was accessed. On an international stage, it is very difficult to formulate common laws in different jurisdictions, and perhaps even more difficult to police them when pornographic images can travel the world in seconds from a multiplicity of potentially shifting sources.

Racism on the Net is a similarly disturbing issue. For example, Thiesmeyer (1999) traced the rapid rise of neo-Nazism in recent years. He argued that, although it is impossible to know whether the Net has been the chief cause of this, it is certainly its chief tool. Anyone with a browser can access the extreme-right movements of at least 20 nations, according to Thiesmeyer, each with an average of a hundred subgroups. Now, of course, there are many other benign uses of the Net, and indeed groups opposed to neo-Nazism use the Internet to try to counter its proponents. Nevertheless, an advocacy of total 'free speech' is naive, but as with pornography it is difficult to formulate cross-national laws and policing on these issues.

Returning to the narrower brief of e-commerce, network crime such as fraud is an obvious legal and ethical concern. More subtle but important concerns include areas such as plagiarism and copyright piracy, and privacy. With respect to the latter, Tavani (1999) argued that techniques such as data-mining of Internet usage statistics raises important privacy concerns that go beyond similar concerns in traditional information-retrieval techniques in computer databases. These include the possible use of a single database to extract information about a person, the public nature of much of this information on the Net, and the difficulty in predicting future purposes to which this information might be put. Tavani (1999) argued that such issues are not covered by existing data-protection guidelines and privacy laws.

The need to formulate appropriate policies and laws is evident even from this brief discussion of ethical issues with respect to the Internet. This has not gone unnoticed. For example, Doyle and Morris (1999) produced a detailed set of policy recommendations derived from rethinking the regulatory role of the nation state in the global electronic economy. This publication was produced by the Fabian Society, a think-tank with significant influence on the Labour government in the United Kingdom. However, whilst welcoming such publications and their role in influencing policy, there is a need for a much wider public debate. The Internet is very new and, as with many new technologies, debate on ethical concerns often lags behind the introduction and use of the technology. The meteoric rise of the Net provides a good example of this, and it is extremely important that this new phenomenon and its effects are widely debated from a broader ethical as well as commercial stance.

ANALYSIS AND CONCLUSIONS

This chapter has focused on inter-organizational networks, and the increasing role of inter-organizational systems of various kinds. The Internet and associated web technologies have provided a major boost to these developments in recent times. At one level, these developments can be seen as a response to pressures from global markets, increased competition, and changing product-market structures. One can also turn this the other way round and argue that IOS, and particularly the deployment of Net technology, are in part creating these globalized phenomena. It is, however, best to conceptualize them as inextricably inter-linked, and to analyse the co-evolution of the technological networks and broader organizational and societal change. IOS and the Internet provide very powerful illustrations of some of the globalization themes discussed in Chapter 2, such as Castells' arguments on the role of IT in enabling the pervasive expansion of networking throughout the social structure.

In this final section of the chapter I return to the questions of trust and power relations in inter-organizational networks that were raised in the introduction. They have been discussed already to some extent in the empirical examples given, but this section aims to synthesize some

Table 7.1 *Trust in electronically mediated interaction*

Need to maintain personal relations for complex interactions based on trust	• Unlikely to be achieved solely through electronic media • Related to sophisticated improvisation and complex situated local action • Need for thoughtful media balance
Trust-based value chain may provide good context for IOS implementation	• Of potential benefit to the supply chain as a whole • Although persuasion may be based on latent power of one of the partners
The maintenance of trust is a key role for managers of network boundaries	• Delicate, risky and time-consuming knowledge work • Such tacit skills are not amenable to being 'captured' in computers

insights from all the material of the chapter. In addition, in the concluding sub-section, other human and organizational issues are discussed with specific reference to the global networking role of the Internet. A summary of key points in this section is provided in Tables 7.1–7.3.

How are Inter-Organizational Trust Relations Affected by Electronically-Mediated Interaction?

The basis of trust between the representatives of different organizations is crucial to organizational partnering, and this can be disrupted in some cases by electronically-mediated interaction. In the London Insurance Market, the communication and knowledge-sharing between underwriters and brokers, concerned with the crucial risk negotiation process, was weakened by the use of the electronic system, at least in the eyes of most of the Market participants. The complexity and importance of the task was not suited to communication at-a-distance, but needed good personal relations between the underwriter and broker to be maintained through face-to-face contact. Another way of expressing this is to say that the job of both parties required sophisticated improvisation and complex situated local action, using the concepts introduced in Chapter 3. The electronic placing system did not support this adequately.

There are of course many areas where electronic interaction is indeed adequate. For example, ordering a book over the Internet does not require personal interaction with the supplier, provided one is confident that the firm will deliver. More generally, there is a need for a thoughtful balance between the use of technology, and more conventional methods of human interaction such as face-to-face meetings. Even in the case of Dell computers, using new technology more than most, Michael Dell noted the importance of 'old-fashioned' methods of human contact. Our ability to 'understand' and 'trust' other people has been largely based on face-to-face contact throughout human history. It seems highly unlikely that we can build a new world in the space of a few years that overturns these deep-seated aspects of human nature.

The computerized reservation system in the JAL case provides an example of a relatively simple transaction system where the organizational partners did not require face-to-face contact. However, issues of trust were still important, in that the organizations in the keiretsu-based value chain needed to believe that the IOS was of benefit to them. Although this acceptance may have required no explicit exercise of power to persuade members of the chain, there must have been a latent influence from JAL related to its dominant position in the chain.

However, it seems that trust was maintained in the network sufficiently for the IOS to function effectively.

The maintenance of trust is a key role for managers who act on the boundary between the interests of their organization, and those of an inter-organizational network of which their organization forms a part. They are engaged in a particularly 'delicate, risky and time-consuming type of knowledge work' (Knights, Murray and Willmott 1993), since they must face both ways to some extent. Such tacit skills are not amenable to being 'captured' by computers, or shared through computer-based systems, providing a good example of the difficulties of knowledge conversion as discussed in Chapter 3. The arrival of the Internet does not remove the need for such skills either, particularly in relatively complex business-to-business interactions.

How is Power Implicated in Network Relationships?

As implied in the discussion above, power and trust in inter-organizational networks cannot be neatly separated, and indeed they are inextricably interlinked. For example, the use of coercive power may be effective in producing short-term compliance, but may harm trust relations in the network to everyone's longer term disadvantage. As outlined earlier, Hart and Saunders (1997) discussed ways to mitigate this, including the concept of a 'hearts and minds' campaign to persuade suppliers of the value of EDI. In the theoretical terms introduced in Chapter 3, this can be viewed as an attempt to create a new 'regime

Table 7.2   *Power in inter-organizational networks*

Power and trust in inter-organizational networks are inextricably interlinked	• Use of coercive power may harm trust relationships • Although various actions can be taken to try to mitigate this
IT-enabled networks are deeply implicated in shifting power relationships	• Changing identities and roles • Changing market structures • Power over suppliers/partners • Power relations between supply chains
Conflict around IT-based change is potentially high for networks of autonomous or semi-autonomous organizations	• Based on complexity of reciprocal relationships • Resistance often easier in such contexts due to relative autonomy

of truth' concerning the value of EDI to everyone in the network. At a more detailed level, Hart and Saunders described how the firm in their case study tried to maintain trust relations, alongside its exertion of power over suppliers, by using industry-approved rather than proprietary standards.

It is clear from all the case study evidence in this chapter that IT-enabled networks are deeply implicated in shifting power relationships. For example, in the London Insurance Market case this included changing identities and roles for the brokers and underwriters, and potential future changes in market structures, through processes such as disintermediation. Barrett and Walsham (1999) linked these issues to the location of knowledge in the Market and power–knowledge relations. They argued that knowledge in the London Market has traditionally been held with broker or underwriting firms, and power–knowledge relationships were mediated through personal relationships. The shift to an electronic placing system places a high value on the explicit representation of knowledge in electronic documents on the network, and past information stored in computers. However, these imply uncertain shifts in power–knowledge relations, and resistance to the EPS system can be seen in part as reflecting participants' concerns regarding their future autonomy, prestige and control.

With respect to the case of supply chain networks, rather than the network of autonomous organizations of the London Insurance Market, we have already seen that power over suppliers and partners was a key issue in all the cases considered. Holland (1995) hypothesized that competition in the future, in IOS-mediated supply chains, would tend to occur between supply chains rather than between individual units. The truth of this assertion is by no means obvious, however, for example in the context of the Internet, where suppliers and customers may have more flexibility in shifting between supply chains.

Different views on the merits of IOS may not result in open conflict in the case of supply chains, due to fear of sanctions on the part of the weaker parties. The situation is rather different in the case of autonomous or semi-autonomous organizations, where resistance is easier, as we saw in the London Insurance Market case. A further reason why conflict may arise in these latter circumstances is that the reciprocal relations in such networks are often highly complex, implying that an IOS-based approach may be seen to be beneficial to some, but of less value or even detrimental to others in the network. It is clear that IT-based approaches need to be based on a substantial consensus in such cases, rather than being imposed on a reluctant constituency.

What Human and Organizational Issues Arise from the Spread of Global Networking Technologies, Particularly the Internet?

The Internet offers a unique vehicle for the development of global networking, and in particular for the inter-organizational networks that have been the focus of this chapter. In examining the potential of the Net, it is important to try to balance the new features and opportunities that it offers, with a recognition that human behaviour remains relatively stable over long periods of time. Thus the human and organizational issues associated with IOS, for example, will still be of some relevance to the 'new' domain of e-commerce, although they make take somewhat different forms. In other words, what can we learn from the old that is relevant to the new, and what has changed?

Business-to-business (B2B) electronic interaction is increasingly being carried over the Internet, and forms the largest part of the e-commerce boom, although not the most widely reported in the popular press at the time of writing. In what ways is B2B a new phenomenon? It certainly offers the potential for cheaper, more reliable and sometimes innovative ways in which communication and collaboration between organizational partners can be maintained. However, the issues of trust and power relations between partners, discussed above for IOS, are still of key relevance. Even if the electronic placing system in the London Insurance Market had been carried over the Net initially, the human and organizational issues described earlier would have remained a stumbling block to its acceptance and use.

Table 7.3   *The Internet: some human and organizational issues*

E-commerce has new features, but much can be learnt from earlier experience	• B2B offers cheaper, reliable internal and external communication • But issues of power and trust between partners are still important • B2C offers a direct low-cost channel to consumers • But customers need to trust business sellers
Extensive use of the Internet raises many crucial ethical issues	• Privacy, pornography, racism • The digital divide • Whose interests are served?
Analysis of the potential of the Internet in non-Western cultures must address issues of local specificity	• Will not follow US model in a simple way, but geared to local histories and contingencies • Need for understanding of cultural and cross-cultural issues

In the business-to-consumer (B2C) sector, web-based information and purchasing offer a new direct low-cost channel to consumers, or at least to those who are on-line. However, trust still matters, as it does with conventional sales, and issues such as the value of respected brand names are crucial. Indeed, they are probably more important in a context where the goods will be delivered later, and trust is needed at the time of purchase. As we saw in the case of Spanish-speaking Latin America, Davis (1999) argued that there is in general no strong service orientation from companies in the region, so that consumers are often suspicious of on-line goods and services, for example the likelihood of goods being delivered within a reasonable time.

In addition to the specific business issues related to B2B and B2C, the extensive use of the Internet raises many important ethical issues of global relevance. Privacy, pornography and racism are examples that were discussed briefly earlier in the chapter. The most crucial of all is perhaps the 'digital divide', where Internet access and use may further separate the people of the Fourth World, using Castells' term for the disadvantaged as introduced in Chapter 2. Taking an actor-network perspective, the Net and its users may constitute a stable network of exclusion, based on a narrow definition of self-interest and ignorance or lack of concern for the silent voices of those on the outside.

Although the Fourth World includes the disadvantaged within the economically advanced countries, and does not include the elite in the developing countries, nevertheless it is largely made up of the citizens of the non-Western countries, excluding islands of prosperity such as Japan. So what is the potential of the Internet in these non-Western cultures? In view of their different histories and local contingencies, it is unlikely that they will follow a US-type model in any simple sense. For example, in Latin America, Davis summarized that in 1998 Internet technologies were being used mainly by the large corporates for marketing and internal communication, with selling over the web being a relative novelty. Davis argued that there were special problems for e-commerce in this region based on issues such as security of payment, poor telecommunications infrastructure, and the trust issues discussed above.

Looking to the future of the Internet outside the Western region, both business-to-business and business-to-consumer success, and more generally issues such as education through the Net, must surely rely on an understanding of local cultures. The approach to purchasing, and the types of items purchased, will be different in Bombay and Bangkok, or Singapore and Saigon. It could be argued that the international elite who travel between such cities may form a homogeneous and wealthy consumer base, the globapolitans in Castells' terms, but large local markets will still exist. Business-to-business transactions, even more than consumer purchasing perhaps, imply the need for an understanding of local norms and values and cross-cultural issues when working between countries. These cultural issues, related to the use of IT, are the central focus of Part 3 of the book.

Part 3
Different Worlds

8
Culture as Context

The case studies in the book so far have mostly focused on the use of IT in the economically advanced countries of Western Europe and the United States. This can be justified on the grounds that technology use in these countries is more widespread, of a more advanced nature, and more influential on global economic activity than the use of IT in the rest of the world. Nevertheless, processes of globalization have seen IT penetrating all countries of the world at least to some extent, and it is likely that this trend will continue. Indeed, emphasis on global markets and the global economy implies the need to take the use of IT in these 'other' countries seriously, even if one adopts a narrow economic viewpoint. If one considers the wider perspective that these countries include the great majority of the world's population, the case for considering them in some detail becomes even stronger.

We have already seen that there are significantly different issues to consider when analysing the introduction and use of information technologies in countries with cultures far removed from those in the Western world where the technologies originated. For example, in Chapter 3 I discussed the limitations of adopting a Western view of decision-making in the very different context of Egypt. In the same chapter, the role of information in Nepal was seen to be at odds with the perceived need in Western countries for the active externalization of meaning. In Chapter 4, the case study of GIS in India discussed the problems of introducing such systems in a country where its citizens do not generally adopt a map-based approach to the conceptualization of space. In Chapter 7, the different characteristics and constraints of Spanish-speaking Latin America were used to analyse the effect of local contingencies on the global e-commerce phenomenon. The purpose of the current chapter is to expand this consideration of the appropriation of information and communication technologies in non-Western cultures, and three key questions will be addressed:

- How does culture relate to IT use and how may culture be understood?
- How should appropriate IT adoption in different cultural contexts be facilitated?
- Can the excluded of the Third World be brought into the global network society?

The empirical material of the chapter discusses three specific case studies, one taken from each of the world regions of Asia, Latin America and Africa. The first concerns the introduction of a material requirements planning system into a manufacturing company in Thailand. The second case study analyses the growth of an information-based company in Mexico. The third case involves the development and use of district health information systems in South Africa. The final section of the chapter will return explicitly to the key questions listed above, drawing on all the case material in the chapter.

THAI VALUES AND AN MRP SYSTEM

This case study concerns the introduction of a material requirements planning (MRP) system into a manufacturing company in Thailand, called Quickfood. The description is based on a longitudinal field study carried out over the period 1995–97, and reported on in Rohitratana (1998, 2000). The principal method of data collection was through semi-structured interviews, conducted in the Thai language, with a range of organizational participants involved in the process of MRP implementation. Interviewees included users, system developers, consultants and senior managers. In addition, the researcher had a number of informal discussions with key personnel. All 39 formal interviews were transcribed, and 25 of these were translated by the researcher from Thai to English. I was the research supervisor for this study, but I do not speak Thai, and therefore I had access to the English material only.

Quickfood was considered to be a large company in the food industry in Thailand, with three sites and about 2200 employees at the time of the research study. It manufactured three products, namely bread, cheese and ice cream, primarily at the main production site in Rachada province where the field research took place. The head office was located in the capital, Bangkok, and a further new production site for bread was opened in 1996 in Sesami province. The company had an overall Managing Director (MD) supported by three Vice Presidents (VPs), one responsible for the Rachada production site, and two at head office concerned with accounting/computing and purchasing/administration/human resources, respectively. Figure 8.1 shows an outline organization chart and the names of some key senior managers, whose family relationships are discussed below.

Simon was the first MD of the company, and he assigned Sam to the position of VP of the Rachada branch. In 1984, Simon brought his son, Keith, into Quickfood and promoted him to be VP responsible for accounting and computing. This situation remained the same until Simon's death in 1992. The MD position was then filled by a new appointment, Peter, who came from the overall holding group. Peter brought his daughter, Pam, into Quickfood in 1994 as R&D manager in the Rachada branch. No long after that, Sam was transferred to China to explore new market opportunities, leaving Pam to act as VP at Rachada in his absence. This did not work out well since many staff were uncomfortable with her management approach and, following a major strike threat, Sam was brought back from China to rescue the situation. As a final note in this saga of family connections, Peter promoted his son, Paul, to the post of production manager at the new Sesami site in 1996, reporting to the production VP, Sam.

Computers in Quickfood

Although Quickfood had used computers on an IBM platform to manage various administrative systems at head office from 1988, the Rachada branch had continued to use manual systems to control production activities. Stock cards were used to monitor inventory levels, production plans were made using a calculator, and raw materials were ordered using judgement based on experience. Keith, as VP responsible for computing in the late 1980s, felt that the manual production system was inefficient and introduced too much human error, and in 1991 the use of computers for production was approved by Quickfood management. The company decided to buy an MRP system, called Plus, to run on an AS400 minicomputer platform. Keith suggested that there were two main reasons for this choice. First, it would be easy to link and convert data due to compatibility between the IBM and AS 400 platforms. Second, Keith took advice from an external consultant, who had implemented Plus for other companies.

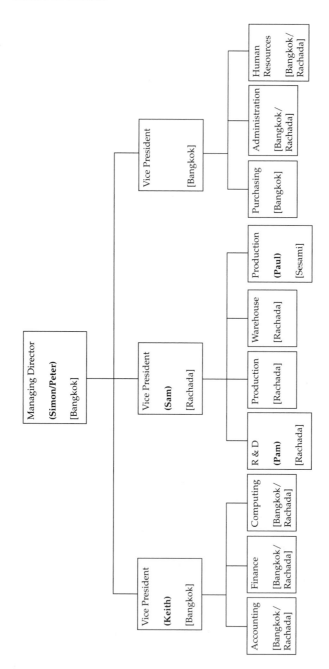

Figure 8.1   *Quickfood: organization chart. Adapted from Rohitratana (2000) with permission from Ashgate Publishing Ltd*

The Plus system was purchased from Advance Ltd, who had a monopoly for that system in Thailand, and Advance also supplied all the necessary consulting services, such as tailoring the software to fit Quickfood's particular characteristics. Quickfood decided to buy 11 modules of the MRP system, separated into the three groups of accounting, production and logistics. The project started with the inventory module, and two members of the computer department were sent to Advance to learn how to set up and maintain the system. In October 1991 the computer department started setting up the code, with help from Advance, and in January 1992 the inventory module was run on the Plus system in parallel with the manual system.

From this promising beginning, the implementation of the MRP system for production purposes progressed very slowly indeed over several years. Although various modules were 'implemented', such as the Master Production Schedule module in the ice cream factory in 1996, evidence from the case study suggested that these did not normally replace the pre-existing manual systems. The management problems at the Rachada production site, referred to above, created further delays. Negotiations regarding full implementation of the MRP system were still taking place between the production managers and the computer department at the end of the research period in March 1997.

The Influence of Thai Culture

In trying to analyse reasons for the slow and fragmented MRP implementation process, Rohitratana (2000) described some 'Thai values' that had a strong influence in her view, based on her extensive field research and knowledge of Thai culture. First, and not surprising in view of the earlier description of family relationships in the top hierarchy of the firm, she argued that the importance of kinship in Thailand was crucial. For example, the initial priority of the MRP project derived partly from Keith's position as son of the managing director at that time, Simon. After Simon died in 1992, the new MD, Peter, promoted his daughter, Pam. After the trouble at the Rachada site, and Sam's return, Pam suggested a new production-oriented project that was enthusiastically supported by Peter in order for her to gain respect amongst the employees. The MRP project, which needed similar resources in terms of manpower to Pam's new project, was largely disregarded.

Rohitratana developed her analysis of Thai values further, using the concept of *bunkhun*. Komin (1990) defined this as: '... the psychological bond between two persons: one who renders the needy help and favours out of kindness and other's remembering of the goodness done and his ever-readiness to reciprocate the kindness, not bound by time or distance'.

Creating this bond is called *saang bunkhun* and this may be used to build up an entourage or empire of people who gain protection and benefits from a powerful person, but who in return will not question that person's authority. With respect to the MRP project, Rohitratana argued that Sam had built up this type of power base in his many years at the Rachada factory. It was difficult for Pam to take over Sam's position in this respect, and indeed he was brought back from China when major employee resistance occurred. All of this diverted attention from the MRP project itself, and Pam then needed some other way of promoting her own position which, as discussed above, was largely at the expense of the MRP project.

What was the attitude to the MRP project of employees lower down in the hierarchy, such as key users? Rohitratana argued that *criticism avoidance* was a crucial consideration here. This value originates from the difficulty in a Thai context in separating the opinions from the person holding those opinions. A person whose opinions are criticized can perceive themselves as insulted, leading them to lose face. A key user explained this attitude and its effect on the MRP system as follows:

> . . . we realized that the system may be useful, but may not be appro-priate to our company. As you know, we were only the subordinates, we had to do whatever the bosses ordered. How could we refuse to operate the system? We decided to keep quiet until the problem explicitly appeared. Otherwise, the boss may have thought that we were resisting using the system. It would be too risky to do so.

It is not that users were unaware of the limitations of the computer systems, but that they felt it unwise, and contrary to values implicit in Thai culture, to speak the truth, since it would be perceived as criticism of a person or persons. So, in trying to analyse why the inventory module was unsatisfactory, since it did not accord with actual stock levels, the following quote reveals almost a conspiracy of silence:

> Every month we discuss the difference between the actual inventory on hand, the inventory in the book, and the inventory on the screen. The VP will ask the warehouse for the reasons [for discrepancies]. His reply is always 'that the raw material sack/bin was broken' or 'that the raw material is stuck in the sack/bin'. He used these reasons,

which were not true, as an excuse every month and everyone realized that. No one wanted to criticize him, even the VP, because making a person lose face is equal to making an enemy. It may lead to difficulty in getting cooperation from that person and also from his department. Also, if you get into trouble in a meeting some time, he will not speak against you in return. It is a good deal, isn't it?

A rather deeper explanation of attitudes such as criticism avoidance is the concept of *kreng jai*, concerned with interpersonal behaviour patterns amongst Thais. Komin (1990) explained this as the need to be considerate, to take another's feelings into account, or to take every measure not to cause discomfort or inconvenience to another person. This concept is to be observed by all—superiors, equals and inferiors—with a difference only in terms of degree. Rohitratana noted that the people involved in the MRP project at Quickfood were concerned about this value at all times. Many employees explained to the researcher that they decided not to tell top management about negative implementation results using explicit mention of this attitude. For example, one interviewee in this category argued that this is essential as a form of 'social glue' in Thai society:

I think it is normal for us to feel *kreng jai* and pay respect to the superiors because they are higher than us in terms of knowledge, status, education and power. They can protect us in most critical situations, not only at the workplace but also at home. When we have been working together for a long time, we feel like a relative or a cousin. The superior can be compared to the elder relatives to whom we have to pay respect in any situation. If there is anything we can do for them, we would do it as best we can because we realize that they will never harm us. I think these kinds of values keep us together.

Some Implications

The simple message from the above analysis is that Thai culture was an important factor in the history of the MRP project in Quickfood. It provided the set of shared norms and values which all the participants could be thought to have internalized in various ways through their social conditioning in Thai society, and these influenced the forms of cultural interaction and power relations between the participants in the case study. Of course, socio-political analyses of the introduction of computer-based information systems are not new, with this book having given many such examples already. The difference in the Quickfood study is the use of specific features of Thai culture in the analysis.

An interesting footnote to Rohitratana's study is that she presented this work at an international conference in Thailand in 1998, at which I was also present. In the discussion of the work after the presentation, a Thai participant at the conference argued that the specific 'Thai values' used by Rohitratana were less relevant to the contemporary world, since Thai culture was changing, due to increased contact with foreign cultures through the activities of multinational companies for example. A shift in cultural values in Thailand is no doubt taking place, but it is worth noting that neither side in the above debate was arguing against the importance of Thai culture in influencing events, but rather about the specific form that such an analysis should take.

Following on from this point, there is a well-established tradition in international management, developed from the work of authors such as Hofstede (1980, 1991), to analyse cultural differences between countries using variables such as power-distance and degree of individualism. On the positive side, this type of work is helpful in alerting us to cultural differences, and in providing some 'universal' measures with which to analyse them. On the negative side, such measures are crude in that they sweep the subtleties of cultural difference under the universal carpet. Concepts such as *bunkhun* and *kreng jai* cannot be subsumed under Western-centric universal measures without a considerable loss of understanding. In addition, the analysis developed by Rohitratana, and presented here, is based on the view that an understanding of IT adoption in particular cultural contexts should draw on locally relevant concepts, and show how they were implicated in the evolving process of IT acquisition and use.

This is a process-oriented approach in contrast to the static feel of cultural 'measures'. The globalization pressures of contemporary society are leading to technologies like MRP systems being introduced into countries such as Thailand, and it is crucial that we gain a better understanding of how to analyse the process of local appropriation of such technologies. The Quickfood case study provides one example of how to develop such an analysis.

AN INFORMATION COMPANY IN MEXICO

The second case study in this chapter shifts us from Asia to Latin America, and the description of the case is based on a research study reported by Jarvenpaa and Leidner (1998). The case concerns three companies in Mexico, called the Group, running two newspapers and an on-line financial information service, respectively. The case is of the 'heroic' variety, in that it describes the successful way in which a dynamic leader, Alejandro Junco, transformed the company that he inherited from his grandfather into an information group. A key point made by Jarvenpaa and Leidner is that much of the literature on IT in less-developed economies emphasizes the importance of adapting organizational approaches, including the use of IT, to local cultural values and practices. In contrast, they argue that resourceful managers can not only shape their own company, but also the broader economic and social system around them.

Their study was based on semi-structured interviews with 40 people, including 32 employees of the Group, five academics with collaboration or consulting relationships with the company, and three customers of the Group's products. Two-thirds of the interviews were conducted in English, and the rest in Spanish via a translator. The interviewees provided, in the words of the authors themselves, 'retrospective accounts of events'. In addition to the interviews, the authors gathered data from a range of other secondary sources such as marketing material, annual reports, newspapers and Internet sites.

Case Description

In 1973, Alejandro Junco took over control of the newspaper *El Norte*, the highest circulation paper in Monterrey, a Mexican industrial city with about five million inhabitants. During the 1980s, Junco decided to redefine the company as an information company rather than a newspaper company and he adopted the motto that 'IT provides the way for market advantage'. The first major new project was to make a large electronic database of material about Mexico that was being published on paper around the world. This database also included government-based statistical information on the economy. In April 1987, a product called InfoSel En Linea was launched, providing on-line access to the database using the national telephone system. The service was not a financial success, and in 1990 it was discontinued. One reason given for the failure was the inadequate Mexican telephone system in terms of service quality.

In November 1990, InfoSel Financiero was launched, an on-line information service focused specifically on the financial sector. Instead of relying on telephone lines, the company partnered with FM broadcast stations throughout Mexico. This new service was very successful. By

1993 it was earning US$8 million in revenue, and a network product had been launched, allowing organizations to have one subscription but many users. By 1995, revenues were US$12 million and the product contained a wider range of information from local and foreign financial markets. As of 1997, some 3500 organizations were using the system, both nationally and internationally. A senior executive of the company said: 'InfoSel Financiero is the standard for Mexican financial news and information. All the banks, all the brokerage houses, all major corporations are subscribers to our service.'

International competitors, such as Reuters, remained viable in niches that provided foreign market information to Mexican-based firms, but InfoSel was dominant in the provision of Mexican financial information, with an estimated 80% market share reported in 1997.

In 1995, InfoSel launched an Internet access dial-up service, and by 1997 had some 25 000 clients. However, although it had a strong position as an Internet access provider, management saw the company as primarily a value-added information service. One of the managers explained the strategy as: 'Our slogan is that anywhere in the world, if you want information on Mexico, go to the InfoSel web site.'

In parallel with the development of InfoSel, Junco's information group expanded its activities further in 1993 with the launch of a new newspaper called *Reforma* in the capital of Mexico, Mexico City. At that time, this city of some 25 million people had between 25 and 30 existing newspapers, each with a low readership. Junco aimed to enter this market with a different type of product: '. . . changing the nature of information delivered in Mexico so that the information was trustworthy and so that the presentation of the information was superior'.

By 1995, despite various difficulties with unions and government, *Reforma* had a daily circulation of 86 000 and 39 000 subscribers. Early in that year, in conjunction with InfoSel, *Reforma* opened a web site to distribute news on the Internet, and by 1996 there were 20 000 on-line subscribers, many from overseas. By 1997, *Reforma* was the second largest newspaper in terms of circulation in Mexico City, but the first in advertising revenue because of the higher average purchasing power of its readers.

Overcoming Constraints

The way in which Jarvenpaa and Leidner analysed the relative success of the Group was through describing the process of 'overcoming constraints', these being classed as cultural, technical or political in nature.

I will outline this analysis here, but I also include some of their material on key resources and capabilities that were brought to bear by the Group, including aspects such as leadership, the Group's internal culture and the development of external networks.

The authors described cultural constraints in Mexico as including a lack of a work ethic amongst journalists and a lack of an information culture in the country. With respect to how the Group tackled the first of these, the launch of *Reforma* used 'fresh new people that had never been journalists', recruited directly from the universities and then gave a six-week training programme taught by US journalism professors. *Reforma* also deliberately sought female journalists. According to Junco, it was: '. . . very important that women were entering our newsroom. Women journalists were less susceptible to the old practices than men'.

A second cultural roadblock, according to the authors, was the general lack of interest in 'objective' information on the part of Mexican readers, and this needed to be stimulated through aggressive marketing coupled with encouragement to the reporters: 'Our instructions to reporters specifically encouraged avoidance of adjectives. We strive to be direct, objective, well quoted and void of fabrication. Of course, we have our critics who think we violate the Mexican tradition of flowery language, politeness and genteel etiquette.'

All of this sounds like trying to make Mexico similar to the United States, but anyone with any familiarity with this country will know that Mexicans are generally very patriotic and fiercely independent. This is addressed in the article when discussing the way in which the Group tried to emphasize Mexican values in its own organization. First, Mexican traditions were celebrated. For example, the headquarters of *Reforma*, although newly built, reflected Mexican architectural tradition with a European neoclassical facade, and an interior representing a combination of pre-Columbian construction and a colonial house. Architecture that celebrates the past is highly prized in Mexican culture, representing the symbolic harmony of the past and the present.

A second way in which Mexican aspirations were appealed to was through an emphasis on the need for the Group to disseminate information about Mexico to Mexicans in order to enable them to compete against large multinational companies. A manager explained that: 'What motivates me is to make Mexico competitive.' Jarvenpaa and Leidner argued, in summary, that the Group had selectively combined US cultural values with those of Mexico.

In terms of technical constraints, the authors identified a weak national IT infrastructure, poor in-house technology in customers' premises, and a shortage of qualified technical staff. As we have seen, InfoSel Financiero side-stepped the first of these using FM radio stations. Over time, InfoSel built the largest private satellite-based information network in Mexico allowing the release of wide area network (WAN) versions of its products. It was this private network that it leveraged to become an Internet access provider. Customers of InfoSel, such as the banks, were helped to develop their own in-house technical resources by close collaboration and the provision of 'nearly unlimited' training. The Group developed an alliance with a leading technological university to recruit qualified staff, and invested heavily in technical training.

This emphasis on leading-edge IT was a long-term vision of Alejandro Junco, as stated earlier, and the stability of his leadership over a long period of time enabled this vision to be translated into action. For example, it took from 1986 until 1994 for InfoSel to become profitable, but it then created the basis for future expansion. Indeed, Jarvenpaa and Leidner argued that this placed InfoSel in an enviable position *vis-à-vis* its foreign competitors. The Group had developed a viable low-cost and expandable technological infrastructure, whereas its competitors required a large shift from their normal infrastructure to operate efficiently in Mexico.

Finally, the article discussed political constraints, including the opposition of the Newspaper Vendors Union, and confrontations with the government over issues such as criticism of its policies and its honesty. With respect to the first of these, the Group created its own distribution channel in the end, having failed to reach agreement with the Union. Some history of the Group's turbulent relationship with the Mexican government is given in the article, although such a complex matter could no doubt be the subject of a much larger analysis. It is worth noting that Junco 'relentlessly pursued partnerships with other firms and organizations that share the same values'. These included Mexican organizations such as the Monterrey Institute of Technology, but also foreign companies such as Microsoft, Dow Jones and Business Week. In addition, alliances with elements of government were formed, and with customer organizations. A company with such a network of alliances is in a more powerful position to negotiate with any potential opposition, including the government of its own country.

Implications and Limitations

Jarvenpaa and Leidner stated that the primary contribution of their paper was the extension of the resource-based theory of the firm to a developing country context. This extension in their view was to environments where the firm has to shape the environment itself, not just proactively respond to it. This is an interesting perspective, and a nice contrast with most studies where the broader environment of the firm is taken to a large extent as given. The article is optimistic in tone, with the 'hero', Alejandro Junco, triumphing over difficulties and opposition, and seeing his IT-driven vision of transforming a newspaper company into a powerful information group coming to fruition. Two limitations of the research study and the published paper are worth noting here.

First, the paper is uncritical of the management of the Group, and Junco in particular, except perhaps for the early financial failure of the InfoSel operation. Even this is presented as a step to the eventual success of InfoSel Financiero. The authors mainly interviewed Group employees, supplemented by academics with collaboration or consulting relationships with the company. Three customers of the Group offered the only possibility of a non-Group view. Most of the interviews were in English, and thus with relatively well-educated and privileged Mexicans. One suspects that a rather different story might have been told by government officials, union representatives and competitors, particularly if the interviews had been conducted in Spanish with no tape-recording, when interviewees would have been more likely to express controversial views. Lower-level employees of the Group themselves might also have had more critical things to say if no translator had been present. This limitation of the study should not be taken as totally invalidating its analysis or conclusions, but as a word of caution in interpreting the heroic tale of Alejandro Junco and his Group.

A second limitation of the study is referred to directly by the authors themselves: '... another limitation of the study is that we analysed the case data via a theoretical lens developed in the United States. The emphasis was not on understanding the events using Mexicans' own management thinking, terms and constructs' (p. 358). This approach is understandable in terms of the ready availability of theoretical schema from the United States, and indeed justifiable as a way of testing those ways of looking at the world in different national contexts. The problem, as alluded to by the authors, is that the study has a 'distanced' feel about it in some ways, since the richness of any culture, including that of Mexico, can only be properly appreciated using its own terms, constructs and language.

Despite these limitations, the researchers tried hard to blend Mexican and non-Mexican elements, with some substantive discussion of the latter, despite the US emphasis of much of the theory and methodology of the study. One further implication from the study, of more general relevance than solely to Mexico, is that the indigenous information group was able to use its local knowledge, access and alliances to compete successfully with the powerful US-based multinationals centred north of their border. The InfoSel marketing manager described the basis for this as follows:

> Compared with Reuters, we have a little bit of an advantage because no one has more accurate information than the people who live and breathe it. We have some ventures with official government entities that put us up ahead of the game. Our reporters have close communication ties with government and bank officers who are typically the first to be aware of important news in the financial sector and this network has given InfoSel an advantage over Reuters and the other US-based firms trying to tap the Mexican market.

There are some signs of encouragement here for the development of competitive IT-based industries outside the rich Western countries.

DISTRICT HEALTH INFORMATION SYSTEMS IN SOUTH AFRICA

The third case study in this chapter is drawn from Africa, and this section is based on work on district health information systems in the Republic of South Africa reported on in Braa (1997), Braa, Heywood and Shun-King (1997), and Braa and Hedberg (2000). The focus here will be mainly on the period 1994–97, but a brief update to the year 2000 will be given later in the section. Jørn Braa is a Norwegian researcher who spent a total of about two years in South Africa during the period 1994–97, collaborating in action research projects with others from both Norway and South Africa. By 1997 the work had been formalized into the Health Information Systems Pilot Project (HISPP), as part of an initiative by the South African Ministry of Health to develop guidelines for district health and management information systems. The project was funded by the Norwegian government through the aid agency NORAD.

The work is interesting in a number of respects, not least that it reports on computer-based information systems in the African continent, an area of the world about which such published material is scarce. In addition, the publications discuss the attempt to apply Scandinavian-type participative design approaches to systems development in the very different cultural context of an African country, and with a focus on the vitally important health sector. Finally, South Africa is a complex country with a difficult history and an uncertain future, but it is regarded by many as of great importance to the development of the African continent as a whole. Compared with the rest of sub-Saharan Africa, South Africa has a relatively well-developed infrastructure and economic base, and a successful South Africa could be one of the engines of growth for the whole continent.

Following an armed struggle and international pressure, the notorious apartheid system was ended in South Africa in the early 1990s. A democratically-elected government of national unity was formed in 1994 under the leadership of Nelson Mandela. The government brought with it a new policy agenda, and health was regarded as an important sector. Government health policy stated that the health system would focus on districts, sub-divisions of the country containing between 50 000 and 500 000 people. Within the districts, the primary health care approach was to be adopted. The precise meaning of this term is unclear, since it can be taken to imply something very comprehensive, or more limited in its focus. Braa (1997) described it as: 'Essential health care should be made accessible to individuals, families and communities by means acceptable to them, with their full participation, and at a cost that they and their country could afford' (p. 23). More limited definitions of primary health care focus on selective approaches and specific programmes such as oral rehydration, breast-feeding and immunization.

Regardless of the precise definition, a key goal of primary health care programmes is local empowerment. In terms of information and related computer-based information systems, this translates into the need to create, analyse and use data at the same level at which it is collected. The concept is local information for local action, rather than data being seen as going up the hierarchy to higher-level decision-makers. Braa and his co-workers tried to implement this type of approach in a variety of locations and types of area within South Africa. In view of space constraints, only one detailed example will be provided here.

Mitchell's Plain

Braa, Heywood and Shun-King (1997) described Mitchell's Plain as a commuter town on the outskirts of the major city of Cape Town. It was created in the 1970s for 'coloured' people, this being a label for people of mixed race, a significant group in the Cape Town and Western Cape Province areas. The population of Mitchell's Plain was estimated as between 300 000 and 400 000 people at the time of the research. The incidence of tuberculosis was possibly the highest in the world, and unemployment, gangsterism and violence were rampant. Health services were run on fragmented lines with four major authorities running the various services.

After the election in 1994, representatives from the different service providers came together to try to build a unified management structure for health provision at the district level. The Mitchell's Plain Primary Health Care Forum was an umbrella organization with representatives from grass-roots and community-based organizations in addition to the service providers. One of the first priorities identified by the embryonic district health-management team was the need for adequate information. They requested help on this from a local university, and Braa and his co-workers described the results of a survey that was carried out in response to this request. A questionnaire was handed out to all health services in Mitchell's Plain to identify staff attitudes to collecting and using data. Responses were analysed and results were presented to staff in meetings at health clinics and the day hospital. Focus group discussions were held to get direct input from staff, and to promote discussion, with the aim of 'empowering staff to use information'.

The results on the existing use of data were almost wholly negative according to the researchers. For example, data were kept on most activities ranging from in-patients, antenatal care and immunization, home visits and community health activities. The researchers reported that nobody found the statistics useful in their daily work, with the opposite being more usual: 'Keeping stats is a waste of good time.' Despite this perception, large amounts of data were collected, with an estimated 20% of staff time being spent on this process.

Other findings were that data were sent upwards to different head offices, but nowhere in the district were they coordinated in one central location. There was a 'general sense of helplessness amongst staff about information collected'. No goals or targets were related to the statistics, and staff never saw any results from their hard statistical work. Feedback was minimal from higher officials, and usually only negative. No staff had any training in data collection, analysis or use. The researchers noted that the survey results 'painted a grim picture' of the information systems at that time. They argued that the information systems were developed to support the centralized and vertically organized health service of South Africa's past, which was close to the antithesis of a district-oriented approach.

Following the survey and the subsequent discussion, a new step-by-step process to the creation and use of information systems was initiated. This was described as follows:

A project has been set up to provide information support to district management by developing health and management information systems at both institutional and district level. A main focus is on developing an 'information culture', building capacity and empowering health workers and community. The project applies a participatory design approach using techniques such as prototypes, maps and wall charts.

All of this sounds worthwhile in principle, but it is not an easy task to implement these goals. For example, 'developing an information culture' implies a complete change in attitude and approach on the part of local health workers of all races in South Africa, who had traditionally operated under a centralized apartheid regime.

In a later practitioner-focused document, provided as an appendix in Braa (1997), the researchers discussed some of the problems in forming a team of committed local people. They listed three major problems that needed to be overcome. First, they noted that enthusiasm and participation had fluctuated on all their projects, including Mitchell's Plain, with people being active for a time but then not attending. A second problem had been inappropriate representatives from the health service providers, these often being the senior people from those organizations who had no time to actually work on the project. Finally, but not least in view of the community-oriented goals of primary health care programmes, community involvement had been problematic, with decreased levels of activity after the initial phase of the projects. The researchers gave reasons for this as including the differences in perceived goals and background between people from the community and the health service providers. Community representatives had felt 'sidelined', for example when technical medical or information systems language was used.

Despite such difficulties, the HISPP project went ahead in three districts, including Mitchell's Plain. The other two districts were a black shanty town with about 300 000 inhabitants, and a small industrial town with a population of around 70 000. Some progress had been achieved by 1997. New health forms had been designed in collaboration with those involved, and they had later been piloted, evaluated and changed. Databases had been designed, and training provided to local personnel in their development and use. A process of putting together annual reports for each of the districts had been initiated, and monthly reports were set as a new goal.

Braa and Hedberg (2000) provided an update to the process described above. Following the pilot study in the three districts, in early 1999 the South African Department of Health agreed to adopt the strategies, processes and software developed in the pilot districts. The project was re-named the Health Information System Programme (HISP), dropping the term 'pilot', and the programme was to be rolled out to all districts in the country in the period 1999–2001. In addition, similar initiatives had been started in Mozambique, and some other sub-Saharan African countries were investigating whether the approach could be adapted to their requirements.

Implications and Discussion

Braa (1997) discussed lessons that he felt he had learned from his years in South Africa, and related experiences with health information systems in Mongolia. Participative information systems design in Scandinavia has normally focused on people in a specific workplace location, and IT has often been seen as a potential threat to workers' jobs or job satisfaction if not integrated through participation. Braa argued that these experiences need significant adaptation for the different contexts of developing countries:

> There I have learned that the lessons from Scandinavia are indeed important, but they need to be adapted and *cultivated* in third world contexts. First of all, in the 'shanty huddles' of township South Africa, system development, *learning* and *empowerment* need to address the *community* rather than the workplace. Another important difference to the Scandinavian approach is that deprived communities are not threatened by technology, they are threatened by being ignored and sidelined by the technology (italics in the original) (p. 2).

The metaphor of 'cultivation' of information systems is an interesting one. The argument is that particular information systems may be planted in specific locations, so that the seeds are similar, but that local growing conditions are infinitely variable. Thus the developing plant needs to be tended and nurtured through people at the local level who have ownership and commitment towards it. Braa argued that a participatory design process is crucial in helping to create such ownership, and thus that a bottom-up approach to information systems development is essential. In the health arena, this is in line with the basic approach of primary health care.

There are over 150 districts in South Africa, and usually they are very different one from another. For example, the black shanty town referred to above as being one of the other locations worked on by the joint Norwegian/South African team, is called Khayelitsha. The population there is primarily from the Xhosa tribe, whereas Mitchell's Plain is inhabited by 'Cape coloureds'. The two groups are described by Braa as being 'as culturally different (from each other) as two groups may be'. This may be something of an exaggeration in global terms, but nevertheless makes the point that the implementation of appropriate health information systems in all South African districts will require different local adaptation in each of them. Braa argued that: '*Diffusion* is thus to spread *replicable processes* (the "similar") and to cultivate them in each district (the particular and "different")' (p. 13).

This approach ties in well with the cultural perspective that we have focused on in this chapter, although there is a relative absence of detail with respect to local cultural perceptions and issues in the work reported on by Braa and his colleagues. Although we are told details, such as that representatives tended to be too high level to be useful, or that interest declined after the initial enthusiasm in some cases, no explanation is given from the viewpoint of the people affected. The reader would have benefited from hearing more about what the local participants thought about the various projects, and the broader socio-political context in which they were situated.

It would be inappropriate to end this section with a criticism. The work in South Africa has had important ethical goals of improved health care in deprived areas of an African country, and has emphasized local involvement and empowerment. Some progress had clearly been achieved, and this should be welcomed. Computer-based information systems should not be seen as linked solely to economic returns, and restricted to the privileged parts of the world. The HISP project should be commended for its wider vision.

ANALYSIS AND CONCLUSIONS

This chapter is concerned with IT in non-Western cultures, and the case studies described above have all been from the so-called developing countries. This term embraces a large number of heterogeneous nations in Africa, Asia, the Americas and Australasia, with the ex-communist states of Eastern Europe being included in some cases. There is enormous variety in the social, political and economic contexts of these countries, as is evident from the three cases presented. There is a related large variability between non-Western countries in terms of their current status with respect to information and communication technologies, as reflected in such elements as technological infrastructure, the availability of trained personnel, and current levels of IT usage.

Table 8.1   *Culture and IT*

Need to gain understanding of cultural contexts in order to follow process of IT appropriation	• Case studies show importance of such cultural understanding • Countries often have major internal cultural variety • Applies to developing and developed country contexts
Cultural analysis needs to go beyond simple 'universal' approaches	• Hofstede-type variables may have sensitizing value • But inadequate to investigate IT adoption and use processes
Various ways to gain deeper cultural understanding	• Immersion valuable in principle • But only if accompanied by cultural respect and effort • Reading about culture of value to all, including indigenous people

Thus, in this chapter I have provided illustrative material on what is a highly complex subject. Indeed, due to biases towards rich Western countries, the published literature has largely ignored the subject until fairly recently. The guest editors of a special journal issue (Davison *et al.* 1999) on 'IT in developing countries' described this area as remaining 'something of a Cinderella pursuit'. There are some exceptions to Western-only publications, and readers interested in IT in the non-Western countries can find rather more published material in the 1990s than was available in the previous decade. For example, the International Federation of Information Processing has a working group devoted to the topic of IT in the developing countries, and published papers from their conferences cover a wide range of issues and contexts (Bhatnagar and Bjørn-Andersen 1990; Bhatnagar and Odedra 1992; Roche and Blaine 1996; Odedra-Straub 1996; Avgerou and Walsham 2000).

I return now to the questions asked at the beginning of this chapter on IT and culture in the developing countries. The remainder of the chapter provides some synthesized answers to these questions, using aspects of the case studies in the chapter for illustrative purposes. A summary of key points is given in Tables 8.1–8.3.

How Does Culture Relate to IT Use and How May Culture be Understood?

A key argument of this chapter is the need to gain understanding of cultural contexts in order to trace the introduction, development and use

of information and communication technologies in particular socie
Thai values derive from long-standing attitudes in Thailand that can
considered to form a social glue holding people and society together,
and the Quickfood case demonstrated the importance of these values in
MRP adoption and implementation. Mexican nationalism relates to a
subtle and shifting blend of Western and indigenous values, and these
were integral to the strategy and growth of the information-based company. South Africa has a unique history and the development of health
information systems required high sensitivity to this cultural context.
We saw in earlier chapters how attitudes to information, knowledge,
decision-making and spatial awareness are heavily influenced by cultural
values.

Two further comments can be made about culture as a key context for
IT adoption and use. First, countries often have major internal cultural
variety, and this also needs to be appreciated and taken into account.
The South African case study used the illustration of the 'Cape coloured'
Mitchell's Plain community as contrasting with the black shanty town of
Khayelitsha. Second, it is worth noting that an understanding of the
cultural context for IT introduction is not limited to the areas or countries
of the developing world, but applies equally to the so-called developed
countries. For example, health information systems in the United States
and the United Kingdom need to be designed to take account of the very
different histories and cultural attitudes within those two countries.

If culture is important, how can it be understood and analysed? I
argued in the discussion of the Thai case that Hofstede-type variables
may have limited value as sensitizing devices to cultural difference, for
example for expatriate managers. However, working with IT in a particular context requires a deeper local cultural understanding, and a process-oriented view as to how culture is implicated in IT adoption and use
processes. There are various ways in which cultural understanding can be
developed, not least by living in a particular country, and thus being
immersed in the culture. However, distance is not simply a matter of space,
but also reflects mental attitude. An expatriate manager of a multinational
company, staying in a five-star hotel, may be physically present in a particular country, but may have little access to or interest in local culture.
Understanding through immersion requires a starting point of respect for
local cultural values, and considerable effort to understand these.

Another way to develop cultural understanding is to read extensively
about a particular region or country: its history, geography, social and
religious beliefs. For example, if one is planning to work in an Islamic
country, it is highly desirable to know something about the religion of

Islam, the Koran, and practices such as frequent prayer derived from these beliefs. The benefits of reading and reflection on culture apply to the indigenous people of a country as well as to foreigners, since we can all deepen our understanding of our own country by reflexive reading.

How Should Appropriate IT Adoption in Different Cultural Contexts be Facilitated?

Some of the Western literature on IT in developing countries, whilst recognizing the importance of local cultural understanding, views culture as a barrier to IT adoption. This is an unfortunate assumption in my view. It tends to assign or imply a low worth to indigenous culture, and a correspondingly high worth to Western culture. There is a need for greater respect than this towards the culture of others. This does not imply a blind acceptance of other cultural values, since this type of naive acceptance can be dangerous in giving support to tyranny, for example. However, the foreigner in any country needs to be constantly vigilant when thinking that difference implies inferiority. The worst examples of such an attitude are often provided by people from Western countries

Table 8.2   *IT appropriation in different cultural contexts*

Culture should not be viewed as a 'barrier' to IT adoption	• Such a view often assigns a low value to indigenous culture • Vigilance is needed to avoid equating difference with inferiority
Need for local appropriation of IT	• No society can afford to ignore current technologies • Challenge is to use technology appropriately • Metaphor of cultivation suggests one way
But also need to shift attitudes over time	• Long-term commitment often required to achieve this • Tends to 'drift' over time in response to local improvisation and adaptation
Actor-network theory offers a theoretical basis	• Focuses on values implicit or inscribed in the technology • Also on processes of enrolment of actors through translation of interests

who mistakenly equate high economic living standards with high cultural and ethical standards. The business world often tends to reinforce such values, whereas cultural sensitivity implies the need to see economics as only one aspect of life.

We saw in the earlier chapters of the book, for example in the discussion of the GIS in India case in Chapter 4, that IT may be viewed as an 'actor' with embedded interests reflecting those of its Western-society origins. Does the cultural bias of IT/IS and related methodologies imply that these are inappropriate technologies for non-Western cultures? The answer to this is a resounding no in my view, since no society can afford to ignore these technologies at this time in history. The challenge for Western-origin IT in non-Western cultures is to find ways in which to appropriate and utilize the technologies in ways that are compatible with local approaches, or in some cases in ways that enable subtle changes in local culture over time.

The metaphor of cultivation at multiple decentralized levels, as illustrated in the South African case, suggests one way of approaching the issue of supporting local appropriation of processes and systems, being sensitive to local norms and values, but also trying to shift the 'information culture' over time. The Mexican information group case study also demonstrated aspects of fitting in with local culture in emphasizing respect for traditional Mexican values. However, the company was also active in trying to change attitudes to information in the Mexican media industry and the general public. The company took a long-term approach to this, since deep-seated cultural attitudes are not easily changed, but require sustained and committed effort over considerable periods of time. The efforts of the South African team also demonstrated this long-term commitment.

The work of Madon (1992, 1993) provides further support for the idea that significant change can be achieved over a long period of time, often not as originally planned. Madon spent eight years studying the introduction and use of computer-based information systems to support district-level administration in India, with frequent and prolonged visits to that country. She is a British national, of Indian origin, who speaks Gujarati, the language of the state of Gujarat in western India. Her language capabilities and cultural background enabled her to interact with people at all levels in Indian society, particularly in Gujarat.

Madon and Walsham (1995) summarized some of the concrete results from this work. Very briefly, computers were introduced as a top-down initiative related to a particular system called CRISP, designed to support rural development, but with data sets and reporting procedures set by

central government in New Delhi. The system did not, however,
)ort the work of local agencies in Gujarat, and was seen by local
administrators as a significant burden. Following a change in central
government in 1991, more emphasis was placed on decentralized activities at the state and district levels, districts in India being sub-divisions
of larger states. The State Government of Gujarat, having seen computers arrive through the CRISP initiative, started to encourage their use
for other purposes, through training programmes on the use of packages
such as word processors, spreadsheets and databases. This led in later
years to some simple but valuable computer applications related to local
needs. We see here a gradual evolution of attitudes to the use of computers over time, which a 'snapshot' picture taken at a specific point
would have missed completely. Madon's work provides support for the
view of Ciborra *et al.* (2000) that IT infrastructures tend to 'drift' over
time, deviating from their original planned purpose in response to processes of local improvisation and adaptation.

The ideas of actor-network theory, introduced in Chapter 3, suggest a
theoretical basis for these processes of local adoption and adaptation of
IT. The use of this theory focuses both on the values implicit or inscribed
in the technology and systems, and on processes of enrolment of human
actors over time, through the translation of their interests, into a relatively stable network of aligned interests. For example, Braa and
Hedberg (2000) utilized the theory to argue that the large-scale diffusion
of the HISP approach to all district-level health information systems in
South Africa needed to be carried out through the creation of 'smaller'
actor-networks in each district and province, linked together in the
'larger' actor-network of the whole programme.

Can the Excluded of the Third World be Brought Into the Global Network Society?

The South African case provides an example of an intervention in the
health sector of a Third World country, mostly directed at the poor of
that country. This can be justified on ethical grounds, but also on the
grounds of the need for long-term stability. South Africa provides a
particularly good example of this, with large gaps between the rich
and poor of the country needing to be closed to try to avoid creating
a socio-political environment within which crime, domestic unrest and
political instability flourish.

More broadly, the exclusion of the Fourth World, in Castells' terms,
can be thought of as the contemporary version of neo-colonialism,

Table 8.3 *Including the excluded in the global network*

The exclusion of the Fourth World should be of concern to us all	• On ethical grounds • But also on grounds of long-term societal and world stability • Current form of neo-colonialism is exclusion rather than invasion • Need to use IT to help the disadvantaged and give access to opportunities
Local IT initiatives are possible and desirable	• In public sectors such as health, and in the private sector • May sometimes be small in scope, but there is no viable alternative to starting such initiatives now
Key role for government and inter-governmental agencies	• IT policies on tariffs, infrastructure etc. • IT education and training

whereas the older colonialism achieved its power through the invasion and control of territory. It is imperative on ethical and expediency grounds that we try to include the excluded in the global network society. From the perspective of this book, although the issue is rather broader, inclusion involves using IT effectively to help the disadvantaged, and trying to give them access to the opportunities offered by such technologies.

As we have seen from the case studies in this chapter, local initiatives are possible and desirable, both in public sectors such as health, and in the private sector. It could be argued that the Mexican and Thai cases provide examples, more or less successful, of IT-based applications in the private sector that do not touch the lives of the poor in those countries directly. This is a reasonable point, but effective and efficient manufacturing and information sectors are surely desirable to provide economic growth, job opportunities, and the national financial capability for programmes aimed at the poor.

Just before the completion of this book, I visited a community project in a rural area of South Africa, around the town of Siyabuswa. This project aims to provide additional education to school children and adults, and includes a computer literacy programme (Scheepers and de Villiers 1999). The latter involves basic computer skills and the use of simple word processing, spreadsheet and database packages. There is as yet no Internet connection, but there are plans to obtain one. This initiative is relatively small in scope, and at one level could be considered as offering little hope of closing the privilege gap that exists between these school children and adults, and their counterparts in my home town of Cambridge in the United Kingdom. I do not, however, take such a defeatist view. There is no viable alternative but to start initiatives such as the Siyabuswa project, with the hope that they will lead to bigger projects with a wider scope in the future. The people of the Siyabuswa region, attending the programme in large numbers, clearly supported this view.

Local initiatives such as the Siyabuswa project often receive government support, which raises the broader issue of the appropriate role of government and inter-governmental agencies in facilitating change in national contexts with respect to the introduction and use of information and communication technologies. Specific IT policies that need addressing in all countries include trade issues such as tariff policy, infrastructural needs such as telecommunications systems, and the stimulus of local productive capacity. Perhaps the most important area of all for government policy with respect to IT is education and training. The development of local people's skills and knowledge of IT, including those of the disadvantaged in society, is the only long-term sustainable way to ensure the inclusion of the excluded. This does, however, require a desire on the part of the people of the world, particularly the rich and powerful, to see this happen.

9
Working Across Cultures

This chapter continues the focus of Chapter 8 on IT in non-Western cultures, but with a specific emphasis on cross-cultural working. As discussed earlier in Chapter 2, global interconnection and mobility is increasing, together with the widespread application of common information and communication technologies across the world. This has led to an increase in cross-cultural working, with IT often used to facilitate interaction, or sometimes being the central focus of the work being carried out, such as in the area of cross-border software outsourcing. Cross-cultural working can take a number of forms, such as short visits by foreign teams to particular local contexts for 'technology transfer' projects, or more in-depth collaboration over an extended period of time.

Earlier material in the book, and in particular the previous chapter, has illustrated both the diversity of culture, and the importance of understanding culture in designing and using information and communication technologies. It follows from this that cross-cultural working may be problematic, with different norms and values leading to the possibility of disagreement and conflict. Approaches based on IS and methodologies from the Western countries may be perceived as inappropriate in radically different cultural contexts. Thus, in this chapter, I will address the following key questions:

- What problems exist in knowledge-sharing across cultures?
- Do Western-origin IS and methodologies embed features that inhibit cross-cultural working?
- How can effective co-working with IT in cross-cultural contexts be facilitated?

Three case studies will be examined in detail. The first case concerns Indian expatriates working in Jamaica on a joint software development project in the insurance industry. Secondly, I will describe and analyse a long-term collaborative project on health information systems between staff from Finland and Yorubaland in south-western Nigeria. The third case deals with technology transfer of a management information system (MIS) to China. The final section of the chapter will provide a synthesized response to the key questions listed above.

INDIAN SOFTWARE DEVELOPERS IN JAMAICA

This case study describes a software development project in a Jamaican insurance company, with the cross-cultural element being the local involvement of a team of Indian software developers. The description of the case study is based on papers by Barrett and Walsham (1995) and Barrett, Drummond and Sahay (1996). Barrett, a Jamaican national, carried out the field studies, consisting of 54 semi-structured interviews undertaken in three field visits in the period 1993–95. I was involved in the last of the three field visits to Jamaica in 1995, and carried out seven of the interviews with Barrett, some of the field notes from which are drawn on directly in the description below. In terms of the Indian dimension of the study, I had worked extensively in India, and Sahay is an Indian national. Field interviews were supplemented by data from other primary sources, including internal design documents and strategy plans, and secondary sources such as sectoral studies, trade journals and local newspapers.

Jamaica is located in the high risk catastrophe region of the Caribbean, but the capital base of general insurers in Jamaica is insufficient for high risk insurance cover, such as that caused by earthquake and hurricane. Jamaican general insurance companies thus rely on worldwide reinsurers, who underwrite some of these high risks. From the 1960s to the mid 1980s, the general insurance industry in Jamaica, and to a great extent worldwide, was lulled into a false sense of security. A relatively 'catastrophe-free' period led to overcapacity on the supply side, resulting in fierce competition and low premiums. The stage was set for the reinsurance crisis of the late 1980s and early 1990s, the effects of which on the London Insurance Market have been discussed earlier in Chapter 7. The intensity and frequency of catastrophes during that period multiplied, and major international reinsurers had to pay out large claims, resulting in bankruptcy in some cases. This led to undercapitalization of the market, and created acute problems for local insurance companies to secure adequate coverage for high risk insurance.

In this section I will look at some of the effects of such conditions on a particular Jamaican general insurance company, called Abco, that formed part of a broader Jamaican financial conglomerate, called the Jagis Group. In 1987, the Group Chairman, Jones, had publicly cautioned the general insurance industry of the impending reinsurance crisis. In 1988, his worst fears were realized. Hurricane Gilbert swept through Jamaica, paralysing business activities on the island for a couple of months. At Abco, computer records were lost, and claims were made on policies that did not exist on the batch system. After the hurricane and other world catastrophes, reinsurance not only became a problem to obtain, but reinsurers started to demand better quality information from companies such as Abco on risks and levels of exposure.

In late 1988, Jones led an investigation as to how IT could be used to provide superior quality service to clients through improved claims handling, as well as providing reinsurers with the more detailed risk and exposure information that they required. The decision was made to develop a new general insurance information system, called Goras. A leading management consultancy was commissioned to conduct the requirements study and a group software development company, Gtec, was set up within Abco in order to strengthen existing IT skills. In March 1990 an Indian software expert, Raj, and other experienced Indian software developers were recruited from software houses in India to form the top management group of Gtec. The Jagis Group Financial Controller, who was a Jamaican of Indian origin, argued that the management consultancy company was similarly recruiting expatriates in this way, and then charging very high rates:

> I realized that what they [the management consultancy] were doing was to employ a consultant, mark his wage rate up three times and then charge the client … So, I had the idea to bring skilled people in as they did and replicate it [the management consultancy] in an IT division for the Group. India was an appropriate market with a large volume of IT professionals with experience.

Project History

I turn now to the history of the implementation of the Goras project. Gtec, with its Indian management led by Raj, was selected to carry out the project. However, in the initial stages of development it became clear that additional expertise in insurance systems was needed, and a selected team of Jamaicans from the Jagis Group was seconded to the project as insurance consultants, including the MIS manager of Jagis, Roberts. A member of Roberts' team highlighted an initial team briefing by Jagis Group senior management on their expected role and involvement in the project, and the results of failure to work successfully with the Indian team: 'They were quite direct in their approach ... They explained that [a well-known local company] also used Indians as subcontractors as they had international development experience ... We would either sink or swim with them [the Indians].'

The initial stages of the project were marked by some enthusiasm, at least by team members at the programmer level. Indian developers provided guidance to the Jamaican members on software development issues drawing from their experience on past development projects. There were weekly awards for the 'most helpful member' and 'project champion', and cash incentives for meeting deadlines. A key developer at Gtec reflected later:

Looking back at it now, it was well organized. Every Monday, a memo came out specifying the deliverables and bonus structure for the week. There was a bonus on top of your salary if you met deadlines ... but it was so hard to make your deadlines ... Though teams were compliant, deadlines were rather stringent, if not unreasonable.

As time went by, conflict started to develop between the Indians and the Jamaicans, particularly at senior and team leader level. Raj was viewed by the Jamaicans as having an autocratic approach as he would 'lay down the law which was not to be questioned'. In contrast, the senior Jamaican on the project team, Roberts, viewed an appropriate management style with Jamaicans as being more consensual: 'If there is a problem to be solved, we would sit down and solve it ... It was not a sort of hierarchy ... It was a team effort, meet and discuss each project.'

Resentment by the Jamaican software developers at all levels had deeper roots than specific conflicts on management style, since some of the locals believed that Indians were not needed in the first place. A key Gtec developer expressed this sentiment as follows:

The Abco MIS staff felt the whole project had been taken away from them ... They were the natural group to be utilized to develop a new general insurance system for Abco. Instead [the management consultancy] who were a bag of Indians again were asked to do the functional requirements and the initial design. Later on, Gtec was formed, staffed by Indians in all the senior posts, and responsible for the Goras project ... The Indians had been given power over the Jamaicans.

There are, of course, two sides to these cross-cultural issues. Raj, for example, was critical of the Jamaicans' more laid-back attitude to deadlines, regarding their formal working hours as being all they were prepared to offer to the project:

With the Indians, there is no discussion once the deadline is agreed, they will work until 9 p.m. every night, weekends if necessary to have it on my desk at the stipulated time. However, with the Jamaicans, this is not the case. If the worker recognizes that they cannot meet the deadline, they will call me up and give some excuse as to why they need more time ... they expect me to understand and accommodate.

Raj also felt that there were significant cultural differences in the way that project activities were coordinated. In India, that task was handled by the project manager whose job was 'walking around and seeing how people are progressing, coordinating and administering activities', while in Jamaica project coordination was seen by him to be inherently problematic. Raj attributed this to the Jamaicans' inability to 'link hands and do parallel work'. To illustrate this point, he offered an analogy of Jamaica's performance at international athletics events: 'They are fantastic runners ... they only miss out on medals at international relay races because at the interchange of the baton, it is dropped or it is passed too late outside the permitted exchange ... there is no training to coordinate and keep things moving.'

In contrast, a Jamaican member of the software team viewed the Indian approach to coordination as representing an adult–child mentality, related also in his mind to the Indian caste structure:

The strict deadlines seemed impossible, and I was not used to the interpersonal relations of the closely knit teams ... I was reluctant to fully integrate myself into the environment which was different to what we [Jagis MIS staff] were used to ... It was a school room attitude, with someone senior to me telling me to do as he says ... It was hard to relate to their caste system where hierarchy and status were so important.

These comments relate to differences in deep-seated cultural attitudes to hierarchy and authority that were recognized on the Indian side also, but of course with a different emphasis on their merits and demerits. Raj gave his view of Jamaicans' attitudes in these areas as follows:

Everybody treats everybody as equal. The boss is viewed as a supervisor but at the same time they expect to be treated as equal. If something is due at the end of the month, don't intervene [as the boss] ... The attitude is 'I will tell you if the job is done or not, then we reset the date and keep going ... If you feel performance is bad, then fire me with redundancy pay' ... They don't want a monitoring system ... It is demeaning to them if the boss asks about progress of activities in between tasks.

So, how successful was the project itself in this cross-cultural environment? The development of Goras started in 1990. The original plan envisaged a year for completion, but there were significant delays and major project cost overruns. The acceptance testing done by end users showed substantial inadequacies in the design, but the system was finally 'delivered' by Gtec to Abco in August 1992. After further quality assurance, user testing and system modification, a first attempt at implementation was made in December 1992. The implementation was not a success. System performance was poor in terms of time taken to carry out tasks, and users were critical of the restricted functionality of the new system, partly due to incomplete data conversion from the old system.

In January 1993 a new CEO of Gtec was appointed, also an Indian expatriate. Raj stayed on as technical director of Gtec, 'preferring to work on technical issues rather than organizational ones'. The responsibility for further development of the Goras system and user acceptance testing and training was switched to the Jagis group, although Gtec continued to make a technical input. By 1995, at the end of the research period, the Goras system had still not been implemented, but new deadlines were in place for implementation later in that year. An increased emphasis had been placed on user involvement. One of the Jagis IS staff described this as follows: 'Testing started in July [1994] with live data from users. Each module is being tested module-by-module and then issue forms are created which then involve a lot of work on the part of MIS [staff] to implement the required changes.'

Five years after project inception, there was general optimism about successful project implementation within a reasonable time frame of a few months, but it still remained a promise rather than a reality.

Problems and Issues

In trying to assign reasons for the relatively unsuccessful history of the Goras project, at least for its first five years, it is difficult to separate out individual causes from the mesh of interconnecting issues. In talking to a range of participants in 1995, by which time the unsuccessful history was a reality for everyone, various problems were raised that have not already been mentioned above. For example, some participants felt that Gtec 'undersold to get the job' in the first place. In other words, that the original implementation time frame of one year was known to be insufficient by Gtec management, but that they decided to present it in this way to obtain the business. There was also a recurrent theme as to whether project expertise in a technical sense was sufficient throughout the project, and indeed a US consultant was used at a later stage in 1994 to help sort out difficult technical problems.

Issues such as underselling and limited technical expertise occur in a wide variety of contexts of new IS development, and implementation of any IS project would clearly suffer if these were present. Nevertheless, as described in the previous sub-section, there were also major problems for the Goras project related to cross-cultural issues. These can be summarized as a chronic distrust, rivalry and difference in style between the Indian software developers in Gtec and local Jamaican IS personnel. Barrett and Walsham (1995) highlighted how the different cultural backgrounds of the system developers affected approaches to IS development on the Goras project as follows:

> While occupational cultures for Indians and Jamaicans alike originated from software development, the impact of the local work culture at Indian software houses and the insurance company respectively were significantly different. The norms of an Indian software house include high productivity and profitability, the software development being driven from a specification under strict project deadlines. The norms of an insurer's MIS department in Jamaica involve application development by MIS personnel working closely with end users with a backlog of applications being quite acceptable (p. 30).

The new CEO of Gtec appointed in 1993 expressed this clash of cultures in a rather more graphic way when reflecting on the history of the project in 1995: 'When Jagis took over the initiative for implementation of Goras [in 1993], some Jamaican staff saw it as the end of two years of servitude.'

What could have been done to facilitate a better cross-cultural context for the Goras project? There are no 'silver bullets' of course, since difficulties in cross-cultural teams stem from differences in deeply held norms and values that may generate conflict when the members must work together for a common purpose. Nevertheless, on the Goras project no effort at all seems to have been made in the first instance to try to reconcile the difference in approach, or at least to forge some compromise. Telling the Jamaicans that they must 'sink or swim' with the Indians is unlikely to be successful in keeping the whole party afloat. A serious effort to discuss issues of style and approach by the different nationalities may have been helpful, and senior management of the Goras Group could have provided some leadership for this to take place. By the end of the research period some uneasy cross-cultural compromise had been reached, largely through changes of personnel at the top of Gtec, and a reduction of the role of the expatriate Indians.

COLLABORATION BETWEEN FINLAND AND YORUBALAND

The second case study on cross-cultural working involves a Finnish–Nigerian collaborative project on the development and use of computer-based information systems in Nigeria, with a particular emphasis in this section on health information systems. The material here is based on the work of Korpela (1996). Korpela is a Finn who spent 10 months in south-western Nigeria in 1989, participating in the development of a very basic, relatively low-cost patient information system for the teaching hospital of the Obafemi Awolowo University (OAU) in Ile-Ife. Close collaboration between Korpela and other Finns, and Nigerian colleagues in the hospital and the OAU computer science department, continued throughout the 1990s in the form of a joint IS project. The clinical benefit achieved was 'not as much as was planned and aspired for', but Korpela (1996) drew on the long-term project to develop some interesting analyses and conclusions for the development and use of Western-origin information technologies in developing country contexts, with a primary focus on black Africa. He also derived some lessons for cross-cultural collaboration in such contexts.

Korpela challenged what he saw as the predominant view that organizational obstacles to IT in developing countries are related to local cultural values. In particular, he cited literature that summarizes such cultures as being authoritarian, top-down and non-democratic. He argued that, if this is the case, three possible conclusions can be reached: IT should be introduced in traditional societies by authoritarian, non-participative means; or Africans who appreciate their traditional culture should abandon IT; or that in order to benefit from IT, Africans should abandon their culture.

In contrast to the above, Korpela argued that the traditional culture of the Yoruba people in south-western Nigeria could not be simply classified as anti-democratic, top-down and authoritarian. However, elements of such an approach were introduced into Nigeria in pre-colonial times, particularly through the slave trade, continued during the British colonial period, and were maintained by 20 years of post-colonial government based on the 'barracks model of administration'. Korpela concluded that what is needed to use IT effectively in Yorubaland is to reject this 'dependency' culture, and to return in some senses to the older traditional roots of Yoruba culture: 'Both IT development and traditional cultures suffer from dependency, and the core remedy for both is popular participation and democracy' (p. 37).

I will now investigate in more detail how Korpela derived his arguments and arrived at this conclusion.

Yorubaland and the Yoruba

Korpela cited Hofstede (1991), whose work I critiqued in the previous chapter, as taking West Africa, an area equal in size to Europe, as one 'culture' characterized by Hofstede's usual aggregate variables such as low individualism and a high acceptance of an unequal distribution of power. However, Korpela pointed out that the country of Nigeria, for example, is a colonial creation and contains many different groups with 'sharp cultural discontinuities'. One such group is the Yoruba people, numbering some 20 million in the 1990s. Although there are of course differences within this large group, Korpela drew on the extensive literature on the Yoruba to highlight five aspects of the Yoruba cultural heritage that are distinctive, and should be considered in his view when discussing the social context in IS development in Yorubaland.

First, the Yoruba are distinctive among all the forest peoples of Africa in their ancient urban way of life. In the period of the ninth to the eleventh centuries, a great number of towns and cities were established that functioned as independent but interacting political units. Agriculture has remained the primary occupation, even up to the present day, but people have always preferred to live close to each other in the town, and to go to their farms only for as long as work is required.

The gender division of labour is a second aspect that has differentiated the Yoruba from many other African peoples. Most Yoruba wives did not work on the farm, except during harvest time. Instead, Yoruba women have traditionally engaged in crafts and trade, both local and long-distance. This gave them a fairly independent financial position, which was reflected in their legal and professional status as well. In many 'modern' occupations, Korpela noted that women were still striving after their traditional autonomy, but that aspects of contemporary society have created 'severe obstacles' in some cases. For example, about one in four computer science students is female, but they are confronted by unequal opportunities and contradictions between their familial and professional roles.

Yoruba arts and crafts include world-famous brass and terracotta sculptures, and a wide range of other activities such as ironwork, beadwork, carpentry, weaving and dyeing. Craftsmen and women were organized in guilds. There was no restrictions on the entry into a trade, but a three to seven year apprenticeship with a master was required. Korpela noted that the tradition of guilds or professional associations is very much alive today. Not only do the traditional professions of market women, dyers or carpenters have their organizations, but so also do some of the new professions, such as motor mechanics. The apprenticeship mode of training is still commonplace.

In terms of the political system, the Yoruba developed a kingship model more than a thousand years ago. There was a hierarchical structure of authority from the head of the smallest settlement through lesser kings up to the overall king, *oba*, who had an important religious role. His position was not hereditary, but he was elected from a royal lineage by a council of high chiefs. Elsewhere in Yorubaland the political system was characterized by a hierarchy, a set of checks and balances among the rulers, and a mixture of hereditary and elective elements. The models were never stagnant, with new forms evolving over time. Today, traditional rulers have no official power, but have considerable informal authority.

Finally, in Korpela's five cultural characteristics of the Yoruba, comes religion. Yoruba traditional religion comprised a large pantheon of named gods, and a distinctive cosmology. The latter divides the universe into two related realms: the visible world of the living, and the invisible world of ancestors, gods and spirits. The world is regarded as a journey/market-place that we visit during our lives, whereas the other world is home. Nowadays, nearly all Yoruba are Christians or Moslems, but Korpela argued that the traditional philosophical world view, derived from the ancient religion, remains influential.

This very brief summary of Korpela's synopsis of cultural character-istics obviously does an injustice to the complexity and subtlety of Yoruba culture. However, it is hoped that it succeeds in demolishing naive concepts that attempt to describe culture through simplistic aggre-gate variables. For example, Korpela discussed the concept of 'hierarchy or otherwise' based on his cultural characteristics. He argued that Yoruba cosmology pays attention to a multivocal setting in which the units of the whole are discrete and share equal value with other units. The *oba* is supreme and distant, but everyday life is governed by a balanced set of holders of chieftancy titles. There is a trait of hierarchy, but simultaneously a counterbalancing trait of consensuality. Korpela continued:

The latter aspect [consensuality] should not be misinterpreted as homogeneity and harmony. Rather it is a recognition of the exis-tence of independent, different and often conflicting actors. Several studies appear to suggest that the colonial and post-colonial era has consistently strengthened the individualist, hierarchical aspect, but the consensual aspect continues to survive in forms like professional associations and a remarkable tolerance of religious differences (p. 35).

In contrast to the complex counterbalancing of hierarchy and commu-nity values in traditional society, Korpela argued that the legacy of colonialism and neo-colonialism is an individualist and often violent influence. Thus the effect of the slave trade was indirect and struc-tural—the external exploitation relation created an internal structure of a middleman economy that reproduced, amplified and perpetuated a process of gradual underdevelopment. This was continued under colonial rule where politics was a power struggle unmediated by consensual norms, and administration was effected through an unresponsive central bureaucracy. This approach has been continued by the post-colonial African rulers. Korpela argued that:

In this view, the administrative culture of bureaucracy, 'lack of aware-ness' and 'politics' is a dependent form of a 'modern' society, not something created by the various traditional value systems of the indigenous peoples. Correspondingly, 'participation' and 'democ-racy' are not seen as alien European values, but a *sine qua non* for a return towards genuine development (p. 37).

Problems With IT Development

Returning now to the specific focus on IT, Korpela and his colleagues identified five complexes of problems that have hindered the effective use of computers in Yorubaland, and Nigeria more generally. Korpela related these problems to the earlier cultural analysis to ask whether, and to what extent, IT problems could be ascribed to traditional Yoruba cultural values, or to other aspects of Nigerian life, including the legacy of colonialism, and its predecessors and followers of the slave trade and military rule.

The first set of problems was environmental, such as those caused by the hot and humid climate in this part of the world, resulting in technical problems with computers and related technologies. Although Korpela says that these cannot be ascribed to social conditions, it could be argued that the poor performance of computers in such contexts relates to Western-oriented technologies that were not built to perform in typical African conditions.

Problems with infrastructure such as electricity supply, telecommunications availability and quality, and transportation routes were the second set. The third set were problems of finance. Korpela considered that neither of these sets could be ascribed to traditional Yoruba cultural values. Instead, he saw them as related to inefficient and corrupt practices in aspects of industry and government in Nigeria. He argued that such practices derived from the dependency culture of neo-colonialism, resulting in some greedy people maximizing their personal economic advantage at the expense of the development of the country:

> ... it is reasonable to assume that corruption and greed are attributable to the introduction of monetary relations in an 'underdeveloped' middleman economy where hard work does not pay. The problems of infrastructure and supporting activities are also a logical expression of an economy which is geared towards 'modern slave trade' instead of production for domestic needs (p. 37).

Korpela made a related point when addressing the fourth set of problems that hinder IT development, namely bureaucracy, 'politics', and 'lack of awareness'. In the hospital information systems project, as in other such projects in Nigeria, the administrative culture is highly hierarchical, which poses major problems. People shy away from making decisions, decision-making is delegated upwards, and horizontal cooperation across sectoral boundaries is discouraged. However, Korpela argued that this derives from the dependent form of a 'modern' society, not something created by the various traditional value systems of the indigenous peoples. For example, he noted with respect to bureaucracy:

Seniority in traditional Yorubaland was not a mechanical function of age and birth, but partly achieved by one's personal performance. In the 'informal sector' today, seniority is observed, and there can be inefficiency in management, but hierarchical bureaucracy is not an issue. The bureaucratic ills are present in the 'modern' organizations shaped according to foreign models (p. 36).

The final set of contextual problems for IT development was a tendency for hardware and software vendors to have a 'sell and run' strategy, based on aggressive selling without significant after-sales support. Again, Korpela considered that this could not be laid at the door of 'traditional' Yoruba culture. Whilst this has emphasized the 'good life', such a life is seen as one in which materialistic possessions are to be achieved and enjoyed in harmony with the community. Korpela argued that this traditional attitude is in conflict with greedy materialism.

Implications

Korpela concluded from his analysis that what was needed for the development and use of IT in Yorubaland was a 'return' to traditional values rather than their rejection, the rejection of IT itself, or the imposition of IT in a top-down manner. The hospital information systems project has continued and, more generally, Korpela and colleagues (Korpela *et al.* 2000, Soriyan *et al.* 2000) are trying to develop 'made-in-Nigeria' systems development methodologies that are appropriate for the severely constrained conditions in most of black Africa, and in tune with local cultural characteristics. With respect to the specific work in Yorubaland, Korpela (1996) summarized this objective as follows:

... if and to the extent that IT activities in Nigeria can be liberated from the shackles of dependency, a genuine 'Yoruba brand of systems development' could emerge, a brand which would purposefully exploit the conducive aspects of traditional culture. The same is true for all traditional cultures in Nigeria (p. 38).

Korpela also drew some interesting conclusions on the need for sensitivity towards 'culture' in systems development work, or more generally IT introduction. He argued that cultural learning is an inevitable part of all systems development work, since the developer needs to 'learn' about the culture in which he or she is trying to work, even if it is within their own national context. He explained this as follows:

> An *oyibo*, whiteman, from Finland will inevitably make 'cross-cultural mistakes' and face 'cross-cultural obstacles to understanding' when conducting systems development in Nigeria, and the same would apply to a Nigerian systems developer in Finland. A Yoruba systems developer in Hausaland (another part of Nigeria) will also need to engage in some cultural learning, even more so if female. However, the same is true when a male, technically educated, upper middle-class systems developer of any ethnicity enters a hospital in order to interact with mostly female, humanistically educated, lower white-collar nurses of *the same ethnic culture* (p. 38).

This argument has some validity, but the degree of learning necessary when dealing with cross-cultural collaboration between Finland and Nigeria is not likely to be of a similar magnitude to that of an intra-Finland project.

It is possible to criticize elements of Korpela's analysis. He could be considered too idealistic in that he tends to emphasize only the positive aspects of Yoruba culture in his written work, whereas there are doubt-less aspects of traditional values of less merit. In addition, the separation of Yoruba traditional values from those deriving from the legacy of colonial dependency is somewhat artificial in practice, since individuals, groups and communities in Yorubaland will have been influenced by both sets of values. Present-day Yoruba culture will be a hybrid, making a 'return' to traditional values infeasible even if desirable. However, despite these comments, Korpela's work reflects a refreshing approach to cross-cultural collaboration, displaying a deep level of cultural aware-ness and sensitivity. In addition, his work and that of his colleagues provides a counter to the argument that Africans should adopt Western approaches and culture since they are 'better' than their own, or should reject IT altogether, or should impose IT top-down to match local cultural characteristics. Korpela drew a final 'simplified proposition' regarding the practice of IT introduction in developing countries:

> If one is going to practise systems development in a given cultural setting, one needs to know how to behave in that culture; either by being raised within it or by studying the cultural traditions in question. If one is going to study the factors affecting systems

development in a given country, one needs to pay more attention to the political economy and the material conditions of the country within the world-system. In developing countries, both researchers and practitioners need to take into account wider contextual issues and pay more attention to participative, empowering methodologies than in the industrialized countries (p. 40).

WESTERN MIS IN CHINA

In this section I will examine cross-cultural collaboration in a rather different context, namely the development of a management information system (MIS) for a financial agency in China, based on a technology transfer project funded by a Western donor agency. China can be considered to be a particularly important cultural setting for the use of IT. The Chinese component of the world includes the People's Republic of China, and other parts of Asia where ethnic Chinese form an important part of the economic and social life, such as Malaysia, the Philippines, Indonesia and Singapore. It is of enormous size in terms of population, numbering well over a billion people, and most commentators expect its importance in the world economy to increase over the coming years. In the next sub-section I will describe some work that seeks to explain the role and value of MIS in Chinese business culture. I will use this analysis to critique aspects of the case study described later in the section.

MIS in Chinese Business Culture

The material in this sub-section is based on an article by Martinsons and Westwood (1997). The article was written by two Western authors with extensive work experience in Hong Kong, now an integral part of the People's Republic of China. Their paper drew extensively on the literature on China, from both philosophical and empirical perspectives. Their particular focus was to explore the reasons as to why 'Chinese managers make remarkably limited direct use of computer-based information systems'. Their explanation for this phenomenon goes back to the roots of Chinese society in Confucian values and behaviour which distinguish Chinese managers and workers from their Anglo-American counterparts. For example, the authors emphasized personalism, paternalism and high-context communications as critical in the Chinese context, and they suggest that these characteristics tend to be in conflict with explicit Western-origin MIS. I will now examine their arguments in more detail, with Table 9.1 providing a summary of the analysis.

Table 9.1 *Chinese business culture and MIS use*

Chinese cultural characteristic	Nature of constraint on MIS use
Personal relationships are the preferred sources of business information	• Reliance on informal (primarily verbal) rather than formal (written) communications
Centralized decision-making	• Reduced need to exchange information between managers
Information is a major instrument of personal power	• Relatively little information is broadcast or made accessible
High context communications	• Data and information are perceived to lose much of their meaning if they are encoded
Decision-making based on intuition and experience	• Reduced need for data collection and analysis
People should adapt to the environment rather than attempt to control it, in order to maintain harmony	• Reduced need for business planning and scenario development/analysis

Taken from: Martinsons and Westwood 1997. Reprinted from *Information and Management*, vol. 32, 1997, pp. 215–228, with permission from Elsevier Science.

The first attribute noted by the authors concerns the importance of personal relationships in Chinese business culture. Chinese societies are based on networks of relationships, and one is first and foremost a member of a collective. The very concept of self is relational, and the needs of one's group, including one's family, supersede individual aspirations and their fulfilment. Martinsons and Westwood described how they saw this relational approach playing out in the context of Chinese organizational behaviour:

Private meetings rather than written memos or reports are the primary means of communication. The face-to-face contact sensitizes the boss to the opinions and feelings of his [sic] subordinates. Employees will compete for the privileged confidence of the boss and manoeuvre to get close to him so that they can better understand his intentions. The amount of information they receive will reflect the degree to which they are trusted ... New business is often generated by introductions and personal referrals rather than more formal marketing activities (p. 222).

This emphasis on informal face-to-face communication, and not on written-down information, implies a limited role for explicit MIS, at least when addressing important or sensitive issues.

A second feature of traditional Chinese society has been paternalism, relating to the importance of the family with the father figure at the centre, combining discipline and benevolence. This is reflected in Chinese firms having more centralized structures than their Anglo-American counterparts. Key decisions are made mostly by the proprietor, and if not by him, then often by a relative. There is often no explicit dependence in decision-making on subordinates, nor a responsibility to adopt a team approach. This reduces the need to exchange information between Chinese managers, certainly of a formal kind, and thus calls into question the role of an MIS in decision-making.

A related point is that information is seen as a major instrument of personal power, and is fundamentally a personal asset rather than an organizational resource. Martinsons and Westwood described the structure in a Chinese organization as perhaps being best represented as 'a series of concentric circles with the patriarch in the centre'. Power is maintained by carefully controlling key information. Most management information is for top managers only, and remains in a soft form in the mind of the manager. Key details, ideas and knowledge are selectively passed on to chosen individuals. The concept of broadcast and fully accessible information in an MIS, or through the Internet for example, goes against this philosophy.

Another way of looking at the traditional Chinese approach to communication is focused on the actual form of messages when they are written down, the number of words being relatively small 'so that the suggested ideas are limitless'. The assumption is that the words will be read and used in 'high context' face-to-face situations:

> Chinese messages are comparatively terse in words, but rich in meaning. Subtle cues are used to enrich the explicit content. Audible clues, such as tone, dynamics and any hesitation in response, together with facial expressions and body language, must be perceived and interpreted in order to fully understand the words being communicated (p. 220).

Thus for the Chinese, if we accept this model, little value is seen in codifying business information into a standardized form, especially if its context would be lost. Decision-making is not only personal and centralized, but also relates to the view of knowledge as the subtle accumulation of experience absorbed over many years. Thus high value is placed on intuition by the powerful and experienced leader rather than in a Western-style 'rational' analysis based on openly available data and criteria.

Finally, Martinsons and Westwood discussed the Chinese view of the 'environment', or the outside context within which business must function and decisions must be taken. Traditional Chinese philosophy emphasizes the need to accept the environment as 'given' at any particular point in time, and the need to seek harmony with it. Thus, rather than trying to project and control the future, the tendency is to focus on responding to present contingencies. Again, if this view remains valid in contemporary Chinese business culture, it would explain to some extent the lack of interest in Western-origin techniques of scenario planning and various other forms of forecasting models.

Some qualifications need to be made on the material in this sub-section. Any attempt to characterize any culture, Chinese or otherwise, is doomed to failure to some degree, and the ethnic diversity of China makes the task particularly problematic. The reader with knowledge of any Western culture will have noted that such aspects as the importance of personal relationships, the withholding of information as a political device, and the use of intuition in decision-making are not limited to Chinese organizations. However, the argument in the paper reviewed above is that they are more central and emphasized in a Chinese context, and that this view is helpful in explaining the relative lack of interest in computer-based information systems in China. A final important qualification is the argument that Chinese society is changing, particularly in the era of globalization, and thus that the hold of traditional values is weakened. Martinsons and Westwood accepted this argument in part but caution the following: 'The trend towards globalization will undeniably blur the boundaries and distinctions between societal cultures ... However, the management systems of the Chinese are likely to reflect the inertia of their deeply-rooted values for many decades to come' (p. 223).

Logical Frameworks: a Chinese Case Study

I look now at a specific case study, described by Bell (1998), to develop an MIS for a Chinese Financial Analysis Agency (CFAA). The project was funded by an unspecified Western donor agency. Bell is a British academic, who was the lead facilitator of the project team brought in to carry out the project planning. They made extensive use of a project planning tool, called the Logical Framework approach, or Logframe for short. Bell noted that this tool is very popular in development agencies such as the British

Department for International Development and the World Bank. He ascribed this popularity to the framework's conceptual simplicity and the need in project planning for an approach that can be rapidly applied.

Logframe consists of broad goals to be achieved, purposes at a more micro level, outputs as the specific results from the planned project, and activities that need to be undertaken to produce the outputs. Each of these elements are measured by Verifiable Indicators (VIs), a subset of which are Critical Indicators (CIs). Means of Verification (MOVs) are the sources of data necessary to verify the status of the various indicators. The final piece of the framework is assumptions, which are defined as important events, conditions or decisions 'outside the control of the project', necessary for the achievement of the project goals, purposes, outputs or activities.

Even this brief description of the framework is enough to show a sharp contrast between the Logframe approach and traditional Chinese business culture as described in the sub-section above. This can be illustrated by the first assumption that was made by Bell's project team, namely that 'people (will) want and make use of the information (from the project)'. This assumption is not discussed any further in Bell's paper, but as we saw above, the desirability of open and freely available data for logical decision-making purposes can be thought to be an invalid assumption, at least in a traditional Chinese business context. More generally, Logframe itself has a rigid, Western feel about it, with steps and indicators and measurement variables, rather than projects being seen as proceeding intuitively in 'high context' personal interactions based around powerful, knowledgeable leaders.

Even though the project team used the Logframe approach, possibly on the insistence of the donor agency, Bell was aware of the dangers of such Western-oriented methods: '... the possibility for the "methods and mindsets" of Western theory to become a tyranny, disempowering local people in development projects and imposing a dominant orthodoxy often irrelevant to the lives of people in developing countries' (p. 17).

Bell quoted Chambers (1997), who had this to say about the local 'acceptance' of a forerunner to the Logframe methodology: 'Ultimate consensus has been assured by verbal dominance, exhaustion and the bottom line that donors have the money' (p. 44).

But how valuable is this form of 'consensus'? Although the local actors may concede at the project planning or technical implementation stages, the project may well fail after the foreign project team get back on the plane and go home.

One of the tools used by the project team at CFAA to gain an understanding of the Chinese context was the 'rich picture', an element of the action research approach known as soft systems methodology (Checkland 1981). Whilst not wishing to argue that the rich pictures had no value for contextual understanding, it is important to note the strong Western cultural bias of such tools. Bell described their use in the project as follows: 'The rich picture is a fairly unstructured tool for summarizing everything which you know about a situation ... You do this by building a cartoon-type representation of it ... The objective is to capture the richness of the context' (p. 17).

A number of elements in this statement contrast sharply with traditional Chinese views of the world, as portayed earlier. Context is not an object to be 'captured' by a cartoon-type diagram, but knowledge of context is something deeper, more intuitive and experience-based. You cannot summarize 'everything you know' in a diagram, or words for that matter, since ideas are limitless and negotiated in an ongoing interactive process.

Bell and his colleagues were very concerned about participation in the CFAA project, particularly by those at lower hierarchical levels in the agency. However, this does not appear to have been achieved in any full sense since 'scope for inclusion was limited by the terms of reference of the project and the time available'. Bell concluded that the project would have benefited by more emphasis on 'canvassing opinion from those who the project would affect'. Without wishing to argue against participation as such, this improved approach as envisaged by Bell could be considered infeasible, at least in a traditional Chinese business context, if one takes the concentric ring model of Chinese business organization seriously. Those in the outer rings would not see it as their place to engage in open participative debate.

The purpose of this sub-section is not to condemn the work carried out by Bell and his project team, nor to doubt the sincerity of their intentions. The reason why the case is presented here is that it represents, in my experience, a fairly typical information technology transfer project undertaken by the Western development agencies. Not only do the technologies themselves embed Western values in some senses, but the project planning and implementation tools are strongly culturally biased. Much emphasis in such projects is often placed on training, and the CFAA project was no exception: 'A lot of time and effort went into designing training schedules and contents. The assumption arose from a conscious recognition that poor and insufficient training in the past had been critical in previous IT-related project failures' (p. 25).

But training does not normally produce significant change in deeply held systems of belief and mindsets. Training will be a failure if the gap is too great between these beliefs and those implied by the use of IT as conceived by its Western donors and implementers.

I sent an earlier version of this case study description to Bell for comments. In addition to expressing doubts on the validity of the description of traditional Chinese culture as summarized in Table 9.1, Bell felt that the CFAA work had not been conducted in a 'traditional Chinese culture' anyway. I would certainly accept this point, since agencies such as the CFAA in an era of globalization reflect a complex and shifting hybrid of Chinese and Western cultural values. However, I will end this section with a short quotation from my reply to Simon Bell, with which he said he was in complete agreement:

> I *do* think that Western-origin methodologies such as Logframe *are* often inappropriate for radically different cultural environments. I have had many years experience of failed Western-driven technology projects in Third World countries. Whilst these cannot be put down simply to a particular methodology, they often reflect an unwillingness on the part of Western aid agencies and others to take due account of different attitudes to fundamental issues such as conceptualizations of knowledge, politics, information sharing etc. Training is often the mantra, but training does not touch more fundamental cultural attitudes ... My argument in a nutshell is the need to take culture *seriously* (personal communication from myself to Bell).

ANALYSIS AND CONCLUSIONS

The three case studies presented in this chapter are a small selection from the immense potential variety of cross-cultural work involving IT. However, the material presented here has demonstrated the complexity of the issues involved when people from different cultural backgrounds work together, the need for an understanding of culture by expatriates working outside their own context, and the problematic nature of 'technology transfer' from Western countries to the developing world. The analysis in the remainder of the chapter develops some conclusions on such issues, using the key questions given at the start of the chapter as a framework. Summaries of the main points in this section are given in Tables 9.2–9.4.

What Problems Exist in Knowledge-Sharing Across Cultures?

We saw examples earlier in the book that showed how the very nature of knowledge itself is constructed differently in different cultures. For

Table 9.2   *Problems of knowledge-sharing across cultures*

Different conceptualizations of knowledge	• Nature of knowledge, e.g. as accumulation of experience versus explicit models • Knowledge-sharing
Different views of appropriate personal and power relations	• Hierarchy or consensus • Closely knit teams or personal autonomy • Paternalism
Different attitudes to IT development	• Job coordination • Time-keeping • Following methodologies or intuition and experience

example, the Indian GIS case in Chapter 4 demonstrated that there are different forms of spatial awareness, with Indians not normally being dependent on the map-based ways of knowing that are common in Western countries. This chapter has provided further examples. Martinsons and Westwood (1997) argued that knowledge in a traditional Chinese context is seen as the subtle accumulation of experience absorbed over many years, rather than knowledge based on Western-style analysis using openly available data and criteria. In the context of Yorubaland, Korpela argued that traditional religious views remain an important philosophical knowledge base.

The nature and form of knowledge-sharing also varies between cultures. In Chapter 3 we saw that Lam (1997) described engineering knowledge in Japan as being shared in intensive human-network-based communication rather than being coded and structured in explicit procedures, guidelines or computer systems. In this chapter, knowledge-sharing in a traditional Chinese business context was argued to take place through face-to-face communication with favoured subordinates. Knowledge-sharing in traditional Yoruba culture recognizes the existence of a multivocal setting of independent, different and often conflicting actors.

All consideration of knowledge-sharing has a related power dimension, and there are widely different views of appropriate forms of personal and power relations in different cultures, which can lead to cross-cultural conflict in some cases. The Indian software developers in Jamaica were used to operating in a strongly hierarchical context, whereas the Jamaicans with whom they were working favoured more consensual styles. The Indians worked as a closely knit team, whereas the Jamaicans were used to a culture of relatively high levels of personal autonomy. Paternalism was argued to be a marked feature of traditional Chinese business contexts, with the father figure at the centre combining discipline and benevolence. This would be relatively alien to Westerners working in China on technology transfer projects. Korpela described traditional Yoruba culture as having traits of hierarchy, but counterbalancing traits of consensuality. Finns working in such contexts need to be sensitive to differences from their own culture in this regard.

These different world views provide a problematic context for cross-cultural projects on the development and use of IT. They result in different styles and methods of working, and contrasting attitudes to issues such as job coordination and time-keeping. These were areas of major contention in the India/Jamaica case. In the context of the Chinese CFAA case, the Western team followed methodologies such as Logframe and soft systems methodology. In a traditional Chinese business context, emphasizing intuition and experience, such an approach appears problematic. This issue of the cultural content of methodologies is discussed more generally in the following sub-section.

Do Western-Origin IS and Methodologies Embed Features that Inhibit Cross-Cultural Working?

I argued in Chapter 8 that actor-network theory offers a theoretical basis for thinking about values implicit or inscribed in particular information and communication technologies. Similarly, Western methodologies can be taken as actants which embed assumptions related to the cultural background from which they originated. For example, the Logframe methodology has a strong Western-society feel to it, based on explicit goals, purposes, outputs and activities, and quantitative measurement indicators.

Table 9.3   *IS, methodologies and cross-cultural working*

Western-type IS and methodologies as actants with embedded features	• Explicit goals and quantitative measurement indicators • Surfacing of assumptions through pictorial diagrams
There is a need for adaptation and compromise on both sides in cross-cultural work	• To adapt methodologies • To compromise on working styles • To understand the expectations of the other
Requires an attitude that 'other' cultural values are not necessarily negative	• Not seeing one's own society as an ideal type • Opportunities for continuing hybridization

However, the more qualitative soft systems methodology also embeds cultural assumptions, with its cartoon-like rich pictures and explicit surfacing of assumptions. I am not arguing that such methodologies are necessarily inappropriate in cultural contexts different to those from which they derived. Rather, in terms of the focus of this chapter on cross-cultural working, that Western practitioners and consultants need to be aware of the cultural bias of their techniques and methods.

Thus there is a need for adaptation on both sides in cross-cultural working. In the Nigerian case, we saw the effort to produce a 'made-in-Nigeria' systems development methodology, but the input of the Finnish team no doubt gave this a hybrid cultural flavour. In some cases, disagreement will remain as to appropriate approaches, and forms of compromise need to be developed. I described the situation at the end of the research period in the Jamaican case as one of uneasy cross-cultural compromise.

In order to be in a position to compromise, it is necessary at least to have a good understanding of the expectations of the other party. An interesting discussion of this issue is provided by Sahay and Krishna (2000) when describing a case study involving global software outsourcing from a North American multinational, called Global, to an Indian software house, called Shiva. The article discusses how the radically different cultural base of the partners was handled, not always in an amicable way. For example, in the early phases, Shiva resisted the introduction of monthly progress reports, a practice that was routine in Global. More generally, Global attempted to make Shiva conform to a range of their standard practices. Later, Sahay and Krishna argued that the relationship 'showed signs of maturing' based on both sides gaining an increased understanding of the other's problems. The earlier state of 'speaking past each other' had changed and people were listening. The authors concluded that, in the later stages, there was a sense of concreteness to the expectations of the other, even though there may not have been agreement on the appropriateness of the expectations.

In order to listen seriously to people from other cultural backgrounds, there is a need to see that one's own society is not an ideal type to be aspired to by other cultures. Unfortunately, much of the Western literature on information and communication technologies seems to make this assumption, normally implicitly. For example, Hill et al. (1998) reported on a qualitative study they had made on Arab culture and IT transfer. Their research was based on focus groups of young Arab adults recently arrived in the United States, interviews of experienced Arab–American business people, and a field study of Arab knowledge workers in Jordan, Egypt, Saudi Arabia, Lebanon and the Sudan. Their results contain much of interest to anyone concerned with IT transfer to the Arab world, or in cross-cultural working with Arab communities based in any country. However, everything that is listed as 'impediments for information technology transfer' has a negative connotation, and is often linked to deeply held Arab values. For example, 'impediments' include religious values and loyalty to national traditions. In contrast, all 'impetus for information technology transfer' has a positive connotation, and is linked to Western values, particularly those of the United States. These include action rather than rhetoric, linkage to the world system, and keeping business competitive. Although Hill and co-authors could reasonably argue that this is what their respondents said, and that they were merely reporting these responses, the manner of reporting suggests a world view that Arab culture is a barrier to IT adoption that needs to be overcome. The authors did conclude that there was a need for 'culturally appropriate IT design and implementation', but the implicit model comes across strongly that Arab culture should be viewed as a negative, at least in terms of IT adoption.

I am not making the argument that all aspects of traditional Arab culture should be viewed positively, and that any change that compromises traditional values should be opposed. Rather, I am arguing the case for sensitivity to what is good in existing cultures, rather than the assumption that any aspects that conflict with one's own cultural values are necessarily bad. With a more open-minded approach to cross-cultural working, there are many opportunities for new forms of hybridization of methodologies, systems and people. Diversity is a survival feature of living organisms, enabling adaptation to a changing environment. Diversity can in principle be preserved by isolation, but this is increasingly infeasible in our globalized world. Diversity through different forms of hybridization and cross-cultural intermingling is a more feasible avenue for the future.

How Can Effective Co-Working With IT in Cross-Cultural Contexts be Facilitated?

The Finland–Nigeria case study provided a good example of the development of computer-based information systems and related methodologies which were sensitive to the indigenous context, and a project concerned with changing the lives of the people in the Yoruba region, and Nigeria more generally, in a positive way. The issue of culture was taken seriously in a long-term project of committed cross-cultural

Table 9.4   *Facilitating effective cross-cultural working with IT*

Developing indigenous IS and methodologies by committed cross-cultural collaboration	• Taking culture seriously • Addressing local problems • Changing the local in a positive way
Designing appropriate cross-cultural teamworking styles and methods	• Forms of interaction and knowledge-sharing • Vital issue for global 'virtual' teams
The Internet may offer new opportunities	• Multicultural interaction • But preserving and valuing elements of local diversity

collaboration. The work also addressed other local issues such as environmental, infrastructure and financial problems, and difficulties with hardware and software vendors. Korpela argued that there is a need to undermine the impact of the post-colonial dependency culture in Nigeria at the local level through information systems that empower local workers in areas such as health provision. He further argued that this represents, in some sense, a 'return' to traditional Yoruba cultural values.

In cross-cultural working, we have seen that clashes of style and approach, and attitudes to knowledge-sharing, may lead to lack of understanding and sometimes conflict. Appropriate cross-cultural teamworking styles and methods need to developed through joint efforts and compromise. In the Jamaica–India case, where major problems arose in this area, no effort was made initially to address this issue. It was only later, after these issues had severely hampered the project, that some belated attention was paid to achieving acceptable forms of working.

The main case studies that I have used in this chapter have all involved cross-cultural working where the workers were co-located in the same site or region, at least for significant periods of time. Interesting new issues in cross-cultural collaboration arise when considering global 'virtual' teams, whose members have to transcend both cultural and physical barriers. The paper by Sahay and Krishna (2000), cited in the previous sub-section, addressed this issue. These authors argued that the need to coordinate the Indian–North American team working across space created tensions with the human preferences of the software developers for proximity in space.

Practical approaches to address such problems are offered in a paper by Maznevski and Chudoba (2000), who described a substantial longitudinal case study that they had carried out on three 'virtual' teams, with parts of the teams in the United States, Europe and Asia. The paper concluded that team interaction was composed of a series of communication incidents, with effective interaction blending regular face-to-face incidents interspersed with less intensive shorter incidents using various media. The implications of the cross-cultural aspect are less clearly developed, partly due perhaps to less research access to the non-US respondents. Nevertheless, the authors argued that cultural issues were important, and gave an example of one of their cross-cultural teams having different attitudes to responsibility, requiring members to use telephone or face-to-face meetings to discuss such issues rather than fax or e-mail. They also made an interesting remark concerning cross-cultural sensitivity, or rather the lack of it, in one of the teams with an Asian component. Members of the East Asian site preferred a sequence of a faxed agenda for discussion, informal discussions over the phone, and then faxed confirmation of decisions made during the discussions. However, the researchers saw no evidence that the non-Asian members tried to accommodate these preferences.

Finally, what of the role of the Internet in shifting forms of cross-cultural collaboration and teamworking? It is too early to have much empirical evidence on this, but cross-cultural working through the Internet may offer opportunities for enhanced multicultural interaction but without suppressing local diversity. The Global/Shiva partnership could be taken as providing an early example, since much interaction in this case took place over the Net. As described in Chapter 2, authors such as Beck and Castells have argued that IT, and in particular the Internet, have the potential to aid political involvement. The Net also has the potential to support increased cross-cultural sensitivity, knowledge-sharing, and teamworking. Whether this will happen depends, however, on the approaches and attitudes of its information suppliers and users.

Part 4
Conclusions

10
Designing for Diversity

In reviewing major writers on contemporary society in Chapter 2, I argued that four broad themes could be synthesized from such work. First, that the world is undergoing major processes of change and, second, that information and communication technologies are deeply implicated in the transformations taking place. Many people would accept this broad picture, but the third theme is more contentious, namely that the change processes are not uniform, and that individuals, groups, organizations and societies will remain distinct and differentiated, although increasingly connected.

The empirical material in Parts 2 and 3 of this book has illustrated this theme of diversity, a counter-argument to the image of global homogenization and the ideology of rule by the world market. I have tried to unpack some of the subtlety and variety of what constitutes the globalized individual, group, firm, network or culture. I have done this mainly through the use of in-depth case studies, each of which has shown some small part of the immensely varied mosaic of the world as a whole.

The fourth theme from Chapter 2 was that there is an increasing need for reflection and action on the part of individuals, groups and societies in the new 'Information Age'. I hope that the book has provided the reader with much material for reflection, but what about action? In each of the empirical chapters I posed some key questions and provided some synthesized answers. However, practice is always situated in a unique historical context, and must take full account of local contingencies and opportunities. No simple blueprint for action is possible, but it is hoped that the book has been helpful to the thoughtful practitioner in raising themes, issues, concepts and theories of relevance to the effective use of IT in his or her own context.

In this final chapter I offer some conclusions on three topics concerned with future action. First, I revisit the four analytical areas introduced in Chapter 3 on 'Computers at Work', which aimed to provide constructs to examine IT in society at the micro-level, and I synthesize some overall conclusions in each of these areas. Second, I look at the role of the researcher on IT in the contemporary world, and I outline a future agenda for relevant research. Last, I offer some personal views on the question as to whether we can make a better world with information and communication technologies.

COMPUTERS AT WORK

The four conceptual areas concerned with IT in society that were introduced in Chapter 3 were: data, information and knowledge; the role of information technology; improvisation and appropriation; and power and politics. Each of these areas is revisited below, with a focus on synthesizing some broad conclusions derived from the empirical material of the book. The empirical chapters of Part 2 were organized for analytical purposes at various levels of analysis, namely the individual, group, organizational and inter-organizational levels. The material in Part 3 looked at culture as a context for IT, and cross-cultural working. However, the themes from Chapter 3 cut across all these chapters and topics, and similarly this section will blur the somewhat arbitrary boundaries of the empirical chapters by looking at the conceptual themes in the light of all the empirical material of the book.

Data, Information and Knowledge

Data and information were discussed briefly in Chapter 3, but a particular focus throughout the book has been on the issue of knowledge and knowledge-sharing. The meaning of the term 'knowledge' is problematic, and the first question to ask in a specific organization is: What forms of knowledge are particularly important in that context? One particular classification is Blackler's (1995) summary of the different views of knowledge in the literature as embrained in individual conceptual skills or cognitive abilities, embodied in the person as in expertise in sport, encultured in shared group norms, embedded in routines, or encoded in books, databases or web sites. This is only one way of breaking down knowledge types: others are feasible, but the classification challenges simplistic notions of knowledge as a commodity that is easily transferred.

Not all knowledge can be 'extracted' from an individual and stored in an encoded form. Embrained, embodied or encultured knowledge tends to be tacit, and often not codifiable. In addition, when we say that knowledge is extracted from an individual, in the form of a book for example, we are seeing only a snapshot representation of aspects of that person's knowledge, rather than the sum total of his/her understanding of the subject addressed. Its 'reuse' by someone else will not have exactly the same connotation as for the original generator of the knowledge representation.

This gap between knowledge in practice and that represented in computer systems was exemplified by some of the representations of work that we looked at in the case studies in this book. For example, the ConsultCo systems administrators, described in Chapter 4, carried out their work in a hands-on subjective way, but were required to represent their work as distanced and objective through precise documentation. Similarly, the Comco hardware repair agents, described in the same chapter, were pulled between the computer-based representation of their work in terms of meeting precise deadlines, and the perceived need on the part of some of the agents for good customer relationships.

Knowledge-sharing is not, therefore, merely a matter of coding information into computer systems of various forms, including databases and web sites, and making this accessible to others. In addition to the limitations of what can actually be captured in this way, knowledge-sharing between people requires a climate of trust. The majority of the brokers and underwriters in the London Insurance Market case in Chapter 7 argued the need for face-to-face contact in the critical insurance placing transaction in order to negotiate effectively and to maintain trust in their relationships. Their resistance to the potential elimination of personal interaction and its replacement by electronic communication should not be seen primarily as an anti-technology stance, but a healthy awareness of the realities of human interaction.

Of course, not all knowledge-sharing can take place in face-to-face mode, and indeed much can be achieved through electronic media. Maznevski and Chudoba's (2000) research on global virtual teams, outlined in Chapter 9, concluded that team interaction in their case studies was composed of a series of communication incidents, with effective interaction blending regular intensive face-to-face dialogue with less intensive shorter incidents using various electronic media. The challenge for the future in all organizational contexts is to choose an appropriate media blend, including the crucial face-to-face mode, in order to facilitate effective knowledge-sharing and interaction in a cost-efficient way.

Any consideration of knowledge-sharing has a related political dimension. In any context, individuals may see personal advantage to be gained through their own knowledge, and they may not wish to share this with others. For example, Neil in the Comco case in Chapter 4 drew on his expertise to legitimize the evasion of the controls that he saw the organization trying to place on him, and he certainly had no interest in sharing his know-how with others who he saw as potential competitors. Even in contexts where the individuals saw some value to themselves in knowledge-sharing, such as the sales reps in the Compound UK case in Chapter 5, surveillance of their interactions limited the degree to which they felt able to share personal knowledge. This led to the suggestion of the need to create 'safe enclaves', electronic or otherwise, where people at lower and higher hierarchical levels can feel able to communicate in a relatively open way.

What are the influences of different cultural attitudes to knowledge? Lam (1997), as discussed in Chapter 3, described engineering knowledge in Japan as being shared in intensive human-network-based communication rather than being coded and structured in explicit procedures, guidelines or computer systems. This created major difficulties in knowledge-sharing between British and Japanese engineers when trying to collaborate on a joint product development project. The Indian GIS study in Chapter 4 provided a further example of the cultural specificity of knowledge, with maps not being the normal way to conceptualize space in an Indian context. Such cultural differences in terms of ways of knowing have immediate implications for the acceptability of Western-origin computer systems such as GIS. In Chapter 9 we saw further examples of the problems of knowledge-sharing across cultures in the context of IT projects, in the Jamaica–India and Chinese MIS cases.

The Role of Information Technology

Examples of the problems of cross-cultural transfer of IT, such as those in Chapter 9, lead directly to the second micro-level theme that I introduced in Chapter 3, namely: How should we conceptualize the role of information and communication technologies? I have argued throughout the book that IT should not be conceptualized as a neutral resource. Rather, it should be seen as both reflecting and forming the attitudes and aspirations of its designers and users.

Actor-network theory has been used in a number of places throughout the book as a theoretical way of conceptualizing the role of technology as an 'actant' in actor-networks of humans and non-humans. For example, the theory was referred to explicitly in the descriptions of the GIS case in Chapter 4 and the SAP case in Chapter 6. In addition, the later work of Braa and Hedberg (2000) uses the theory explicitly to conceptualize the role of the district-level health information systems in South Africa, as discussed in Chapter 8. The theory can be considered valuable, however, in any context of IT introduction and use. It focuses attention on norms and values inscribed in the technology, and also on the processes of enrolment and translation whereby human and non-human actors do or do not form relatively stable networks of aligned interests.

It is not only the technology that has a non-neutral role in social and organizational activity. Approaches and methodologies for IT introduction can also be considered as actants. For example, traditional values in Thai society, as we saw in Chapter 8, do not encourage the questioning of implementation approaches, and thus methodologies such as participative design are not well-aligned to Thai values. The approach of the Finnish–Nigerian team to this issue, as discussed in Chapter 9, was to produce a made-in-Nigeria systems development methodology, designed to be appropriate for the severely constrained conditions in most of sub-Saharan Africa, and in tune with local cultural characteristics. This contrasts with the use of Western-oriented methodologies such as Logframe as described in the Chinese MIS case in the same chapter. I argued there that such methodologies are often inappropriate for radically different cultural environments.

The method of analysis through an examination of shifting actor-networks of people, information technologies and methodologies is also highly relevant in Western contexts. Technologies such as enterprise systems embed views of work practice, and thus may 'impose' such practices as discussed in the SAP case in Chapter 6. The metaphor of electronic concrete suggests concerns about the lack of flexibility that may be inherent in such solutions. Similarly, methodologies such as BPR had inscribed notions of 'obliteration' of existing organizational forms embedded in them, and were ostensibly concerned with goals such as empowerment and a more customer-focused organization. In practice, as I argued in Chapter 6, BPR had complex and varied effects in different organizations, related to the history and context of its implementation, and the way in which the change programme was designed, implemented and appropriated by organizational actors.

What can be said about the role of the Internet, a very important IT 'actant' at this point in time? Tapscott (1998) argued that the Internet is unique in three respects that make it vital to the future of the world economy. The first characteristic is ubiquity, namely that the Net can be in an indefinite number of places at the same time and has the potential therefore to be 'everywhere'. Secondly, the bandwidth of communication is large, and constraints on this are diminishing rapidly due to advances in technology, so that in principle any size of electronic object can be sent around the world almost instantaneously. Thirdly, the Net has a unique multi-purpose capability, with the capacity to carry data, text, sound and images in any combination.

Tapscott's three characteristics provide a neat summary of its key technical advantages over earlier electronic media. However, three alternative words can be put forward as qualifications to the message of ubiquity, bandwidth and multi-purpose, namely people, context and diversity. As discussed throughout this book, seamless electronic communication does not imply seamless human communication. The case studies that I have described have shown the variety in the way that people communicate and interact in a specific context with all the diversity implied by the specificity of particular individuals, groups, organizations and societies. Certainly the Internet is important, and it is right to focus on utilizing the potential of electronic media such as the Net to enhance our businesses, educational institutions or leisure activities. However, we also need to recognize the critical importance of an understanding of human beings in diverse contexts; the way that we think, communicate and act. The role of the Internet in these human processes will exhibit great variety. For example, as argued in Chapter 7, Internet usage and impact in different societies will not follow the US model in any simple way, but will evolve in response to local histories, contingencies and actions.

Improvisation and Appropriation

The above focus on local specificity of Internet usage leads directly to the third general theme on IT in society introduced in Chapter 3, namely improvisation and appropriation. The first of these refers to the non-routinized nature of work practice, and the second to the way that information and communication technologies are appropriated to support that work practice. The case descriptions and analyses in the book have illustrated both of these themes, and I will now summarize some conclusions from this material.

A first conclusion is that IT is often introduced to support order and control, but not improvised work practice. For example, in the Comco case in Chapter 4, the Traveller and Dispatch systems were used by the company to try to monitor and control the work of the hardware engineers, but they were not designed to support the more improvisational aspects of the situated practice of the engineers. This caused resentment on the part of some of the engineers and led, in some circumstances, to deliberate manipulation and evasion of the constraints implied by the system. Similarly, in the ConsultCo case in the same chapter, one worker was reminded that she must not go outside the constraints of the work as imposed from above, even though that involved helping users.

The enterprise-wide approaches to organizational change mediated by IT, described in Chapter 6, were all strongly related to control. The LA system in UK Bank was rolled out to the whole organization with the goal of better control of the bank's lending activity. The centralization of the back office activities in Probank can also be seen as increasing management control. The SAP system in Norsk Hydro was designed to integrate and control their disparate European operations. I argued in that chapter that organizations need, however, to be concerned with innovation and autonomy, as well as with order and control, since otherwise sources of learning, growth and effective change may be blocked. There needs to be a balance between control and autonomy, and computer-based information and communication systems should not be designed primarily as central control mechanisms, but rather as support for effective local work practice.

A positive example of the design and use of a system to support local work activities is provided by the Zeta case, described in Chapter 5. There was a focus here on the need for the continuous management of process in the introduction of groupware systems. The different approaches to change were labelled as anticipated, emergent and opportunistic, with the latter two taking place after the introduction of the technology in response to local initiative and experience. This relates to Ciborra's (1996b) argument that groupware technology needs to 'drift' in practice away from its original design if it is to support improvised work practice effectively. An emphasis on improvisation is valuable, although some work activities do have strongly routinized elements that also need support. For example, I am glad as a passenger that the systems on an aeroplane support the normally relatively routine tasks of taking off, flying and landing the plane. The important point for both routine and improvised activity is that the information or communication technology is able to be appropriated in such a way as to support local work practice effectively.

Approaches to aid local IT appropriation are vital in all contexts, but the material in Part 3 of the book especially has shown the particular difficulty of this in non-Western contexts. As discussed above when considering the role of technology, many computer-based systems have been designed and developed in Western contexts, and non-Western work practices and attitudes may not be closely aligned to those embedded in the technology. However, the Mexican information company case in Chapter 8 provided a largely positive illustration to the development of approaches and systems geared to local contingencies. An important point from that case was that supporting local appropriation does not only involve adaptation of the technology and systems to local conditions, but also in some cases efforts to change those conditions and local attitudes over time.

Two other cases in Part 3 provided additional ideas and concepts concerning local appropriation of IT in non-Western contexts. The metaphor of cultivation was used in the South African case reported on in Chapter 8. Seeds of the health information systems were planted in the individual districts, but the argument was that their growth needed to be closely monitored and tuned to local climatic conditions. This has some similarity with the made-in-Nigeria systems development approach described in Chapter 9. These two cases emphasized the opportunistic and emergent elements of computer-based systems rather than their planned nature. I would like to say, clearly, that information systems of all sorts, computerized or not, can and should be planned to achieve certain goals, and indeed that these goals are sometimes achieved as planned. However, this is by no means the whole story, and the cases in this book have illustrated that much thought and effort needs to be put into what was not planned, but emerges in a continuous process of local learning and adaptation.

Power and Politics

The emphasis on concepts such as knowledge and culture in the material above highlights the dimensions of meaning and norms rather than that of power relations (Giddens 1984). However, the three are inextricably interlinked, and I will now revisit the final theme of Chapter 3, namely power and politics. Some references to the theme have been made already in this conclusions section, for example in noting that all considerations of knowledge-sharing have a political dimension due to the inseparability of power and knowledge in human relations. I have also discussed surveillance through computer systems and its links to control and thus power. Some further conclusions on this theme are now summarized, drawn from the empirical chapters of the book, but first I give a brief personal view on the nature of power and politics themselves.

Power relations are endemic to all social activity, and politics is concerned with the use of resources, through the exercise of power, to achieve particular ends. The economic, social or moral judgement lies not in the question of whether political action is necessary, since it is present in all social action, but whether the means or ends are justified. The answer to this question is of course difficult in any particular context, and it is often contested. This does not imply that it should, therefore, be ignored. I have tried throughout the book to bring out aspects of power and political action in all the cases, since it is essential in my view to stimulate debate on the role of IT from this particular human perspective.

A negative view of the use of IT in contemporary organizations sees it as implicated in coercion and excessive control. This view was discussed, for example, in the use of groupware systems in the Compound UK case in Chapter 5. Many of the pharmaceutical sales reps saw themselves as having being coerced into using systems that were often inappropriate to their job. Also, in what many of them saw as a relatively non-supportive formative context, they were not willing to share knowledge with others in an open way for fear of reprisals. Ironically, this had the effect of reducing effective knowledge-sharing which was a key goal for the system as conceived by management. It was argued in Chapter 5 that there is a need for 'safe enclaves' for knowledge-sharing, where those at lower hierarchical levels can share views in a below-the-line way, rather than being exposed to senior management surveillance in above-the-line systems. I noted in Chapter 5 that this conclusion also applies to intranets. Although intranets offer a new form of cheap and easy intra-organizational communication, power and politics remain key human issues. It is still necessary to try to ensure a supportive formative context, attention to issues of situated local practice, appropriate approaches to surveillance and control, and reward systems that encourage knowledge-sharing.

Willmott (1993), as discussed in Chapter 4, argued that workers in contemporary organizations often self-discipline themselves to conform to espoused organizational values, not solely due to the type of coercion discussed above, but due to the need to create and maintain a personal identity linked to local values. Elements of this could be seen in both the ConsultCo and Comco cases in that chapter, although individuals could be seen to be on different 'trajectories of the self', and there was much scope for personal resistance in the ConsultCo case, with many of the hardware engineers clearly not identifying with the company. Similarly, the cases in Chapter 6 could also be analysed from this identity perspective, with some evidence that managers who stayed on in the UK Bank case, for example, tried to adapt themselves to the 'new' bank manager identity of a computer-supported lending agent. However, again, there was much diversity, and some scope for both overt and covert resistance.

In Chapter 7 I argued that power and political action are of key importance in the context of inter-organizational relations. In situations where partners cannot be coerced into action, such as the group of semi-autonomous organizations that make up the London Insurance Market, high levels of trust are needed to make things work. The electronic placing system was seen as inappropriate by many underwriters and brokers in not effectively enabling the maintenance of trust relations. IT-enabled networks are deeply implicated in higher-level power relations in such contexts, affecting whole firms and industries through market restructuring for example. In the context of the London Insurance Market, this could be viewed as a threat, either by a broker concerned with IT-enabled disintermediation, or more radically by the whole market if it fails to retain its globally competitive position *vis-à-vis* other world insurance markets.

Part 3 of the book was also concerned with power and politics, and IT could be seen in its worst light as an agent of Western imperialism and coercion of the less-developed countries. I would not wish to argue this strongly, with cases such as the Norwegian–South African collaboration on health systems in Chapter 8 as an example of broadly positive efforts to use IT effectively to the benefit of poorer communities in that country. Nevertheless, inappropriate IT transfer projects remain common in developing countries, and there is a need for more openness and willingness to learn on the part of those introducing such systems in non-Western contexts. I am discussing this here, under the power and politics theme, since the reason that such projects tend to continue reflects the asymmetric power relations between the richer and poorer parts of the world. But power should be accompanied by responsibility, and I will return to the issue of ethical responsibility in the final section of the chapter.

THEMES FOR RESEARCHERS

The case material drawn on for this book was generated by research studies, and through the efforts of many researchers around the world. In this section, I would like to explore what future research could be undertaken to further and deepen our understanding of the role and value of information and communication technologies. First, I will discuss methodological approaches, and the role of theory. Second, I will consider what specific topics might be chosen to gain high benefit from future research.

Methodology and Theory

My view on methodology for future research on IT in a global context is that we need more in-depth interpretive case studies or action research projects of the type reported in this book. My rationale for this view is that many important human issues associated with IT cannot be accessed in detail in any other way. For example, such issues include power and political actions, perceptions and feelings, and cultural norms and values. All of these have a major influence on the design, development and use of IT in organizations around the world, and they warrant further and wider study. Unfortunately, power relations and political imperatives in academia sometimes work against in-depth studies, since they are very time-consuming and publication tends to be delayed until years after the start of the study. It can be much easier to carry out a quick survey, perhaps using student subjects for simple access, and to produce a publication to be used for tenure or promotion purposes. There is a current imbalance in the literature towards such approaches, and in the future we need more in-depth contextual research to gain deeper and richer insight.

Is there a role for other methodological approaches, such as 'representative' surveys of individuals or groups with particular roles, or organizations in particular industries or sectors? I would say yes, but the purpose must necessarily be somewhat different. Surveys can provide a wider picture of organizations across a whole sector for example, but they normally lack depth of insight on complex human issues. They are better at reporting on what people in organizations are doing, rather than why they are doing it. Similarly, interviewing people in particular roles across a range of organizations provides a broader picture than a single in-depth case study, but loses the multi-vocal, contextual element. A major problem I tend to have with careful survey-type approaches is not, however, with their content as such, but with the implicit or explicit assumption that what is being presented is truth. Surveys should not claim this any more than in-depth case studies, since the nature and style of questions, methods of analysis, and presentation of the results require a subjective filter by the researcher. All studies are interpretive, viewed from this perspective, and results from them should be reported in ways that bring this out.

What is the role of theory in future research studies, and which theories offer promise in exploring the role of IT in the world? First, I believe that the writers on contemporary society, such as those reviewed in Chapter 2, provide thoughtful material on the broad context of the contemporary world. This is a valuable sensitizing device for researchers, enabling them to see a wider picture within which their own research study is located. The weakness of such theories is that they are very general, producing what I described as 'themes from a plane' in Chapter 2. There is a need to get down to ground level to explore IT in detailed circumstances, and this has been the primary approach of this book.

In exploring the case studies described here, I used elements of the micro-level theories of 'computers at work' introduced in Chapter 3, and I revisited these theories in the previous section of this chapter. I believe that theories of knowledge, actor-network theory on the role of technology, theories of improvisation and appropriation, and conceptual ways of looking at power and politics have proved valuable in exploring the detailed material in this book, and that they offer promise in future studies. However, I do not see these as a complete set in any sense, but rather as potentially helpful ways of viewing the complexity and variety of real world applications of information and communication technologies.

I would argue that researchers should always be trying to supplement their theoretical schema, since locking in to one theory or a limited set of theories is a way of blinding oneself to other perspectives. In this book, I have drawn on some theoretical ideas which did not fall neatly in any of the categories discussed above. For example, in Chapter 4, theories of identity were used to explore the changing work identity of the hardware engineers in Comco. Other theories drawn on in Parts 2 and 3 include theories of culture, organization, time and space, trust, and risk. A detailed treatment of any of these would require a book in itself, so necessarily my use of theory in these areas has been rather limited.

So theory has been used throughout this book, but depth of treatment through specific theoretical approaches has been lost to some extent by the format employed here. What has been gained? Drawing in an eclectic way on a wide range of theories has enabled a broad canvass to be explored, including multiple levels of analysis, and different cultural contexts throughout the world. This 'broad brush' treatment has meant some loss of depth on specific issues, but I hope that what has been gained is breadth and interconnectivity of levels and contexts. Most work in the future, including my own, will tend to be about a specific issue in a particular context, and it will include an attempt to generalize through explicit theoretical treatment, often using only one theory. The broad use of a range of theories in this book provides a wider backdrop for such detailed pieces of work.

Future Research Agenda

This leads directly to the question as to what the specific focus of such pieces of work should be. In other words, what future research agenda would be valuable to pursue to extend our understanding of the role and value of IT in the world? I address this question now, using multiple levels of analysis from individual to society, whilst recognizing that all research issues necessarily cross these boundaries. At each level I discuss the current coverage of work, give a brief linkage to globalization themes, and identify some future research topics. A summary of key points is given in Table 10.1. A full treatment of this topic is provided in Walsham (2000).

Despite studies such as those reported in Chapter 4, the topic of shifting identity linked to the use of information and communication technologies remains under-researched. However, key theorists of the contemporary world and globalization, as we saw in Chapter 2, invariably emphasize shifting personal, professional and societal identities, whilst not normally providing substantial empirical examples of this. There are clear agendas here for future research on exploring shifting identity linked to IT in a wide variety of contexts. These include obvious domains such as organizations in the Western world, but also different cultural contexts, and in home as well as work life.

There is a good body of literature on the use of groupware systems, as reported on in Chapter 5. However, there is very little that addresses the issue of the use of groupware in multicultural contexts, although this is often hinted at as a 'problem' in the existing literature. More generally, 'virtual' teams are becoming more common as organizational and inter-organizational networks are stretched across wider reaches of time and space. There are major research agendas here concerning the benefits and limitations of electronically mediated communication for these teams. A special and interesting case of this is where the virtual teams cross major cultural boundaries. A further area for future research at the group level concerns the use of intranets. Intranets are one way in which organizations aim to support intra-organizational teams working across time and space, but as yet there are few 'critical' studies in the literature, namely those that try to investigate both advantages and disadvantages of intranets in specific contexts.

Studies of IT/IS at the organizational level have been carried out over many years, and there is much interesting work here, some of which has been reported on in this book. Global initiatives and approaches, such as BPR and enterprise systems, have been common in recent years, and it seems likely in the era of globalization that fashionable approaches such as these will continue to diffuse rapidly across the world. The Internet is the current fashion, in the Western world at least, and I will comment on this below. However, our track record in predicting new IT innovations has been dismal in the past, and it seems likely that this will continue,

Table 10.1 *Future research agenda*

Level of analysis	Current depth of coverage	Linkage to globalization themes	Future research agenda
Individual	Very limited	Major shifts in personal and professional identity in contemporary world	• Explore shifting identity linked to IT in a wide variety of contexts
Group	Good work on groupware	Groups need to communicate across time–space	• Groupware in multicultural contexts • Global 'virtual' teams • Critical studies of the use of intranets
Organization	Much interesting work here	Global initiatives and approaches such as BPR, enterprise systems	• Research on contemporary global organizational themes, e.g. the Internet
Inter-organization	Growing literature	Networking for global reach	• Critical in-depth case studies of inter-organizational systems • Major work needed on e-business
Society	Under-researched, particularly in contexts of developing countries	Ironic under-representation in the age of globalization	• Role of IT in different cultures: anti-ethnocentricism

meaning that future fashions cannot be easily predicted. Researchers will need to respond to new themes when they arise, the rationale for working on them being their importance to world affairs, rather than necessarily their intrinsic merit.

There is an extensive and growing literature on inter-organizational networking, and the role of IT in this process, reflecting the global reach that is aspired to by many contemporary organizations. Some examples of work on this area were provided in Chapter 7. However, there remains a shortage of critical in-depth case studies. A crucial area for future studies is e-commerce, or more generally e-business. Despite the enormous hype and interest in the use of the Net for business-to-business and business-to-consumer applications, it is currently hard to find in-depth case study material that takes a balanced academic view of e-business, analysing both opportunities and limitations of this medium for consumer sales or inter-business transactions and relationships. Major research work is needed in this area.

It is ironic that, in this age of globalization, many societies in the poorer parts of the world remain under-researched. In addition, specific aspects of the culture of such regions and countries are often seen as impediments to 'progress', including that brought by IT. Such ethnocentricity is to be deplored, and it is hoped that the multicultural emphasis of this book makes a small counterbalancing contribution to the literature. However, much more is needed. An understanding of the use of IT in cultures other than those of the Western world can perhaps be justified on economic grounds alone, in terms of increasing understanding of global markets and supply chains. A deeper ethical rationale is that we should all be concerned about the world as a whole, and not just some subset within which we happen to be located or to work though accident of birth or background.

MAKING A BETTER WORLD WITH IT?

I sometimes describe my professional interests as encapsulated in the following research question. Are we making a better world with IT? Most people around the world seem to relate easily to this question, and a common response is to ask a question in turn. Well, are we? At this point, I tend to slide off into the professional academic's response of 'on the one hand, yes, and on the other hand, no'. Let me try to give a more specific answer to end the book. As already noted above, the world, in my view, should include the whole world.

What is meant by a 'better' world? Do we mean better in purely economic terms, or related to a wider global agenda of social or spiritual welfare? I think we should mean the latter, but this makes the issue more complex. A computer-based information or communication system might make economic activity more efficient, but suppose that there are major negative consequences such as excessive work intensification or devastating job losses. In which case, is this a good thing? Simplistic market-driven economics would have us believe yes, and people who stand to gain economic benefit in the short term often state that this is the only sensible way to view the world. But we all know deep down that the world market is unfair. If you are born in a Bombay slum, your opportunities for sharing in the wealth of the world are likely to be more limited than those of the child of an affluent Westerner. The social benefits that flow from economic efficiency are not equally or fairly shared. In addition, social or spiritual welfare does not equate simply to material welfare. So, there are wider issues than simple market economics, and at the very least we should try to include these in our agenda for a better world.

The case material presented in the book does not, however, enable us to answer the question simply, even in specific cases. It was probably clear to the reader where my sympathies lay with respect to particular economic and social issues raised in the various cases in the book. However, in any particular case the issues are complicated, and we all need to make our own judgements. My judgements are no more or less important than yours. The crucial point is that we attempt to make some judgements in this world of different shades of grey, based on the broad agenda of improving the world, seen in our own terms.

So, my final message is a processual one. The important thing is to try to assess on a continuing basis, and case by case, how, why and in what ways IT is being used, and whether it is making the world better. There are no simple answers, but the important action is to continue addressing the question with all the vigour at our disposal. Information and communication technologies are important actants in the making of the contemporary world.

This is still a world of difference, and many aspects of this difference are to be welcomed in my view, such as differences of gender, religion and culture. However, judgements also need to be made on aspects of difference that are not acceptable, such as stark asymmetries of wealth, power and the consequent ability to lead a full and rewarding life. We should all be trying to use IT to overcome such problems, and thus to make a world of difference that we can all celebrate.

References

Appadurai, A. (1996) *Modernity at Large: Cultural Dimensions of Globalization*, University of Minnesota Press, Minneapolis.

Attewell, P. (1991) Big Brother and the Sweatshop: Computer Surveillance in the Automated Office, in: C. Dunlop and R. Kling, eds, *Computerization and Controversy: Value Conflicts and Social Choices*, Academic Press, Boston.

Avgerou, C. and Walsham, G., eds (2000) *Information Technology in Context: Implementing Systems in the Developing World*, Ashgate Publishing, Aldershot.

Barrett, M. (1996) Information Technology and Innovation: Transformations in the London Insurance Market, PhD Thesis, The Judge Institute of Management Studies, University of Cambridge, Cambridge.

Barrett, M. (1999) Challenges of EDI Adoption for Electronic Trading in the London Insurance Market, *European Journal of Information Systems*, **8** (1), 1–15.

Barrett, M. and Walsham, G. (1995) Managing IT for Business Innovation: Issues of Culture, Learning and Leadership in a Jamaican Insurance Company, *Journal of Global Information Management*, **3** (3), 25–33.

Barrett M. and Walsham, G. (1999) Electronic Trading and Work Transformation in the London Insurance Market, *Information Systems Research*, **10** (1), 1–22.

Barrett, M., Drummond, A. and Sahay, S. (1996) Exploring the Impact of Cross-Cultural Differences in International Software Development

Teams: Indian Expatriates in Jamaica, in: J.D. Coelho, W. Konig, H. Krcmar, R. O'Callaghan and M. Saaksjarvi, eds, *Proceedings of the 4th European Conference on Information Systems (ECIS)*, Lisbon, Portugal.

Barrett, M., Sahay, S. and Walsham, G. (1996) Understanding IT and Social Transformation: Development and Illustration of a Conceptual Scheme, in: J.I. DeGross, S. Jarvenpaa and A. Srinivasan, eds, *Proceedings of the 17th International Conference on Information Systems*, ACM, New York.

Beck, U. (1992) *Risk Society: Towards a New Modernity*, Sage Publications, London.

Beck, U. (2000) *What is Globalization?*, Polity Press, Cambridge.

Beck, U., Giddens, A. and Lash, S., eds (1994) *Reflexive Modernization: Politics, Tradition and Aesthetics in the Modern Social Order*, Polity Press, Cambridge.

Bell, D. (1973) *The Coming of Post-Industrial Society: A Venture in Social Forecasting*, Basic Books, New York.

Bell, S. (1998) Managing and Learning with Logical Frameworks: The Case of an MIS Project in China, *Human Systems Management*, **17** (1), 15–27.

Berg, M. (1998) The Politics of Technology: On Bringing Social Theory into Technological Design, *Science, Technology and Human Values*, **23** (4), 456–490.

Berliner, P.F. (1994) *Thinking in Jazz: The Infinite Art of Improvisation*, University of Chicago Press, Chicago.

Bhatnagar, S.C. (2000) Getting Value from IT Investments: Experiences from Two Organisations, in: C. Avgerou and G. Walsham, eds, *Information Technology in Context: Implementing Systems in the Developing World*, Ashgate Publishing, Aldershot.

Bhatnagar, S.C. and Bjørn-Andersen, N., eds (1990) *Information Technology in Developing Countries*, North-Holland, Amsterdam.

Bhatnagar, S.C. and Odedra, M., eds (1992) *Social Implications of Computers in Developing Countries*, Tata McGraw-Hill, New Delhi.

Bijker, W.E. (1993) Do Not Despair: There is Life after Constructivism, *Science, Technology and Human Values*, **18** (1), 113–138.

Bijker, W.E. (1995) *Of Bicycles, Bakelites and Bulbs: Toward a Theory of Sociotechnical Change*, MIT Press, Cambridge, MA.

Bijker, W.E., Hughes, T.P. and Pinch, T.J., eds (1987) *The Social Construction of Technological Systems*, MIT Press, Cambridge, MA.

Bikson, T.K. (1996) Groupware at the World Bank, in: C.U. Ciborra, ed., *Groupware & Teamwork: Invisible Aid or Technical Hindrance?*, Wiley, Chichester. (Out of print)

Blackler, F. (1995) Knowledge, Knowledge Work and Organizations: An Overview and Interpretation, *Organization Studies*, **16** (6), 1021–1046.

Bloomfield, B.P. and McLean, C. (1996) Madness and Organization: Informed Management and Empowerment, in: W.J. Orlikowski, G. Walsham, M.R. Jones and J.I. DeGross, eds, *Information Technology and Changes in Organizational Work*, Chapman & Hall, London.

Bloomfield, B.P., Coombs, R., Cooper, D.J. and Rea, D. (1992) Machines and Manoeuvres: Responsibility Accounting and the Construction of Hospital Information Systems, *Accounting, Management and Information Technologies*, **2** (4), 197–219.

Boland, R.J. (1987) The In-formation of Information Systems, in: R.J. Boland and R.A. Hirschheim, eds, *Critical Issues in Information Systems Research*, Wiley, Chichester.

Boland, R.J. and Schultze, U. (1996) From Work to Activity: Technology and the Narrative of Progress, in: W.J. Orlikowski, G. Walsham, M.R. Jones and J.I. DeGross, eds, *Information Technology and Changes in Organizational Work*, Chapman & Hall, London.

Boland, R.J. and Tenkasi, R.V. (1995) Perspective Making and Perspective Taking in Communities of Knowing, *Organization Science*, **6** (4), 350–372.

Bowker, G. and Star, S.L. (1994) Knowledge and Information in International Information Management: Problems of Classification and Coding, in: L. Bud-Frierman, ed., *Information Acumen: The Understanding and Use of Knowledge in Modern Business*, Routledge, London.

Braa, J. (1997) Use and Design of Information Technology in Third World Contexts with a Focus on the Health Sector: Case Studies from Mongolia and South Africa, PhD Thesis, Department of Informatics, University of Oslo, Oslo.

Braa, J. and Hedberg, C. (2000) Developing District-Based Health Care Information Systems: The South African Experience, in *Proceedings of the IFIP WG9.4 Conference on Information Flows, Local Improvisations and Work Practices*, Cape Town, South Africa.

Braa, J., Heywood, A. and Shun-King, M. (1997) District Level Information Systems: Two Cases from South Africa, *Methods of Information in Medicine*, **36** (2), 115–121.

Brigham, M. and Corbett, J.M. (1997) E-Mail, Power and the Constitution of Organisational Reality, *New Technology, Work and Employment*, **12** (1), 25–35.

Brown, A.D. (1998a) Narrative, Politics and Legitimacy in an IT Implementation, *Journal of Management Studies*, **35** (1), 35–58.

Brown, J.S. (1998b) Internet Technology in Support of the Concept of 'Communities-of-Practice': The Case of Xerox, *Accounting, Management and Information Technologies*, **8** (4), 227–236.

Büscher, M. and Mogensen, P.H. (1997) Mediating Change: Translation and Mediation in the Context of Bricolage, in: T. McMaster, E. Mumford, E.B. Swanson, B. Warboys and D. Wastell, eds, *Facilitating Technology Transfer Through Partnership: Learning from Practice and Research*, Chapman & Hall, London.

Callon, M. (1986) Some Elements of a Sociology of Translation: Domestication of the Scallops and the Fishermen, in: J. Law, ed., *Power, Action and Belief: A New Sociology of Knowledge?*, Routledge & Kegan Paul, London.

Callon, M. (1991) Techno-Economic Networks and Irreversibility, in: J. Law, ed., *A Sociology of Monsters: Essays on Power, Technology and Domination*, Routledge, London.

Castells, M. (1996) The Information Age: Economy, Society and Culture. Volume 1: *The Rise of the Network Society*, Blackwell, Oxford.

Castells, M. (1997) The Information Age: Economy, Society and Culture. Volume 2: *The Power of Identity*, Blackwell, Oxford.

Castells, M. (1998) The Information Age: Economy, Society and Culture. Volume 3: *End of Millennium*, Blackwell, Oxford.

Catudal, J.N. (1999) Censorship, the Internet and the Child Pornography Law of 1996: A Critique, *Ethics and Information Technology*, **11** (2), 105–116.

Chambers, R. (1997) *Whose Reality Counts? Putting the First Last*, Intermediate Technology Publications, London.

Chatfield, A.T. and Bjørn-Andersen, N. (1997) The Impact of IOS-Enabled Business Process Change on Business Outcomes: Transformation of the Value Chain of Japan Airlines, *Journal of Management Information Systems*, **14** (1), 13–40.

Checkland, P. (1981) *Systems Thinking, Systems Practice*, Wiley, Chichester.

Checkland, P. and Holwell, S. (1998) *Information, Systems and Information Systems*, Wiley, Chichester.

Choudhury, V. (1997) Strategic Choices in the Development of Inter-organizational Information Systems, *Information Systems Research*, **8** (1), 1–24.

Ciborra, C.U. (1996a) Improvisation and Information Technology in Organizations, in: J.I. DeGross, S. Jarvenpaa and A. Srinivasan, eds., *Proceedings of the 17th International Conference on Information Systems*, ACM, Baltimore.

Ciborra, C.U. (1996b) *Groupware & Teamwork: Invisible Aid or Technical Hindrance?*, Wiley, Chichester. (Out of print)

Ciborra, C.U. (1999) Notes on Improvisation and Time in Organizations, *Accounting, Management and Information Technologies*, **9** (2), 77–94.

Ciborra, C.U. and Patriotta, G. (1996) Groupware and Teamwork in New Product Development: The Case of a Consumer Goods Multinational, in: C.U. Ciborra, ed., *Groupware & Teamwork: Invisible Aid or Technical Hindrance?*, Wiley, Chichester. (Out of print)

Ciborra, C., Braa, K., Cordella, A., Dahlbom, B., Failla, A., Hanseth, O., Hepsø, V., Ljungberg, J., Monteiro, E. and Simon, K.A. (2000) *From Control to Drift: The Dynamics of Corporate Information Infrastructures*, Oxford University Press, Oxford.

Clark, I. (1997) *Globalization and Fragmentation: International Relations in the Twentieth Century*, Oxford University Press, Oxford.

Coombs, R., Knights, D. and Willmott, H.C. (1992) Culture, Control and Competition: Towards a Conceptual Framework for the Study of Information Technology in Organizations, *Organization Studies*, **13** (1), 51–72.

Cooper, R.B. and Zmud, R.W. (1990) Information Technology Implementation Research, *Management Science*, **36** (2), 123–139.

Davenport, T.H. (1993) *Process Innovation: Reengineering Work Through Information Technology*, Harvard Business School Press, Boston.

Davenport, T.H. (1998) Putting the Enterprise into the Enterprise System, *Harvard Business Review*, July–August, 121–131.

Davis, C. (1999) The Rapid Emergence of Electronic Commerce in a Developing Region: The Case of Spanish-Speaking Latin America, *Journal of Global Information Technology Management*, **2** (3), 25–40.

Davison, R., Harris, R., Vogel, D.R. and de Vreede, G-J. (1999) Editorial Preface, *Journal of Global Information Technology Management*, **2** (3), 1–4.

Doremus, P.N., Keller, W.W., Pauly, L.W. and Reich, S. (1998) *The Myth of the Global Corporation*, Princeton University Press, Princeton NJ.

Doyle, C. and Morris, H. (1999) *The Net Effect: Rethinking the Regulatory Role of the Nation State in the Global Electronic Economy*, The Fabian Society, London.

Foucault, M. (1980) Two Lectures, in: C. Gordon, ed., *Power/Knowledge: Selected Interviews and Other Writings 1972–1977*, Pantheon Books, New York.

Foucault, M. (1979) *Discipline and Punish*, Vintage Books, New York.

Fruin, W.M. (1997) *Knowledge Works: Managing Intellectual Capital at Toshiba*, Oxford University Press, Oxford.

Fuller, S. (1999) Review Essay: The Information Age by Manuel Castells, *Science, Technology and Human Values*, **24** (1), 159–166.

Gallivan, M.J. (1996) Contradictions among Stakeholder Assessments of a Radical Change Initiative: A Cognitive Frames Analysis, in: W.J. Orlikowski, G. Walsham, M.R. Jones and J.I. DeGross, eds, *Information Technology and Changes in Organizational Work*, Chapman & Hall, London.

Ghosh, S. (1998) Making Business Sense of the Internet, *Harvard Business Review*, March–April, 126–135.

Giddens, A. (1984) *The Constitution of Society*, Polity Press, Cambridge.

Giddens, A. (1990) *The Consequences of Modernity*, Polity Press, Cambridge.

Giddens, A. (1991) *Modernity and Self-Identity*, Polity Press, Cambridge.

Giddens, A. (1999) *Reith Lectures 1999*, at http://news.bbc.co.uk/hi/english/static/events/reith_99

Gopal, A. (1997) Information Technology and Globalization: Exploring the Underbelly, in: M. Barrett, D. Cooper, C.R. Hinings, G. Lowe, H. Krahn and K. Hughes, eds, *Proceedings of Workshop on Understanding Information Technology, Globalization, and Changes in the Nature of Work*, University of Alberta, Edmonton.

Grey, C. and Mitev, N. (1995) Re-engineering Organizations: A Critical Appraisal, *Personnel Review*, **24** (1), 6–18.

Grint, K. and Woolgar, S. (1997) *The Machine at Work: Technology, Work and Organization*, Polity Press, Cambridge.

Hallier, J. and James, P. (1997) Middle Managers and the Employee Psychological Contract: Agency, Protection and Advancement, *Journal of Management Studies*, **34** (5), 703–728.

Hammer, M. (1990) Reengineering Work: Don't Automate, Obliterate, *Harvard Business Review*, July–August, 104–112.

Hammer, M. and Champy, J. (1993) *Reengineering the Corporation: A Manifesto for Business Revolution*, Nicholas Brealey, London.

Hansen, M.T., Nohria, N., and Tierney, T. (1999) What's Your Strategy for Managing Knowledge?, *Harvard Business Review*, March–April, 106–116.

Hanseth, O. and Braa, K. (1998) Technology as Traitor: Emergent SAP Infrastructure in a Global Organization, in: R. Hirschheim, M. Newman and J.I. DeGross, eds, *Proceedings of the 19th International Conference on Information Systems*, ACM, Baltimore.

Haraway, D.J. (1991) *Simians, Cyborgs, and Women: The Reinvention of Nature*, Free Association Books, London.

Harrison, R. (1983) *Bentham*, Routledge, London.

Hart, P. and Saunders, C. (1997) Power and Trust: Critical Factors in the Adoption and Use of Electronic Data Interchange, *Organization Science*, **8** (1), 23–42.

Hayes, M. (2000) Engineering Work, Identity and the Role of Information Systems: Two Case Studies of Business Process Re-engineering, PhD Thesis, The Judge Institute of Management Studies, University of Cambridge, Cambridge.

Hayes, M. and Walsham, G. (1999) Shifting Customer-Engineering Relationships: Archetypes of Identities and the Role of Information Systems, Working Paper WP 25/99, The Judge Institute of Management Studies, University of Cambridge.

Hayes, N. (1998) Sharing Knowledge Within and Between Boundaries: The Role of Groupware Technologies, PhD Thesis, University of Lancaster, Lancaster.

Hayes, N. and Walsham, G. (2000a) Safe Enclaves, Political Enclaves and Knowledge Working, in: C. Prichard, R. Hull, M. Chumer and H. Willmott, eds, *Managing Knowledge: Critical Investigations of Work and Learning*, Macmillan, Basingstoke.

Hayes, N. and Walsham, G. (2000b) Competing Interpretations of Computer Supported Work in Organisational Contexts, *Organization*, **7** (1), 49–67.

Hill, C.E., Loch, K.D., Straub, D.W. and El-Sheshai, K. (1998) A Qualitative Assessment of Arab Culture and Information Technology Transfer, *Journal of Global Information Management*, **6** (3), 29–38.

Hirst, P. and Thompson, G. (1996) *Globalization in Question: The International Economy and the Possibilities of Governance*, Polity Press, Cambridge.

Hofstede, G. (1980) *Culture's Consequences: International Differences in Work-Related Values*, Sage, London.

Hofstede, G. (1991) *Cultures and Organizations: Software of the Mind*, McGraw-Hill, New York.

Holland, C.P. (1995) Co-operative Supply Chain Management: The Impact of Interorganizational Information Systems, *Journal of Strategic Information Systems*, **4** (2), 117–133.

Holmer-Nadesan, M. (1996) Organizational Identity and Space of Action, *Organization Studies*, **17** (1), 49–81.

Introna, L.D. (1997) *Management, Information and Power: A Narrative of the Involved Manager*, Macmillan, Basingstoke.

Jarvenpaa, S.L. and Leidner, D.E. (1998) An Information Company in Mexico: Extending the Resource-Based View of the Firm to a Developing Country Context, *Information Systems Research*, **9** (4), 342–361.

Jones, M.R. (1994) Don't Emancipate, Exaggerate: Rhetoric, Reality and Reengineering, in: R. Baskerville, S. Smithson, O. Ngwenyama and J.I. DeGross, eds, *Transforming Organizations with Information Technology*, North-Holland, Amsterdam.

Jones, M.R. (1998) Structuration Theory, in: W.L. Currie and R.D. Galliers, eds, *Rethinking Management Information Systems: An Interdisciplinary Perspective*, Oxford University Press, Oxford.

Karsten, H. (1995) Converging Paths to Notes: In Search of Computer-Based Information Systems in a Networked Company, *Information Technology & People*, **8** (1), 7–34.

Karsten, H. (1999) Collaboration and Collaborative Information Technology: What is the Nature of Their Relationship?, in: T.J. Larsen, L. Levine and J.I. DeGross, eds, *Information Systems: Current Issues and Future Changes*, IFIP, Laxenburg, Austria.

Kling, R. (1994) Reading 'All About' Computerization: How Genre Conventions Shape Nonfiction Social Analysis, *Information Society*, **10** (3), 147–172.

Kling, R. and Iacono, S. (1984) The Control of Information Systems Developments after Implementation, *Communications of the ACM*, **27** (12), 1218–1226.

Kluzer, S. (1991) Book Review—Computerization in Developing Countries: Models and Reality, *European Journal of Information Systems*, **1** (4), 293-294.

Knights, D., and McCabe, D. (1998a) When 'Life is but a Dream': Obliterating Politics through Business Process Reengineering, *Human Relations*, **51** (6), 761–798.

Knights, D. and McCabe, C. (1998b) What Happens When the Phone Goes Wild?: Stress and Spaces for Escape in a BPR Telephone Banking Work Regime, *Journal of Management Studies*, **35** (2), 163–194.

Knights, D., Murray, F. and Willmott, H. (1993) Networking as Knowledge Work: A Study of Strategic Interorganizational Development in the Financial Services Industry, *Journal of Management Studies*, **30** (6), 975–995.

Kogut, B. (1999) What Makes a Company Global, *Harvard Business Review*, January–February, 165–170.

Komin, S. (1990) Culture and Work-Related Values in Thai Organizations, *International Journal of Psychology*, **25** (5–6), 681–704.

Korpela, M. (1996) Traditional Culture or Political Economy? On the Root Causes of Organizational Obstacles of IT in Developing Countries, *Information Technology for Development*, **7** (1), 29–42.

Korpela, M., Soriyan, H.A., Olufokunbi, K.C. and Mursu, A. (2000) Made-in-Nigeria Systems Development Methodologies: An Action Research Project in the Health Sector, in: C. Avgerou and G. Walsham, eds, *Information Technology in Context: Implementing Systems in the Developing World*, Ashgate Publishing, Aldershot.

Kumar, K. and van Dissel, H.G. (1996) Sustainable Collaboration: Managing Conflict and Co-operation in Interorganizational Systems, *MIS Quarterly*, **20** (3), 279–300.

Lam, A. (1997) Embedded Firms, Embedded Knowledge: Problems of Collaboration and Knowledge Transfer in Global Cooperative Ventures, *Organization Studies*, **18** (6), 973–996.

Latour, B. (1987) *Science in Action: How to Follow Scientists and Engineers through Society*, Harvard University Press, Cambridge, MA.

Latour, B. (1996) *Aramis or the Love of Technology*, Harvard University Press, Cambridge, MA.

Latour, B. (1999) *Pandora's Hope: Essays on the Reality of Science Studies*, Harvard University Press, Cambridge, MA.

Lave, J. and Wenger, E. (1991) *Situated Learning: Legitimate Peripheral Participation*, Cambridge University Press, Cambridge.

Lévi-Strauss, C. (1966) *The Savage Mind*, University of Chicago Press, Chicago.

Lind, P. (1991) *Computerization in Developing Countries: Model and Reality*, Routledge, London.

Lyon D. (1993) An Electronic Panopticon? A Sociological Critique of Surveillance Theory, *Sociological Review*, **41** (4), 653–678.

Madon, S. (1992) Computer-Based Information Systems for Development Planning: A Case Study, in: S.C. Bhatnagar and M. Odedra, eds, *Social Implications of Computers in Developing Countries*, Tata McGraw-Hill, New Delhi.

Madon, S. (1993) Computer-Based Information Systems for Development Planning: Managing Human Resources, *European Journal of Information Systems*, **2** (1), 49–55.

Madon, S. and Walsham, G. (1995) Decentralised Information Systems for Development Planning in India: Context/Process Interaction, *Information Infrastructure and Policy*, **4** (2), 163–179.

Magretta, J. (1998) The Power of Virtual Integration: An Interview with Dell Computer's Michael Dell, *Harvard Business Review*, March–April, 73–84.

Malling, P. (2000) Information Systems and Human Activity in Nepal, in: C. Avgerou and G. Walsham, eds, *Information Technology in Context: Implementing Systems in the Developing World*, Ashgate Publishing, Aldershot.

Mangham, I. and Pye, A. (1991) *The Doing of Managing*, Blackwell, Oxford.

Markus, M.L. (1983) Power, Politics and MIS Implementation, *Communications of the ACM*, **26** (6), 430–445.

Martinsons, M.G. and Westwood R.I. (1997) Management Information Systems in the Chinese Business Culture: An Explanatory Theory, *Information & Management*, **32** (5), 215–228.

Maznevski, M.L. and Chudoba, K.M. (2000) Bridging Space over Time: Global Virtual Team Dynamics and Effectiveness, *Organization Science*, forthcoming.

Mclaughlin, J. and Webster, A. (1998) Rationalising Knowledge: IT Systems, Professional Identities and Power, *Sociological Review*, **46** (4), 781–802.

Monteiro, E. and Hanseth, O. (1996) Social Shaping of Information Infrastructure: On Being Specific about the Technology, in: W.J. Orlikowski, G. Walsham, M.R. Jones and J.I. DeGross, eds, *Information Technology and Changes in Organizational Work*, Chapman & Hall, London.

Munkvold, B.E. (1997) Challenges of IT Implementation for Supporting Collaboration in Distributed Organizations: Experiences from Four Implementation Teams, in: R. Galliers, S. Carlsson, C. Loebbecke, C. Murphy, H.R. Hansen and R. O'Callaghan, eds, *Proceedings of the 5th European Conference on Information Systems*, University College Cork, Cork, Ireland.

Munkvold, B.E. (1998) Implementation of Information Technology for Supporting Collaboration in Distributed Organizations, Dr.ing Thesis, Norwegian University of Science and Technology, Trondheim, Norway.

Munkvold, B.E. (1999) Challenges of IT Implementation for Supporting Collaboration in Distributed Organizations, *European Journal of Information Systems*, **8** (4), 260–272.

Naipaul, V. (1964) *An Area of Darkness*, Andre Deutsch, London.

Nonaka, I. (1994) A Dynamic Theory of Organizational Knowledge Creation, *Organization Science*, **5** (1), 14–37.

Odedra-Straub, M., ed. (1996) *Global Information Technology and Socio-Economic Development*, Ivy League, Nashua, New Hampshire.

OECD (1999) *The Economic and Social Impact of Electronic Commerce: Preliminary Findings and Research Agenda*, OECD Publications, Paris.

Orlikowski, W.J. (1993) Learning from Notes: Organizational Issues in Groupware Implementation, *Information Society*, **9** (3), 237–250.

Orlikowski, W.J. (1996a) Evolving with Notes: Organizational Change around Groupware Technology, in: C.U. Ciborra, ed., *Groupware and Teamwork: Invisible Aid or Technical Hindrance?*, Wiley, Chichester.

Orlikowski, W.J. (1996b) Improvising Organizational Transformation over Time: A Situated Change Perspective, *Information Systems Research*, **7** (1), 63–92.

Orlikowski, W.J. and Gash, D.C. (1994) Technological Frames: Making Sense of Information Technology in Organizations, *ACM Transactions on Information Systems*, **12** (2), 174–207.

PWC (1999) *E-Business Technology Forecast*, PriceWaterhouseCoopers, California.

Robertson, R. (1992) *Globalization: Social Theory and Global Culture*, Sage, London.

Roche, E.M. and Blaine, M.J., eds (1996) *Information Technology, Development and Policy: Theoretical Perspectives and Practical Challenges*, Avebury, Aldershot.

Rohitratana, K. (1998) MRP Implementation in Thailand: Social and Cultural Issues, PhD Thesis, University of Lancaster, Lancaster.

Rohitratana, K. (2000) The Role of Thai Values in Managing Information Systems: A Case Study of Implementing an MRP System, in: C. Avgerou and G. Walsham, eds, *Information Technology in Context: Implementing Systems in the Developing World*, Ashgate Publishing, Aldershot.

Sahay, S. (1998) Implementing GIS Technology in India: Issues of Time and Space, *Accounting, Management and Information Technologies*, **8** (2–3), 147–188.

Sahay, S. and Krishna, S. (2000) A Dialectical Approach to Understand the Nature of Global Software Outsourcing Arrangements, Working Paper, Indian Institute of Management, Bangalore, India.

Sahay, S. and Robey, D. (1996) Organizational Context, Social Interpretation, and the Implementation and Consequences of Geographic Information Systems, *Accounting, Management and Information Technologies*, **6** (4), 255-282.

Sahay, S. and Walsham, G. (1997) Social Structure and Managerial Agency in India, *Organization Studies*, **18** (3), 415–444.

Sayer, K. (1998) Denying the Technology: Middle Management Resistance in Business Process Re-engineering, *Journal of Information Technology*, **13** (4), 247–257.

Scheepers, H. and de Villiers, C. (1999) Teaching of a Computer Literacy Course: A Case Study Using Traditional and Co-operative Learning, in *Proceedings of the 7th European Conference on Information Systems (ECIS)*, Copenhagen, Denmark.

Schultze, U. (2000) A Confessional Account of an Ethnography about Knowledge Work, *MIS Quarterly*, **24** (1), 3–41.

Schultze, U. and Boland, R.J. (1997) Constructing High Tech Space: Mind, Body and Place in Knowledge Work, in: H.K. Rasmussen, ed., *Proceedings of the AOS Conference on Accounting, Time and Space*, Copenhagen Business School, Copenhagen.

Scott, S. (1998) Computer-Mediated Interpretation of Risk: The Introduction of Decision Support Systems in a UK Retail Bank, PhD Thesis, The Judge Institute of Management Studies, University of Cambridge, Cambridge.

Scott, S. (2000) IT-Enabled Credit Risk Modernisation: A Revolution under the Cloak of Normality, *Accounting, Management and Information Technologies*, **10** (3), 221–255.

Scott, S. and Walsham, G. (1998) Shifting Boundaries and New Technologies: A Case Study in the UK Banking Sector, in: R. Hirschheim, M. Newman and J.I. DeGross, eds, *Proceedings of the 19th International Conference on Information Systems*, ACM, Baltimore.

Sinha, D. (1988) Basic Indian Values and Behavioural Dispositions in the Context of National Development, in: D. Sinha and H.S.R. Kao, eds, *Social Values and Development: Asian Perspectives*, Sage, New Delhi.

Soriyan, H.A., Mursu, A.S., Adegaye, A.O. and Korpela, M.J. (2000) Information Systems Development in Nigerian Software Companies: Methodological Issues and Empirical Findings, in *Proceedings of the IFIP WG9.4 Conference on Information Flows, Local Improvisations and Work Practices*, Cape Town, South Africa.

Stalder, F. (1998) The Network Paradigm: Social Formations in the Age of Information, *The Information Society*, **14** (4), 301–308.

Star, S.L. (1995) Working Together: Symbolic Interactionism, Activity Theory and Information Systems, in: Y. Engeström and D. Middleton, eds, *Communication and Cognition at Work*, Cambridge University Press, Cambridge.

Suchman, L.A. (1987) *Plans and Situated Actions: The Problem of Human–Machine Communication*, Cambridge University Press, Cambridge.

Tapscott, D. (1998) *Growing up Digital: The Rise of the Net Generation*, McGraw-Hill, New York.

Tavani, H.T. (1999) Informational Privacy, Data Mining, and the Internet, *Ethics and Information Technology*, **1** (2), 137–145.

Teo, H-H., Tan, B.C.Y. and Wei, K-K. (1997) Organizational Transformation Using Electronic Data Interchange: The Case of TradeNet in Singapore, *Journal of Management Information Systems*, **13** (4), 139–165.

Thiesmeyer, L. (1999) Racism on the Web: Its Rhetoric and Marketing, *Ethics and Information Technology*, **1** (2), 117–125.

Truex, D. and Ngwenyama, O. (2000) ERP Systems: Facilitating or Confounding Factors in Corporate Telecommunications Mergers?, in: H.R. Hansen, M. Bichler and H. Mahrer, eds, *Proceedings of the 8th European Conference on Information Systems (ECIS)*, Vienna, Austria.

Tsoukas, H. (1996) The Firm as a Distributed Knowledge System: A Constructionist Approach, *Strategic Management Journal*, **17**, Winter Special Issue, 11–25.

Turkle, S. (1996) *Life on the Screen: Identity in the Age of the Internet*, Weidenfeld & Nicolson, London.

Walsham, G. (1993) *Interpreting Information Systems in Organizations*, Wiley, Chichester. (Out of print)

Walsham, G. (1995) Interpretive Case Studies in IS Research: Nature and Method, *European Journal of Information Systems*, **4** (2), 74–81.

Walsham, G. (1997) Actor-Network Theory and IS Research: Current Status and Future Prospects, in: A.S. Lee, J. Liebenau and J.I. DeGross, eds, *Information Systems and Qualitative Research*, Chapman & Hall, London.

Walsham, G. (1998) IT and Changing Professional Identity: Micro-Studies and Macro-Theory, *Journal of the American Society for Information Science*, **49** (12), 1081–1089.

Walsham, G. (2000) Globalization and IT: Agenda for Research, in: R. Baskerville, J. Stage and J.I. DeGross, eds, *Organizational and Social Perspectives on Information Technology*, Kluwer Academic Publishers, Boston.

Walsham, G. and Sahay, S. (1999) GIS for District-Level Administration in India: Problems and Opportunities, *MIS Quarterly*, **23** (1), 39–66.

Walsham, G. and Waema, T. (1994) Information Systems Strategy and Implementation: A Case Study of a Building Society, *ACM Transactions on Information Systems*, **12** (2), 150–173.

Webster, F. (1995) *Theories of the Information Society*, Routledge, London.

Weick, K.E. (1998) Improvisation as a Mindset for Organizational Analysis, *Organization Science*, **9** (5), 543–555.

Willmott, H. (1993) Strength is Ignorance; Slavery is Freedom: Managing Culture in Modern Organizations, *Journal of Management Studies*, **30** (4), 515–552.

Willmott, H. (1994) Business Process Re-engineering and Human Resource Management, *Personnel Review*, **23** (3), 34–46.

Winner, L. (1993) Upon Opening the Black Box and Finding it Empty: Social Constructivism and the Philosophy of Technology, *Science, Technology and Human Values*, **18** (3), 362–378.

Woolgar, S. and Ingram, C. (1999) Memorandum to Parliamentary Select Committee on E-Commerce, http://www.brunel.ac.uk/research/virtsoc/reports.

Wynne, B. (1996) May the Sheep Safely Graze? A Reflexive View of the Expert–Lay Knowledge Divide, in: S. Lash, B. Szerszynski and B. Wynne, eds, *Risk, Environment and Modernity: Towards a New Ecology*, Sage, London.

Yates, J. and van Maanen, J. (1996) Editorial Notes for Special Issue, *Information Systems Research*, **7** (1), 1–4.

Zuboff, S. (1988) *In the Age of the Smart Machine*, Basic Books, New York.

Zuboff, S. (1996) The Emperor's New Information Economy, in: W.J. Orlikowski, G. Walsham, M.R. Jones and J.I. DeGross, eds, *Information Technology and Changes in Organizational Work*, Chapman & Hall, London.

Author Index

Subject Index

Kling R (1996). Computerization &
Controversy : Values , Conflict
& social choices

303 . 4834 KLI